CHRISTIANITY: THE TRUE HUMANISM

CHRISTIANITY: THE TRUE HUMANISM

J. I. PACKER AND THOMAS HOWARD

WORD BOOKS
PUBLISHER
WACO, TEXAS

A DIVISION OF
WORD, INCORPORATED

TO KIT AND LOVELACE

who show us daily
what it means to be
human in Christ

CHRISTIANITY: THE TRUE HUMANISM

Copyright © 1985 by Word, Incorporated, Waco, Texas.

Library of Congress Cataloging in Publication Data

Packer, J. I. (James Innell)
    Christianity : the true humanism.

    Bibliography: p.
    1. Apologetics—20th century. 2. Humanism—Contro-
versial literature. I. Howard, Thomas. II. Title.
BT1102.P23 1985   239   85-3297
ISBN 0-8499-0316-5

Printed in the United States of America

Contents

Preface

This book is a double act, performed in newscaster manner. We who wrote it are twice-born mainstream Christians, evangelicals, servants of God's church, though we locate it differently, and professional academics (teachers and writers). We are also friends, and on many matters visionaries together. But our writing styles differ, and we have not tried to change that. Readers are therefore free to amuse themselves spotting where in the text one of us stops and the other starts, and guessing how we managed it. Our hope, however, is that they will find something better to do, namely, follow the flow of our argument, which is a unity, making as best we can the single point of our title: namely, that historic Christianity humanizes, whereas secular humanism, despite its purpose, does the opposite. A British one-liner runs: "If we had some bacon we could have some bacon and eggs, if we had some eggs." We see ourselves as having contributed the bacon and the eggs respectively to a mix which we now offer with some confidence as a meal.

Both of us are blessed with wives whose love and patience with us are beyond any praise we can muster. Without them neither of us could do what we do at present. We dedicate this book to them as a tiny token of our very great gratitude.

J. I. Packer
Thomas Howard

CHRISTIANITY:
THE TRUE
HUMANISM

1

Introduction and Agenda

"Existentialism is a Humanism"; so claims the title of one of Jean-Paul Sartre's writings. Christianity is a humanism, indeed the only view of life worthy of that name; so our title claims, and so we seek to show in this book.

Secular humanism is a name which modern Western Christians have given to an outlook that calls itself "humanism" without qualification. The reason for its choice of name is that it believes itself to be offering mankind a formula for human fulfillment. When Christians add the adjective *secular*, they imply that Christianity, understood as "sacred" humanism, stands as its rival. They are right; it does. Humanism—whether in Marxist, existentialist, or Western liberal form (these are its main types)—and Christianity are antithetical.

Humanism says: There is no Creator to worship, no Redeemer to love, no image of God to recognize and honor in my neighbor, no future life to prepare for, no heavenly glory to inherit; and you are not inwardly free till you admit this. Christianity says: The worship, love, valuation, and expectation that humanism sweeps away are the rock-bottom realities of truly human living; without them, one's animal energy neither has meaning nor leads to joy, nor are we either free or fulfilled as human beings. Humanism says: Christianity turns men into milksops and mice. Christianity says: Humanism might better be called brutism or animalism, since it tells us to live without knowledge of God, as the lower animals do. Each view sees the other as desperately impoverishing.

Humanism tells us to think of ourselves as having no environment save that which science—physical, psychological, political, social, economic—studies; no life beyond heartstop day; and no rational goals beyond self-discovery, pursuing pleasure, and lessening others' misery here and now. Christianity teaches us to view God as our ultimate environment; to know him in and through the persons, things, and values that surround us; and to see ourselves as immortal beings of infinite worth whose calling for all eternity is to adore the God who has made us and loved us, to love him and our fellowman in return, and to experience joy in so doing. Each view sees the other as ruinously wrong-headed.

Humanism regards religion as hobbling mankind and holds that no one is healthy in spirit till he has left religion behind. Christianity sees this view as an irrational negating of mankind's deepest instincts and intuitions, and detects as its cause the universal infection called sin. Sin is a moral and spiritual allergy, an unfruitful and diseased reaction to the knowledge of God which should nourish us; it is an anti-God disposition of mind and heart which leads us to refuse godliness as our way of fulfillment and to choose instead a self-oriented path that is ultimately self-destructive. The story of the fall in Genesis 3 is the classic, archetypal illustration of this choice, and what results from it. By this light, humanism, which the United States Supreme Court classed in 1961 as a nontheistic religion, appears as a flawed formula for living, just as other non-Christian faiths do. It, like them, answers the crucial question of human happiness incorrectly and needs radical reshaping by the revelation of God in Jesus Christ. Christianity and humanism are at this point heavily judgmental in relation to each other; that is unavoidable, for each sees as poison what the other offers as medicine. It is no wonder that when they meet the fur flies!

This book, however, so far as may be, is pacific and pastoral rather than polemical. We address ourselves not to humanists or humanism as such, but to the question which engages both humanist and Christian minds with equal seriousness, namely, what constitutes the good life—that is, the truly human life—for mankind. It has been said that the best defense of any position is creative exposition of it, and certainly that is the best means of persuading others that it is true. So, after clearing the ground for discussion, we shall concentrate on spelling out the Christian answer to the question of personal well-being. By this means we hope to justify the claim contained in our title. We cannot make it impossible for humanists still to disagree with us, but we shall try to make it possible, indeed natural and easy, to ask, when they do, whether their alternative answer to our question does not overlook some key facts about humanness as a quality of life.

Can human beings live subhuman lives? As Christians, for whom Jesus Christ is the standard of humanness, we have to answer yes; many do. But that is bad news, for when people lapse into subhuman living, it is tragic and ruinous both for others and for themselves. We hope that our book, under God, may keep some from lapsing in this way, and may even reclaim some who have lapsed already. If it has this effect, we shall be thankful and see ourselves as rewarded for the labor of composing it. For we write to help people, not just to score points.

2

Meet Secular Humanism

Our first step is to focus more precisely on the humanism that has called this book into being and to take its measure. That will help us fix our angles for the rest of the discussion.

What Is Humanism?

The secular humanism that we meet today is not the same thing as the Renaissance humanism which one sees in such men as Erasmus and Leonardo da Vinci. (Renaissance humanism, despite some murky streaks, was in essence a plea for a rich and robust Christian culture.) Nor should we equate secular humanism with the humanism professed by those who teach the humanities professionally; nor should we confuse it with the spirit of sympathetic concern for others' welfare which is often called humanism in these days. Secular humanism is neither a professional field nor a character quality, but an aggressive cultural ideology—that is, a set of ideas expressed in programs designed to change people's lives.

It is a recent growth. Like Kleenex and aerobics, it is a product of the consciously civilized modern West. It appears in various forms, but a single conviction animates them all—namely, the belief that current cultural developments, especially those which claim the name of science, show religion to be irrational and hostile to human happiness. The thought is that only those who know they are on their own in the universe, with no God to worship and no concern about the church, will ever take the bold steps that are needed to set their lives straight. From this it is inferred that the way to help people realize their potential is to disillusion them about religion and so free them from inhibiting superstitions and restrictions. Then, by rational reflection on experience, a wiser code can be devised, and a happier generation will be bred.

The heart of secular humanism thus appears as reaction—reaction born, as it seems, of hurt and resentment, outrage and disgust at the tenets and track record of organized religion. In this the humanist spirit is older than Christianity. Buddhist atheism in the East (sixth century B.C.) was its first appearance, and it broke surface in the West in the first century B.C. with Lucretius' long poem *De Rerum Natura* (On the Nature of Things). The Buddha's atheism was a matter of turning away from a polytheistic type of religion that killed the moral concern through which alone, as he claimed, *nirvana* (blissful nonexistence, man's final goal) can be reached. Lucretius wrote to free people from what seemed to him the crippling fear that the gods take notice of men, and to preach to them the Epicurean gospel of a quiet, pleasure-seeking life, devoid of religious concerns. Here is the spirit of modern secular humanism exactly.

Nowhere is humanist reaction currently more visible than in the United States. This is not surprising. In the United States a conversionist folk religion (legalistic, biblicist, revivalist, conservative, credulous, anticultural, authoritarian) has in the past been strong. Such religion naturally prompts reaction among educated and sensitive people. This problem is not, however, unique to the United States, nor to Protestant countries as such. Wherever Christianity has produced what historians call a "popular piety" claiming to be part of the national heritage, anti-Christian reaction among the intelligentsia has followed. In Roman Catholic and Eastern Orthodox countries, where the church has become an entrenched power structure, revolts that started with anti-clericalism, deism, and atheism have ended in Marxism—the embrace of a secular collective juggernaut as a refuge from a sacred one. In England, where the folk religion was a dignified

Anglican formalism, cooler, less intrusive, and more laissez-faire than either Orthodoxy or Roman Catholicism, the humanist revolt, though not negligible, has been less strong, probably because fewer there have been hurt by dehumanizing versions of Christianity to the point of wanting to exterminate it. But in the United States, where a degree of ferocity unmatched in Britain is part of national life, the enforcing of substandard Christianity in homes, churches, schools, and communities has inflicted so much emotional hurt, that anti-Christian reaction is now marked by a strong head of emotional steam. There is more to secular humanism than the fixated reactionary thinking of the traumatized, but not less; and we shall not understand the movement well unless we give full weight to this factor, just as we have to do when feminism is our subject of study.

The purpose of the foregoing paragraph was to give a diagnosis; it was not an expression of disrespect. It would no doubt be easy at this point to launch into a diatribe against reaction, pointing out that the reaction of man rarely works the righteousness of God, highlighting the folly of throwing away the baby with the bathwater, rubbing in the thought that really wise people do not let the abuse of things blind them to their proper use, and implying throughout that being emotionally scarred has made humanists a bit stupid. To dilate on these thoughts would be very easy—and, as we see it, very wrong! For cheap sarcasm rules out deep understanding, and understanding is what we are after at present. We are asking what makes humanists tick, and we are saying that one factor is the psychology of the scarred mind—by which we mean that our thinking about what has traumatized us is regularly negative, adversative, and hostile to the point of obsession. By divine grace Christians sometimes succeed in loving their enemies, but other folk never do. The burnt child, says the proverb, dreads the fire: having been hurt by it, he fears it all his life. This same kind of fear seems to be the reason many humanists are obsessively anti-Christian, just as it is the reason why some Christians, who see humanism as a conspiracy under which they or those for whom they care have suffered, are obsessively antihumanist. It is clear that many humanists in the West are stirred by a sense of outrage at what professed Christians, past and present, have done; and this makes them see their humanism as a kind of crusade, with the killing of Christianity as its prime goal. We cannot endorse their attitude, but we can understand it and respect it, and we would like at this point to say so.

What's that? says someone. You can respect an attitude that seeks the death of Christianity? Yes, we can, on two accounts.

First, we can justify the disillusionment with Christians out of which the humanist murder plan springs. We know what it is like to be hurt, disillusioned, embarrassed, and disgusted at the words and deeds of professing Christians. We, too, have experienced in our own persons damage done by bad Christianity—Christianity that lacks honesty, or intelligence, or regard for truth, or biblical depth, or courtesy, or all of these together. No doubt we have sometimes inflicted this kind of damage, as well as suffered it. (Lord, have mercy!) We cannot, however, think it wrong for anyone to expect much of Christians and then to feel hurt when they treat others in a way that discredits their Christian commitment. Since Christianity is about God transforming us through Jesus Christ, high expectations really are in order, and the credibility of the faith really is undermined by every uncaring and uncompassionate stand that Christians take. Loss of faith caused by bad experiences with Christians is thus often more a case of being sinned against than of sinning and merits compassion more than it does censure.

Second, we honor the humanists' serious purpose of finding the path to human fulfillment and clearing away all that blocks it. This is our own purpose, too; and though we disagree entirely with them as to what constitutes fulfillment and how it occurs, we see their quest as ours and invite them to see ours as theirs.

Meantime, we set on record our conviction that Western humanism, like Marx's Marxism, is best viewed as a prodigal son of Christianity itself. Though it has left its Christian home in search of freedom and fulfillment elsewhere, and though it is driven very obviously by the rebel son's passion to strike the father dead, it has no alternative home of its own, but continues to be nourished by elements of its Christian heritage of goals and values. Since these are now cut off from their roots in Christian faith, it is uncertain how long secular humanism can last before turning into something else. But perhaps the answer is: It will last as long as organized Christianity is there to provoke humanist reaction, keeping humanism in shape, we might say, by being that against which it constantly revolts. Future generations will see—if the world lasts, that is! (Many Christians and many humanists share doubts as to whether it will.)

What does humanism offer in place of Christian faith? The *Humanist Manifestos I* and *II* (1933 and 1973) have told the world, and there was never any in-house disputing about it in the humanist camp. Humanism sets human beings at the center of the universe, maintaining that Nature, of which man is the most highly developed component, is all that exists; that happiness and enrichment of human life now is all that we should aim at; that scientific reason is the only tool needed for the task; and that religion hinders the enterprise rather than helps it. Working hypotheses (educated guesses, that is) which humanists embrace include the eternity and infinity of the universe; the evolution of man and society as a fact of the past and a hope for the future; the autonomy of man as lord of Nature, to do what he wants with it; the absolute uniformity of Nature, according to the inherent laws of its functioning; utilitarian relativism in ethics, whereby anything that promises happy states and feelings becomes right for that very reason; and a belief that there should be shares for all in all good things. The 1933 *Manifesto* presented this high-minded, world-centered, science-oriented ethic as an alternative religion (understanding religion as a "means for realizing the highest values of life"); and, as we have seen, the U.S. Supreme Court recognized it as such in 1961. The 1973 *Manifesto* restated the same view more stringently, with explicit rejection of, among other things, "intolerant attitudes, often cultivated by orthodox religions and puritanical cultures" which "unduly repress sexual conduct."

The most striking difference between the two *Manifestos* is that whereas the first was signed by thirty-four Americans of whom only John Dewey is known today, the second counts among its signatories philosophers Bland Blanshard and Sidney Hook (American) and Sir Alfred Ayer and Antony Flew (British); authors Isaac Asimov and John Ciardi; scientists Francis Crick, Andrei Sakharov, and Zhores Medvedev (the last two being Soviet dissidents); psychologists H. J. Eysenck and B. F. Skinner, with sexologists Albert Ellis, Lester Kirkendall, and Sol Gordon; and feminist Betty Friedan; plus the atypical but well-known Episcopal clergyman Joseph Fletcher, fount of "situation ethics." These are, to use the British phrase, top people. The humanist support base has become more impressive. Over forty years, humanism has gathered strength.

The common humanist hypothesis about the human condition is evolutionism (the idea that by inevitable progress mankind gets better and better, provided that no one throws a monkey wrench into the works). Politically, most Western humanists embrace some kind of egalitarian socialism. Where Marxism subordinates the individual to community interests and existentialism dissects and mocks him as a passionate absurdity, Anglo-American humanism treats personal welfare as the ultimate value and leaves each individual as free as possible to define welfare for himself in egoistic terms—comfort, convenience, aesthetic pleasure, affluence, self-improvement, sexual satisfaction according to taste, and so on. The inborn aptitude of the human individual for devising a lifestyle which the rest of us will recognize as good and wise is taken for granted; in this regard, humanism is a reintroducing of Rousseau's natural savage in modern dress. Moral values education which, instead of teaching standards, seeks to draw out of children whatever values are in their minds already is a latter-day expression of this philosophy. No doubt some embrace humanism because it offers an escape from religion, or allows them behavior which religion forbids, and they never become conscious of the radiantly optimistic view of our nature which humanism assumes; but the assumption has to be there, or the humanist approach to morals would not make sense. To Christians and others who reject this optimism, humanist permissiveness does not make sense; it seems to them nightmarishly crazy, a canonizing of irrationality and irresponsibility in a way that invites both personal and cultural disaster. But humanists seem happy to give individuals their head, however kinky or kooky the results, because they are quite sure of the innate goodness and wisdom of man.

Or are they? Closer inspection reveals disturbing ambivalence at this point. Humanist leaders prove again and again to be profound pessimists, aristocratically contemptuous of human nature as it is and optimistic only about their plans for changing it. Those who start by echoing the second *Humanist Manifesto*—"the preciousness and dignity of the individual person is a central humanist value"—end up as social engineers devaluing all individuals who do not measure up to their ideal. The notorious willingness of some humanists to justify and recommend abortion, infanticide, euthanasia, and the sterilizing or killing of the physically handicapped and mentally limited, as the Nazis did, is clear evidence of the direction in which their basic attitude takes them. Nor is this an accident of temperament; it is not just that humanists are arrogant and unfeeling, though it seems clear that some of them are; there is a logical inevitability about their impatience with ordinary human beings. After all, when their philosophy starts with permissiveness and aims at a perfectly happy community here on earth, there is no other way for their thoughts to go.

> Morality based on individual sentiment means anarchy and the disintegration of society. Humanists cannot have this, and their writings are filled with fervid arguments in favor of a powerful central state. Autonomous man, they find, needs leadership, and strong leadership is the hallmark of a humanist society. Whether embodied in a committee or personalized in a leader, the elite dominates. Thus, far from being liberation, the anarchy of humanism brings enslavement. The better educated he is, the more likely the humanist is to believe that people are like machines and need to be programmed, and the more likely he is to believe that he should be one of the programmers.[1]

The Marxism of the East, despite its manipulative social policy, calls itself a humanism; the humanism of the West, despite its name, pursues a manipulative social policy; the two ideologies at this point join hands, revealing beneath their surface differences an elitist family likeness. And both contrast with Christianity in the same stark way. Christianity brings authentic personal freedom through submitting to God; acknowledging his standards as absolutes; and accepting his revealed pattern of social order, law, mutual care, and communal restraint as the milieu for each person's individual life. Both humanism and Marxism, however, while proclaiming freedom from all religious bonds, end up enslaving the individual to some communal benefit program which manipulates and ultimately discounts him in the interests (alleged) of the group.

Thus Western humanism, no less than Eastern Communism, dehumanizes and diminishes the individual whose integrity it

---

1. Herbert Schlossberg, *Idols for Destruction* (Nashville: Thomas Nelson, 1983) p. 87.

professed itself so anxious to safeguard and enhance. Inside its velvet glove of tolerance is an iron hand of tyranny; its professed compassion becomes a sanction for cruelty, and its professed humanitarianism a kind of inhumanity. The preciousness and dignity of the individual person is precisely not its central value, and to claim that it is, as humanists commonly do, is really muddleheaded.

But here we need to distinguish between what may be called Enlightenment humanism and Promethean humanism. The Enlightenment was a movement of secular intellectualism; Prometheus was a mythical hero who stole fire from the gods to give to men in order to enrich their lives; and the two humanisms express, respectively, the spirit of refinement and the spirit of revolution. Enlightenment humanism comes from men like Voltaire and Kant, children of eighteenth-century rationalism which glorified cool reasoners; it has always prided itself on maintaining without Christian sanctions a moral code equal if not superior to that of Christianity. That is the humanism of refinement. Promethean humanism, however, stems from men like Feuerbach ("religion means childlike immaturity"), Marx ("atheism is a necessity, since all religions support unjust social structures"), Freud ("religion is an illusion, a wish-fulfillment fantasy"), and Nietzsche ("now that God is dead, everything is permissible"). All these thinkers were products of the nineteenth-century romantic movement, which glorified the heroic rebel. Theirs is the humanism of revolution. Of their ideas and ideologies James Hitchcock has written:

> The new Humanism of the nineteenth century embodied a demonic urge to negate and destroy. As Nietzsche saw clearly, it was not only a matter of not believing in God. Once God had been denied, man could achieve true freedom only by denying all moral constraints on himself and inventing his own morality. The human will alone became sovereign. This type of Humanism has often descended into Nihilism, the urge to destroy and annihilate every accepted good. The older, more genteel type of Humanism has been steadily losing ground to the newer kind, which is in essence profoundly anti-humanistic.[2]

2. James Hitchcock, *What Is Secular Humanism?* (Ann Arbor: Servant Books, 1982) p. 48.

(It is noticeable that whereas the spirit of Enlightenment humanism ran through the first *Humanist Manifesto,* more of the temper of Promethean humanism marks the second. The truculent aggressiveness so often found in current humanist literature suggests that the Promethean spirit is becoming dominant—which in turn makes one wonder whether the humanist movement has not already slid into an irrecoverable decadence. Some decadence is, in any case, inescapable once the relativization of moral absolutes begins.)

Hitchcock's word *demonic* points to a motivation in humanism that is deeper than the merely pragmatic and cultural. The humanist movement, particularly in its Promethean form, expresses the defiance of the Creator's just claims, and the instinct for negating value, which Christianity has always viewed as the image of Satan in fallen man. Viewed from this standpoint, humanism appears as the latest in a series of revolts against Christianity which go back to the first century. In New Testament times the multiform theosophy called Gnosticism tried to swallow up Christianity. At the same time pagan intellectuals ridiculed Christianity's belief in incarnation and atonement, and Rome steadily killed its adherents for the sake of public order. Later, Islam emerged, and Arabs and Turks began to wish Christianity dead. The next revolt against Christianity came with the Renaissance. Unlike Medieval thinkers who sought to integrate all knowledge in a single synthesis shaped by God's revealed truth, the Renaissance belched out a demand to free the arts and, later, the sciences from their Christian moorings. In due course this impulse produced the humanism which we know today.

These were all movements of recoil from the Christian call for unqualified submission to God as finally and definitively revealed in Jesus Christ, whom to know is life and to serve is freedom. In this they matched Satan and the fallen angels, who according to Scripture were the first to refuse to be their Maker's subjects. When all due allowance has been made for the justice of humanist indignation at the sometimes outrageous failings of the Christian church, it has to be said that humanist self-expression often strikes a note of arrogant self-sufficiency and contempt for the very thought of serving God which is the essence of what Christians mean by original sin. Thus behind humanism's real intellectual seriousness we detect a genuine spiritual problem.

Biblical Perspective on Humanism

Humanism, like Marxism, sees itself as pointing the way to an ideal society. It is, in other words, a form of utopianism. That is part of its Promethean character. But Christians know that all utopian dreams, with all the Promethean ventures in self-sufficiency on which they are based, are foredoomed to failure, not only because they lack the spiritual resources needed to gain their goal, but because God himself has resolved that they shall not succeed. When Adam and Eve had defied God by eating fruit from the tree of knowledge, and so yielded to the temptation to seek wisdom (insight and skill for living) apart from God, God said: "'The man . . . must not be allowed to reach out his hand and take also from the tree of life and eat, and live forever.' So the Lord God banished him from the Garden of Eden" and "placed on the east side of the Garden of Eden cherubim and a flaming sword flashing back and forth to guard the way to the tree of life" (Genesis 3:22–24).

The road to Paradise, whether viewed as the way back or the way ahead, is now barred to rebel mankind. The profoundest way to read history is to recognize that the human race has, in effect, been trying to get back to Eden under its own steam all along; the utopian motive has been there, sometimes veiled but always potent, throughout the whole checkered career of humanity. But our fallen race has never managed in this way to reenter Paradise, nor will it ever. No godless heaven will ever be found, or built, on earth, no matter how far we search or how hard we try. God has decreed that utopianism will fail. He has other plans.

We are going to amplify this point, for it is the key to our view of humanism and of all other secular ideologies with it. More than that, it is the key to all true understanding of the Bible and the gospel. The Bible nowadays is a closed book to many who read it, even in our churches; they complain that they cannot understand it, nor see how it hangs together. The gospel of Christ has been widely misunderstood in the West for more than a century and is still misconstrued with daunting regularity by leading Christian spokesmen. The key to understanding both the gospel and the inadequacy of humanism is found in Genesis 3, which shows God dealing with fallen mankind; and it is to this same fallen condition that the gospel declares God's amazing final response in the life, death, resurrection, and promised return of Jesus Christ, through whom he makes all things new. Leaving aside the probably unanswerable questions as to the date of Adam and the geographical location of Eden and what we would have seen and heard had we been there to observe, we read Genesis 3 not only as narrating man's fall from God, but as picturing the continuing human condition as it was yesterday, as it is today, and as it will be tomorrow. Man, as he has been since the fall, is portrayed definitively in the story of the fall. Read thus, as a mirror of mankind's past and present, this chapter shows us the following truths.

1. *From the beginning, man has forgotten that responsive fellowship with God is his highest privilege and dignity.* Like Adam and Eve, we have come to doubt whether depending on and responding to our Maker is really the richest life, and we have let ourselves be betrayed into hankering after the will-o'-the-wisp of independence as if the more independent of God we can be, the nobler we become. This is like saying that the wife's nobility is proportionate to the degree to which she lives independently of her husband. Both sentiments are perverse! Human beings are made for a relationship with God of which total responsiveness in worship and obedience should be the essence, and it is only as we sustain that relationship that real nobility is found in our lives. The supreme proof of this is Jesus Christ, whose nobility sober persons have never been able to deny even when they have failed to see that fellowship with the Father, totally dependent and obedient, was its source. The Promethean attempt in Eden to snatch wisdom in order to live a life that would (supposedly) be enhanced by being independent of God was a recipe not for human nobility but for human degradation. So it proved in Adam and Eve's day, and so it is still. How this works out in humanism we have already begun to see.

2. *From the beginning, man has forgotten that he is finite, limited, and weak.* That he is so is a fact that nothing can alter, but it is a fact that he will not face. "Eat the forbidden fruit," said the tempter, "and you will be like God"—wise enough and strong enough to get on without God, just as God could get on without you. Satan stirs up pride, the desire to be superior to all and inferior to none; and pride prompts in us, as it did in Adam and Eve, the desire to be like God, to play God, to function as God,

and to have everything and everybody revolving round us as all created things should, and do, revolve round their Maker. Pride also leads us to imagine that we have enough strength and wisdom actually to play the divine role, controlling all around us with perfect mastery and glorying in the thought that there is nothing we cannot do. Our whole race suffers from delusions of grandeur, which modern technology serves merely to confirm. The illusion of perfect mastery, like other illusions, is frequently shattered ("Almighty God himself couldn't sink this ship," said the captain of the *Titanic*), but it forms itself again quickly in most minds, for in truth it is wishful thinking, fueled by fancy rather than by fact. We do not wish to face our limitations, so we encourage ourselves to forget them. We like to think of ourselves as God, infinitely wise and resourceful, so we indulge self-exalting daydreams all the time. This spirit is universal, and humanism is in no way exempt; rather, the reverse.

3. *From the beginning, man has made pleasure his prime aim, rather than truth and uprightness.* "When the woman saw that the fruit of the tree was good for food and pleasing to the eye, and also desirable for gaining wisdom, she took some and ate it" (Genesis 3:6). What Freud called the "pleasure principle" became in Eden the typical and dominant human motivation, and such it remains. "It looks good, I want it, I shall enjoy it, I must have it; never mind the consequences, for me or for others; consequences can look after themselves; here it is in front of me, tempting me, and I am going to take it right now"—this mentality and mood are universally familiar, being found not only in society around us but also, as honest people admit, in our own hearts. Though from time to time particular persons and episodes demonstrate to us afresh what it means to be ruled by truth and principle rather than by blind, childish passion, and though we all sometimes make a point of doing what we know to be the right thing, the overall story of our race is of egoistic desire in regular control and of altruism as the exception rather than the rule. There is nothing new (except, perhaps, the degree of openness) in the yielding to selfish, pleasure-oriented, often immoral motivation that is so much a mark of our times; in essence, it has been that way everywhere since the fall.

4. *From the beginning, man has felt that God is against him and has reacted to God in a negative and hostile way.* The form of

Satan's crafty question, "Did God really say, 'You must not eat from any tree in the garden'?" (v. 1), insinuated that the God of the garden was keeping Adam and Eve down; then the statement that followed, "God knows that when you eat of it [the forbidden fruit] your eyes will be opened, and you will be like God, knowing good and evil" (v. 5), was meant to convince them that God was a jealous potentate unwilling to have peers, while they themselves were creatures of great potential, able to become the equals of their Creator. Human thought since Eden has been dyed the color of this conviction. Behind the humanist insistence that religion has been a great hindrance to the progress of our race and that the only way to freedom and maturity is to shake it off, lies the sense of things which was projected by the devil's lie and absorbed at that time into mankind's attitudinal heritage. Since the fall it has never been natural to anyone to love God (or his neighbor, for that matter) with all his heart. Why not? Because, as Paul states, "the sinful mind is hostile to God. It does not submit to God's law, nor can it do so. Those controlled by the sinful nature cannot please God" (Romans 8:7–8). To say that by nature we are all inclined against God, feeling him to be against us, may be startling. As long as our thoughts of God are selective and determined by our own fancy, we may be inclined to protest that it is not so with us. But no "natural man" can contemplate the God of the Bible without finding it in him to wish that God's claims were less stringent and his judgments less severe; and out of this wish will grow hatred of God—hatred that may well express itself in outraged insistence that "God can't really be like that" and outraged censure of Christians for holding that he is. Humanism, in particular, displays this state of mind.

5. *From the beginning, man has thought that he could escape from God and so avoid the consequences of having defied and disobeyed him.* Adam and Eve, we read (Genesis 3:7–8), felt guilty and ashamed the moment they ate the fatal fruit. Their feelings of shame made them want to hide themselves and not be fully seen. This urge found a physical focus, and they donned fig-leaf loincloths, so fulfilling their desire to hide something of themselves from each other. A concealing instinct was part of them now, by reason of their sin. Then they tried to hide from God— tried, because they thought they could do it. But they could not, any more than we can. God knows who we are, what we are, and where we are; and in due course we shall all be called to account.

Retribution for Adam and Eve was drastic. They were expelled from Eden; the land was turned into a paradise for weeds; physical death became their portion, along (presumably) with all diseases that make for death; and their marriage was blighted (vv. 16–19). These inflictions remain part of the human condition, and God has gone on judging sin. The God of Genesis 3 is the same God of judgment whom we meet in every book of Scripture. "You are not a God who takes pleasure in evil; with you the wicked cannot dwell. The arrogant cannot stand in your presence; you hate all who do wrong" (Psalm 5:4–5). "God is a righteous judge, a God who expresses his wrath every day" (Psalm 7:11). Throughout the New Testament, present judgments are acknowledged and future judgment is expected. God the judge is inescapable.

Here, however, we are in another area where fallen human thinking is constantly wishful and unrealistic. Like Adam and Eve at first, people imagine that they can sin with impunity, either because they believe retribution is only a sick fancy and will never really happen, or because they are sure they are not bad enough to be condemned, or because they think they can make up for lapses in one department by spurts of moral effort in another. None of this, however, is true, any more than humanism's venture of thinking God out of existence is true. "Man is destined to die once, and after that to face judgment" (Hebrews 9:27), and this is something which no amount of thinking otherwise can alter.

6. *From the beginning, man has been unwilling to accept responsibility for his actions and admit that he deserves retribution.* The answers of Adam and Eve when God asked them if they had eaten the forbidden fruit show that evading responsibility had already become second nature to them (Genesis 3:11–13). "The woman you put here with me—she gave me some fruit from the tree, and I ate it," said Adam. In other words, it was her fault, not mine! "The serpent deceived me, and I ate," said Eve. In other words, it was not my fault, but his! Reading this, we understand perfectly what was going on in their minds, for it remains one of our most cherished illusions that whatever we have done, we are not to blame; others' influence, or something in our history or our circumstances, should be censured, but not we.

Perhaps the best thing to do with this idea is to laugh it out of court. So we cite the following verses by an anonymous medical man:

I went to my psychiatrist to be psychoanalyzed,
    To find out why I killed the cat and blacked my wifie's eyes.
He laid me on a comfy couch to see what he could find,
    And this is what he dredged up out of my unconscious mind.
When I was one my mommy locked my dolly in the trunk,
    And so it follows naturally that I am always drunk.
When I was two I saw my father kiss the maid one day,
    And that is why I suffer now from klep-to-ma-ni-a.
At three I was ambivalent towards my younger brothers,
    And that's the reason why, to date, I've poisoned all my lovers.
And I'm *so* glad since I have learned the lesson I've been taught,
    That everything I do that's wrong is someone else's fault.

This is a hit particularly at Freudian determinism; but we do well to remember that behind Freudianism and similar views of a behaviorist-determinist sort lies a craving to shift the blame that is as old as Adam. It is to be hoped, however, that honest laughter will shame it into silence.

But it is no laughing matter when we observe how radically, at least in some of its expositors, humanism canonizes this self-excusing instinct. It starts, as we have seen, by abolishing God—the transcendent ground and guardian of right and wrong—which leaves only a social-utilitarian, culturally relative basis for morality. That, however, is only the beginning. It then proceeds to class antisocial behavior as a form of mental illness, to be treated by medical and psychiatric means (up to the point of brainwashing, if need be). It does this as an alternative to understanding wrongdoing in moral terms as a guilty business, meriting punishment. In other words, it abolishes the categories of bearing one's guilt, taking one's medicine, and paying one's debt to society. But this procedure, which is alleged to be kind and humane, actually diminishes and dehumanizes us; for to accept responsibility for our own actions belongs to our dignity as moral agents, however little we like the idea and however much we try to wriggle out of it. Extenuating circumstances there may be, but ultimately we know, and furthermore we know that we know, that those who have done wrong should be made to answer for it, whether to men or to God.

Answering to God for our moral and spiritual shortcomings is in fact inescapable, as we have seen. Nor must this necessarily spell our ruin. Christians know that God in mercy forgives sins, through the atoning death of Jesus Christ. From the recording of

God's promise that the woman's seed should crush the serpent's head (Genesis 3:15) and of his provision of animal skin garments for Adam and Eve (v. 21)—a gesture which involved killing the animals as was constantly done later when sacrificing for sins—we are probably meant to gather that there and then Adam and Eve found forgiveness, though God's curses on this present life remained in force. But forgiveness can only come when sin has been confessed as the guilty thing it is and its hell-deserving demerit frankly faced. This, however, assumes an acknowledgment of God which humanism does not make. We do not doubt that humanists, like Adam and Eve and everyone else, do in fact feel guilt, even after trying to tell themselves that they shouldn't; and it seems clear that in the humanist universe there is no way they can get rid of it. The sad conclusion is that it must stay as an ulcer on their soul all their days, draining love, peace, and good will out of them and souring their spirit, as unforgiven guilt always does. It is a grim prospect.

Is it, then, realistic to imagine that we can, in effect, get back into Eden under our own steam, by careful planning and resolute action? Humanist utopianism, as we have seen, believes that we can, but in this it is wrong. In humanism the revolt of Eden goes on, and the revolt of Eden stands under God's curse. There is, to be sure, a way back to Paradise, but it is not the way of earthbound social utilitarianism steered by sufficiently clever men, as humanism supposes. It is, rather, the way which God in grace has opened, the way of redemption, whereby Jesus Christ the divine-human Mediator brings us our reconciliation to the Father, which he won for us on the cross, and remakes us by the Holy Spirit, whom he sends to us from his throne. Through this redemption we taste the Edenic life of knowing God here and now, though the place where the tree of life now stands (i.e., where the fullness of the life for which we were made is enjoyed) is in a world beyond this (Revelation 22:2). But where the Redeemer and his redemption are rejected, Paradise is missed forever. Scripture is very clear about that. And it is the path of rejection that humanism takes.

So the truth about humanism, which crystallizes as we let the strange old story of the fall speak about it, is as follows: (1) Humanism is one mutation of mankind's continuing bid for independence from our Creator and for autonomous self-sufficiency in personal and community life. (2) It supposes, confusedly and unrealistically, that this is the highroad to happiness and fulfillment for every human being—even, apparently, the unborn and crippled children and the handicapped and elderly people for whom it has in mind a "good death." (3) Its exponents, like the rest of men, take their own wisdom and adequacy for granted and do not consider that it might be beyond the power of man as he is to know what is good for him. (4) Its hostility to any thought of acknowledging and listening to and learning from God the Creator and of exchanging intellectual and moral *autonomy* for *"theonomy"*—in other words, of humbly becoming subject to God's revelation—expresses not only a recoil from unworthy expressions of religious faith, but ultimately the revolt against serving God which started in Eden and is now instinctive to us all. (5) Its refusal to be serious about personal guilt in any form reflects its ultimate unwillingness to allow that we are answerable to a transcendent and eternal Judge—that deep down we are not good but bad, so we really do have something to answer for. (6) It understands freedom in terms, not of contentment in God, but of what the Roman moralist Seneca called slavery to oneself (in his view, "the worst bondage of all"); and the veneer of its professed concern for society conceals the same single-minded, self-deifying egoism into which Adam and Eve were originally betrayed. (7) For its manipulators and those whom it manipulates alike, humanism points away from the human fulfillment which it rightly seeks. (8) It stands revealed as one form of the broad and attractive man-made road that leads to final destruction, above and beyond the immoralities it will commit and the miseries it will cause here and now if given its head. (9) It is from every standpoint tragic folly; the confident kind of folly that has been parading itself as wisdom ever since the world began.

Humanism against Humanism

Our response to secular humanism in this book will not take the form of a general defense of Christianity. We do not plan to argue for each tenet of the faith which official humanism denies. That is not, however, because we doubt if such a defense can be successfully made; we are quite certain that it can. The historic mainstream faith for which we stand—"mere Christianity," as the

Puritan Richard Baxter and, following him, C. S. Lewis called it—seems to us to be supremely and compellingly reasonable, whereas anti-Christianity in all the forms in which we know it seems to us patently unreasonable by comparison. Let us explain.

The unreasonableness of an anti-Christian commitment seems to us to come out in three ways.

First, anti-Christianity fails to face facts. It can neither explain nor explain away the facts of Bible history, centering in the fact of Christ as focused and finding its own center in the fact of his resurrection. Nor can it either explain or explain away the courage of martyrs and missionaries; the compassion of Father Damien or Mother Teresa; the character of men like the apostle Paul, Francis of Assisi, and John Wesley; or the communion enjoyed and attested by millions down the centuries in their life of prayer. It has to proceed as if these realities were never there. But to approve a position that is wedded to this ostrich-like course is surely irrational.

Second, anti-Christianity fails to mesh with life. Its diagnoses and prescriptions do not touch our deepest insights, pains, hopes, and needs. Two millennia of Christian influence, plus a plethora, if not a surfeit, of psychological cross-checking during the past century, has established pretty definitely what these are. We have a thirst for God, a desire for happiness, a need for friendship, minds that want truth, and an instinct for immortality. We need to know that we are loved, that our lives have significance, and that we have something to look forward to; or our happiness, such as it is, flies out of the window. We know guilt as a burden and see death as a threat, and we need to get rid of the burden and transcend the threat, or once again our happiness will fail. Christianity ministers to all these felt needs and relieves all these anxieties. Anti-Christianity cannot do any of this, so the only course it can take is to proceed as if these concerns were not there, or at least were not important. Sometimes it tries to bolster itself up by ridiculing those for whom these concerns retain importance, as if this very fact showed Christians to be poor specimens of humanity. But such posturing cannot stop anti-Christianity itself from seeming forlorn for its inability to rival that which it rejects; nor can it dispel the irrationality of opting for a view which cannot answer our basic questions in preference to one which can.

Third, anti-Christianity in all its forms is arbitrary. We see it to be held together by will-power, energy of assertion, and the turning of a blind eye to awkward facts rather than by force of evidence or cogency of argument. But to embrace a view of which such things have to be said is surely irrational.

If we were proposing to make a comprehensive case for Christianity, we would divide the task into two parts. First, we would labor to vindicate the Christian historical facts—Bible history in general and Christ and the coming of the Spirit in particular— and to justify the significance which Christians ascribe to those facts. With that, we would labor to show that the diagnosis of and the prescription for human needs in the gospel of Christ fit our actual condition as glove fits hand, and we would buttress our claim by appeal to two thousand years of Christian experience. As we went along, we would offer reasons for thinking that our account of Christianity (the "mere Christianity" of which we wrote earlier) is required by the evidence, is adequate to the evidence, and accounts satisfactorily for all relevant data, including the data of eccentric Christianity, reduced Christianity, and anti-Christianity—all three of which have had a very good run for their money in the twentieth century. Explanatory power is, after all, a mark of credibility; as anti-Christianity is discredited by its inability to account for the Christianity that it opposes, so "mere Christianity" is (as we think) rendered more plausible by its ability to account for that which diverges from it and fights against it. Thus we would try to show the complete reasonableness of a Christian commitment. But we shall not attempt anything so ambitious here.

What we tackle in this book is one theme only, that of humanness; and one question only, what being human involves. Our review of secular humanism has given this question a preliminary whirl, but it still needs more precise focusing. We focus it now as follows.

When we moderns—Christian or humanist, theist, atheist, or agnostic—say, "man," what we have in view is a functioning psycho-physical organism, a conscious embodied individual, male or female, who belongs to the human race; or, if we are speaking abstractly, we may have in mind the sum of such individuals viewed as a space-time collective. (In the latter case we might spell *Man* with a capital *M*.) From this standpoint, of course, our humanness is a given fact; only in extreme cases where the mind could not function and personal consciousness had failed would we raise the question whether the physical organism *was*, or *housed*, a human being. (Christians would divide as to which of those verbs they used at that point, though without any major difference of thought. (But now, the life-task for us who *are* human in the psycho-physical sense is to *become* human in terms of our personal quality—our character, emotional maturity, relational empathy, appreciation of value, knowledge of God, inner integration, depth of insight, wisdom, goodness, and love. Becoming human in this sense is what our question and this book are about.

What we shall try to show is that (1) secular humanism, which claims to exalt man, actually impedes his becoming human in terms of these personal qualities, and (2) Christianity, which starts by humbling man as a totally perverse sinner, has a directly humanizing effect on him at all these points. Christianity takes man seriously as an immortal soul whom God is preparing for glory; it gives him a sense of the transcendent; it shows him that eternal issues are involved in temporal choices; it draws him into a love-relationship of praise and thanks, worship and work, with the Father and the Son through the Spirit; it leads him to the discovery that self-forgetful love to God and men is the holiest and noblest disposition there is ("He showed me that all my preaching, writing and other ministry was absolutely *nothing* compared to my love relationship with him," wrote David Watson just before he died).[3]

Furthermore, Christianity sensitizes the sinner to moral realities across the board; it involves him in a work of grace for the renewing of his character in the image of Jesus Christ; it stretches him in sympathy and service manward and in fidelity and aspiration Godward; it gives him a hope beyond this world which sustains and refreshes him in this world; it pitchforks him into grueling fights with himself and the sin that so easily besets him— fights which toughen his moral fiber and deepen his experience of God's power. In short, Christianity makes a man (male or female) of him, a man that without God's grace he never could have been,

---

3. David Watson, *Fear No Evil* (London: Hodder and Stoughton and Wheaton, IL: Harold Shaw, 1984) p. 171.

a man who bears the moral likeness of the Lord Jesus Christ, his Savior, Master, and Friend. By expounding these things we shall make the case for calling Christianity the true humanism, by reason of its humanizing effect. We hope to make it apparent that Christian life is the good life for man.

We shall not say much more about secular humanism as a point of view. Clearly, it is not in the same league as Christianity when it comes to what used to be called "soul-making." It hides from us our eternal destiny, drops God out of our minds, encourages egoism and self-worship, undercuts morality by its relativism and permissiveness, undermines compassion for the weak and helpless who are not socially useful, encourages social programs to manage people as we manage animals, and in all these ways tends to desensitize and dehumanize. If individual humanists are not brash, brassy, arrogant, and insensitive, it will be despite their doctrine, not because of it; it will in fact be because they still bear the impress of the Christianity that they reject. There are, we know, many such humanists, who have been led to their present views not by the kind of mad pride that turned Lucifer into Satan and caused Adam's downfall, but by a compassionate desire to save others from bad experiences of religion like they themselves have had. With regard to the official humanist scheme, we have already said our piece. We would like, however, as we close this chapter, to say a word to this whole class of humanist fellow-travelers.

We say it softly; we know that otherwise we shall not be heard. We are very conscious that we cannot undo their bad experiences and that no apologies from us can cure those sores which we or our heavy-handed fellow-believers have inflicted. Nor can we expect that those who have been thus hurt will quickly cease to suspect that repression, frustration, philistinism, hypocrisy, and cruelty are the natural products of institutional Christianity. Nonetheless, we beg any humanists who see this book to think again, both about what they have let themselves in for and also about what the Christian humanism that stands against secular humanism will yield to any who take it seriously. Humanists are among those for whom we write, and though we do not plan to pull any punches on that account, we shall try to avoid the temptation of playing to our Christian gallery in a needlessly offensive way. (In any case, we could hardly give credibility to an account of Christian virtue by boorishness and discourtesy in stating it.) We shall attempt to write this book in a style that is as persuasive to secular humanists as it is to anyone else.

Having said that, we shall leave secular humanism behind us and move on to our main subject.

3

What Do We Need to Be Human?

If we answered a knock at the door on some freezing night and found a man all blue and shivering on the mat, our first instinct would be to bring him in at once, without asking any questions. If we were to ask, no doubt he would chatter out, "I just want to get warm."

We could plunge him in a hot tub, and this would no doubt do the trick. But it would be odd if we insisted that he stay there. Sooner or later he might venture to ask for a towel. Why? "Well, because I'd like to dry off." "Oh—you not only want to be warm, you want to be warm *and* dry, is that it?"

We can imagine here a sequence of exchanges in which it gradually becomes clear that a man needs to be warm and dry and fed and comfortable (we would not suggest starvation or a bed of nails for him after drying him off). Furthermore, he also needs to be healthy; all of our assistance would seem vain if suddenly he died of a heart attack.

But then we find that things do not stop even there. Here are the police thundering at the door with the news that this man is booked for the guillotine in an hour's time. Despite all that we had done for him, he was a man without hope. Unhappy creature!

A scene like this highlights something about us mortals, namely that the list of things we feel we must have before our lot is bearable is not a short one. In fact it gets longer and longer the more we think about it, without our ever even approaching such luxuries as wealth, fame, power, amusement, influence, pedigree, and so forth. Besides rock-bottom items like being warm and dry and fed and comfortable and healthy and hopeful, we would surely have to include such imponderables as identity ("Nobody knows my name!" is a cry of despair); and freedom (ask a man in Gulag); and companionship (here's an old woman climbing the weary steps to her flat in the West Forties); and peace (what do they want in Beirut or Belfast?).

The list does not stop even here. The more we mull over this business of being human, the more complicated it gets, try as we will to pare it down to simplicity. Sooner or later we will find that concepts like truth and beauty and goodness and love have crept in and refuse to be trimmed away. Truth? Who will urge that it does not matter if a man is sunk in illusion and falsehood? Beauty? Will endless squalor and tawdriness do? Goodness? What cynic will shrug off vice and cruelty as of no account? Love? Need we even raise the question?

On and on goes the list. It covers even such fugitive items as play ("All work and no play makes Jack a dull boy," said the nursery jingle, and what sage will deny it?); conflict (if no flint strikes the steel, there will be no spark); and worship (if I have nothing to adore and extol, how shall I fend off the final disgust and boredom that will make a monster of me?).

Who will tell us when the list is complete? What about esteem? A man can't flourish where he knows that he is thought to be an ass. And joy? Is this the sum of all the other items, or is it something distinct that might still elude me even though I have everything else? And meaning? Suppose I conclude that it all adds up to nothing—what then? Shall I put a bullet through my head?

As far as we know, we are the only creatures who are bedeviled by most of this. Once you get a dog fed he can manage. Give a puffin or a gazelle freedom to range around and it will cope without raising any awkward questions about esteem and meaning. Clearly there is some tremendous abyss that divides us from the other creatures on this planet with whom we share so much in the way of hunger and thirst and bone structure and instinct. They do not seem to be hagridden by all these other things. A dog at the end of his chain may wag his tail more and more feebly as the car disappears down the street, and we may say that he is disappointed. But no dog has ever *reflected* on that experience and written so much as a letter, let alone a sonnet or a drama about it. A dog may sniff at the carcass of its neighborhood playmate, but no dog has ever organized a funeral with palls, hearses, crepe, requiems, and shuttered windows in the wake of the event.

To pursue a line of thought like this is to arrive at the question: Well, then, what sort of creatures *are* we? Clearly zoology will not chase down the full answer since zoology does not deal in data like emotion, hope, despair, and joy. There is something besides bones and fur and habitat that sets us apart from mandrills, chickadees, whales, and all the rest of what used to be called the "lower orders of creation."

What we think about that "something" makes all the difference. A thousand answers have been attempted in the long history of our species. They range from the fears and fancies that lay behind the altars, sacrifices, and amulets of "primitive" religion to the cool fluorescence of New England transcendentalism and Unitarianism, and from the flat nontheism of the Voltaires, Huxleys, and Lord Russells to the bemused and courageous existentialism of an Albert Camus or a Simone de Beauvoir, with every conceivable variation in between.

No book in the world can undertake to sweep away all options except its own when it comes to talking about what human life might mean and how we may best do justice to this baffling topic. Even prophets and apostles did not attempt quite so much. They testified, rather, to what they had seen and heard. If what they said was true, then other options fell away, of course. You cannot have both Baal and Yahweh. Dagon must stoop if God is the Lord. If Billy Graham is right, Carl Sagan and Madalyn Murray O'Hair are wrong. We cannot keep all the options open. But equally we cannot here go through them one by one; nor shall we try.

This book is an attempt to describe the sense in which the Christian religion both undergirds and nourishes all that seems to mark our true humanness. That will seem a strange paradox, no doubt, to some. It is often supposed that to fly into Christianity is to fly away from being human. That is to say people take refuge in religion if they are weary of "life." They run into the shelter of the Church if the winds of sheer reality prove too tumultuous for them. Thinking all will be well, they leave the terrible questions on one side, sublimate their needs in the lovely smoke of the incense that goes up from the altar, and settle their moral uncertainties by taking on the lifestyle of their Christian peers. They inhale the great opiate of the people seeking rest for their souls.

It is easy enough to see why things might look like this from the outside. Christian people have not always been models of courage, integrity, fortitude, and charity, and the devotion which some of them have practiced does seem to have led them away from "life." But most of them would doubtless urge that though they may be doing a poor job of it, nonetheless they believe themselves to be on the path that leads to the fulfillment of all human hopes and potentialities. The faithful of any religion in the world make the same claim, of course; but the task undertaken in this book is to point to what human experience looks like when it is seen in the light of *Christian* vision. And here we face something momentous. If what the saints tell us is true, Christian vision illuminates the whole of our experience with incomparable splendor. Far from beckoning us away from raw human experience, this vision opens up to us its full richness, depth, and meaning.

To be fully Christian, in other words, is to *live*; it is to be fully human. And this is no callow or easily bought testimony. We hear this from some of the most luminous and titanic minds ever to appear on the human scene, as well as from peasants, shopkeepers, kings, hermits, Easterners, Westerners, Africans, Americans, and people of all other sorts and conditions. They all say that to have followed Christ the Savior is to have been brought to wholeness, freedom, and joy, most of them through great struggle and pain. We do not hear from them that to have known Christ is to have escaped from their humanness. On the contrary, it is to have become human, since the One they have followed is, so they say, the one perfectly whole, free, and good man ever to have lived. He was all of that because, they say, he was Immanuel: God with us. He was the "Second Adam," that is, the perfect example of all that humanity was meant to be.

How We Imagine Ourselves

But what were we meant to be? This question has vast ramifications, and we need to open it up. Let us first take soundings from the huge testimony of human imagination. What have we, the human beings in the case, suspected that we were supposed to be? How have we viewed the puzzles that beleaguer our existence?

From the beginning of time we humans have tried to come at this business in a number of ways: in poetry, philosophy, ethical systems, religious systems, and so forth. Perhaps the most vivid of these attempts is seen in art. When you dig up some long-dead city you look for the things that they made, since artifacts give you clues as to how they imagined life. You dig up fifth and sixth century Britain, for example, and find heavy enamel and gold jewelry, whereas in Siam you find very spidery silver jewelry. Delicacy and subtlety, then, were prized more in the latter world than in the former. In ancient Aegean cultures you find little female figurines with immense breasts whereas in the nineteen-twenties in Europe and America, designers went to great lengths to make women look flat-chested. Motherhood and motherliness, one supposes, were valued more in the one culture than the other. In eighteenth century France men's wigs got higher and higher, whereas in the nineteen-forties in America it became popular for men to have very short, stubbly haircuts. Evidently fanciful role-play was thought of as the essence of maleness in the first case, and blunt matter-of-factness in the second. We are meeting here different ideas of ideal life. In truth, everything that we make, whether it is a fertility idol, the hilt of a scimitar, a mantilla, a temple at Karnak, a Morris dance, a spade, a computer, a requiem, or a Cadillac, says something about how we see ourselves. It exhibits something about our hopes, our fears, our standards, our goals, and indeed about the whole scale of good and evil as we see it. Nor is this true of "functional" objects only. Even the sheerest "decoration"—ormolu or linenfold panelling—says, "Down with drabness; it is *worth* decking our life thus."

But of course some things are more important than others when it comes to revealing what we mortals think about ourselves and our life. A pair of spats or a satin slipper will tell us something, but a ziggurat or an icon will tell us much more, for it is in such items as ziggurats and icons that we glimpse all the brightest hopes, deepest fears, and most serene longings of the human soul. One has only to look at the monumental bulls and stiff-bearded giants of Assyria and Babylonia, or the bird-headed men and many-armed dancing goddesses of Egypt and India, or the majestic totem poles of the North-West Indians to see that something unique and arresting is stirring in us mortals—something that inclines us to make these things. The works of man's imagination stir, haunt, thrill, wring the withers, and make us feel that there is far more to life than once we supposed. It is as if we had been asleep till works of imagination stabbed us awake.

Who is this demure madonna, and who is this plump infant on her lap with the orb of the world in his hand? Who are these naked people being prodded along by obscene imps with pitchforks? What are these arches here at Rheims and these trumpets, and voices singing *Laudate et superexaltate eum in saeculo* ("Praise him and magnify him for ever," as the Anglican Prayer Book renders it)? And all this speech and song about sheep safely grazing? Why tell us nightmare tales of Lear and Oedipus, and ravish our minds with the poetry of Eden, the Garden of Adonis, and the Celestial Rose? Why regale us with all of these blisses and abysses? Why not leave us alone? But imagination, once it is stirred into life, will not leave us alone.

If we wiped the slate clean and began again tomorrow morning, it would not be long before we found some boy sitting on a rock somewhere trying to make a whistle out of a reed, and some girl in an empty room pointing her toes, and some old woman mumbling prayers. Human beings simply will not believe it when told that there is nothing there and that consequently everything is absurd and no endeavor is worth making. Or, we may permit our minds to be argued into this, but our imaginations will not come to rest there. Imagination will keep us acting as though there are gods to propitiate, and death to ward off, and serenity to be sought, and love and beauty to be pursued, and harmony and balance and order to be achieved. So it always has been, and so it will no doubt continue. And this is what both art and religion are about, and sometimes politics too.

So Many Schemes

Many schemes for achieving at least some of these goals have been offered, all of them with the promise that here at last is the truth of the matter, or, at any rate, here is the way we must organize our life if we are to find it bearable. Some of the schemes cross the frontier between religion and politics; they give us a theory about our life, and then go on to organize it for us in light of their theory. The theories, however, regularly prove to be too narrow, and the schemes too slick, to be convincing. Fascism, for example, amounts to this: Fulfillment may somehow be found by being caught up in the state. The highest happiness, in other words, is to be lost in a large crowd. This is not the sort of vision to encourage the work of a Jan Vermeer, say, who thought that one small corner of a room might blazon, by its very stillness and domesticity, something of the glory and mystery of human life.

The Marxist ideal often gets to looking like fascism: The bright promise which is held out is couched in great collective terms, with words like "class" and "workers" and "the people" furnishing the vocabulary. Happiness is a new socio-economic order, which you enjoy as part of a large social unit, and that is all the meaning there is in life. It would be difficult for a man like Hamlet to make his troubles seem important to Marxists. All the systems and theologies that promise "liberation" speak in immense, collective terms and hold out to us as being just around the corner, the attractive prospect of earthy and apple-cheeked bonhomie among all simple folk in the world. It is a wonderful vision, but it would not have grabbed Luther in the days of his agony in the monastery when he was seeking a gracious God.

The anarchists, who pop into history from time to time, sing a utopian song also: All will come right if we will only cast off the bonds of law and government and trust everybody's good nature to arbitrate quarrels. This view fails to explain just what it is about us mortals that gives rise to screaming tugs-of-war over the shovel in the sandbox, and to such vengeful tales as Cain and Abel, *The Merchant of Venice*, and the *Oresteia;* but the idea that every normal person is an altruist dies hard, and anarchism remains a hardy notion, with strong appeal to people (and there are always plenty of them) who are fed up with the apparent inadequacies of the established government.

At the opposite extreme to socio-political panaceas stands the dream of solving life's problems by withdrawing into an ideal simplicity of one sort or another. Everyone from time to time wants simplicity and hopes to find in it the key to tranquillity and goodness. Thoreau went off to a pond, and a hundred years later his writing led a whole generation of adolescents to hope that simple life by ponds is the answer to all life's conundrums. The difficulty here is how to get the struggling hordes of Calcutta, say, all off to a sufficient number of ponds. What shall we do about so *many* of us, we might ask. The human race is four billion strong, and rising. There are not enough ponds to go around!

Rural dreams have a powerful grip. No one doubts that a meadow full of buttercups is more soothing than the floor of the Stock Exchange or the Rotterdam docks with their banging tailgates, cursing longshoremen, and hooting klaxons. Wordsworth's nature-mysticism sounds a note that calls us with nearly irresistible sweetness. The thatched roofs and lowing cattle and purling brooks of all romantic primitivism stand far away from the macadam, neon, polystyrene foam, and ersatz coffee cream that surround us now; and the distance breaks our hearts. But the trouble with the thatched roofs is that we in America can't get to them, and if we ever do make a hasty visit to these far-off peaceful scenes, we aren't allowed to stay and bask in them. The tales of Odysseus and Abraham and Frodo and the Flying Dutchman and a thousand others make it sadly clear that willy-nilly, and relationally if not geographically, we must all move *on*. Life is like that. We read these tales and weep, not so much for those heroes as for ourselves.

Sometimes we try to escape into peace by anchoring our hopes beyond this world of change and decay. The imaginative trappings of religion make possible such an escape. Pictures of a cloudless realm of incorruptibility accompany all religion. We need only look at Valhalla, the Happy Hunting Ground, Nirvana, the Oversoul, Paradise, or Heaven to see this. It is a poor religion that obliges you to win, only to tell you that it all leads to nothing in any event.

Some religions tell us to look on our present world as a sort of prison for the soul. It is even urged that the material world, including our own flesh, is not only a prison, but evil as well. Goodness, it is said, will only be found in the spiritual, that is, the nonmaterial, realm. All forms of transcendentalism, Gnosticism, Manichaeism, and Platonism entail some such suggestion, and all mysticism beckons the soul away from the toils of time and sense into a realm of clarity, purity, freedom, and ecstasy. The appeal is almost irresistible; but then we find ourselves wondering how it can have been that this world, with all of its rocks and trees and earth and flesh, can have furnished so much joy to the human spirit and whether we may not see this world as not only cloaking but also revealing something about the eternal realm. Human imagination keeps conceiving, and perceiving, our world to be the herald, not the enemy, of Paradise. Otherwise why does art, and nature with it, seem to present us with the quality that we call sublime? Does the Venus de Milo, for example, suggest something merely gross and corruptible? Is the taste of raspberries nothing? Is the mist on the morning lake only the exhaling of some poisonous fen that we are doomed to inhabit? Is the icon of the Mother and Child picturing only a sordid prison house?

Whatever may be the true answer to all of these questions, we may at least say that all that is most passionately human in us wants the answer to be no. We at least wish that the Venus and the raspberries and the mist and the Madonna were hints of something true and undying. Our imaginations insist that if it all comes to nothing, then existence itself is an exquisite cheat.

There are in fact courageous viewpoints abroad that maintain just this, as our previous chapter began to show. All forms of materialism must come to some such conclusion, since if this world is all that there is, then the taste of raspberries along with all heroic and saintly deeds and all passion and charity will indeed tumble into the endless silence of the grave, and that will be the end of them. With this view it is useless to hunt for "meaning" anywhere since meaning implies some point beyond this realm of decay where all the bits and pieces come home and form a pattern. Or to change the picture, our search for meaning looks for some point where all the tangled threads of life are sorted out and knit into an eternal tapestry. If what we have is only a rat's nest, then life is indeed solitary, poor, nasty, brutish, and short—and worse, a cheat, since it does in fact encourage us to look for some such pattern.

Most of us dodge these terrible notions. Only a few souls have the candor and courage to face the bleak possibility that the rat's nest is all and that there is no point beyond the scrim of time to which we may look for any knitting up of things into any pattern. In our own century we have seen this spirit in the existentialists— such figures as Camus, Sartre, and Simone de Beauvoir. For them, since there is no "outside" point to which the jumble of life may be referred, the only thing a person can do is to make courageous choices in the time-span he has here and thus somehow "authenticate" his existence. Rather than merely bumbling and shuffling through seventy odd years in an apathetic and dispirited way, he can at least rise up, seize the absurdity of it all, and make a clear-eyed choice to live this way or that. This individual will thus have coaxed *some* shape out of the otherwise amorphous mass which is life. Sometimes this desperate view results in a massive cynicism. But then sometimes we find a man—Camus says—who admits that the abyss yawns and that he is going to fall into it, and yet he will not allow that one ought to settle for a barren, self-pitying life of not caring for anything or anyone at all.

The difficulty here for Camus and all of us is this word *ought*. Where did it come from? If nothing means anything then how can we introduce this word into our discussion? We can only have an *ought* if there is some fixed point outside the jumble that suggests that one pattern (selflessness, say) is better than some other (cruelty, say). No one has ever been able to find any footing for *ought* inside the closed circle of present experience. You cannot infer "what ought to be" simply from studying "what has been and is." Camus himself suggested that the only finally serious question is the question of suicide: Either life is worth living or it isn't. If it is, then where in God's name are we to find the locale of its worth? Hamlet appreciated this problem and feared that the answer might lie in "that undiscovered country from whose bourn no traveler returns." Camus felt that we could not allow ourselves to suppose that any such country exists. There is a sort of elegant irony in Camus's death—smashed up in a speeding sports car against a tree. Was this his final act of courage and authenticity or was it an accident? Is everything an accident? Very piquant questions.

But as Camus is the exception among existentialists, so existentialists are the exception among human beings. The anxious certainty that there is "something out there" is almost universal, and always has been. It is certainly what we see at work in the so-called primitive religions. Every tribe and culture we come upon, either in the jungle or under some archaeological mound, seems to have been frantically preoccupied with this question. Altars, sacrifices, amulets, processions, castrations, dances, knives, sacred oaks, sacred bulls, and sacred precincts—who can number the items that show up here? Clearly everyone was trying to get in touch with something or someone outside the circle of the daily pots and pans; and whatever was out there clearly needed to be appeased. Christians have seen this as a smudged racial memory of the Creator's wrath at his creatures' rebellion. During the past century, however, the fashion has been to dismiss it as a bad dream which studied irreligion must cure. In the modern West we have managed fairly successfully to expunge religion's fear, so that community life is now carried forward on a "secular" basis. Decisions on such topics as death and life and morality (abortion, euthanasia, sex, and so on) are sought not from priests or clergy but from judges and psychiatrists and social experts, who do not consult any oracle or make any libations while they are reaching their conclusions.

It is true that you find old women in black babushkas, and young people too, going into church in places like Russia and Poland, where the superstition called Christianity was supposed to have been stopped years ago. Russians were being asked as early as 1917 to wake up from the opiate of religion, but apparently you cannot rouse everyone. In the West the process has been somewhat more gradual. Governments have not suddenly declared that religion is false, but the general flow of popular notions following the wake of science and "progress" implies as much, so that in learned journals and serious discussions and chic parties you cannot assume that everyone who speaks has said his prayers that morning or is forming his opinions on a basis that could be called the fear of the Lord. We have "come of age," they tell us, and we are able to forge our own way of life now without consulting the gods.

The Liberal Temper

It is difficult to find a label for this frame of mind. *Modernism* might do, except that very few people like to think of themselves as modernists, and in any event the term was sullied during the theological battles of the late nineteenth century and has a specific odium attached to it. On the other hand the word *modern* seems harmless enough to most people, although no one quite knows what it means. There is a whiff of snobbism in it since the tacit implication is that modern ideas are more *advanced* than ancient or medieval ones. This may mean that our ideas relate to things that are cleaner or faster or more powerful than their older counterparts; or else that our notions are more useful, as when we conceptualize the Einsteinian universe as over against the Ptolemaic; or that our preferred thoughts are more verifiable, as in the idea that sickness is a matter of bacilli and not of divine judgment. At all events, like Millie in the popular 1967 film, we like to regard ourselves as "thoroughly modern." Even devout people accept most of the modern program and agree to tuck their religion into whatever slots are left over for the As-Yet-Unsolved.

Liberal, as in "liberal arts" and "liberal education," may be the most useful term for this frame of mind that we are trying to define. In its broadest usage the word *liberal* covers more than mere politics. The note it strikes is of a certain urbanity. One is not trapped inside cultic or local prejudices. There is a tolerant elasticity about one's attitudes. One is not easily shocked since one has learned how to entertain a broad spectrum of opinions. One can nod and murmur appreciatively while someone expresses a point of view opposite to one's own. One is not threatened. We might observe this frame of mind at religious congresses where men hum solemn approval of forms of piety and dogma that stand at polar extremes from their own: A thoroughly modern free churchman, in robin's-egg blue polyester or baggy jeans, will applaud some cloaked and grizzled archimandrite from Syria, simply in the interest of good relations. No question arises as to whether either of the two men is in error and ought to change course. No flint strikes against any steel. Everyone is being liberal.

There is, of course, a great deal to be said for this. Amiable congresses are to be preferred to holy wars, inquisitions, and the stake. The difficulty lurking in it all, though, is that to keep the liberal enterprise afloat you must steer past the jagged question of truth. The liberal way is to take this necessity in stride, requiring pacific tolerance as an expression of the modesty which sees that no one has all the truth and anyone may be wrong about anything. So, on liberal principles, a Luddite may feel that machines will destroy us all, and he may be right; but he ought not to come in and smash our wives' sewing machines on that account. A Marxist may think that private property ought to be abolished, but that does not entitle him to blow up Miss Maltby's Seminary for Young

Ladies. A free churchman may believe that ritual is going to strangle all Catholic Christians eventually, but he should not therefore come shouting into mass in an attempt to set them all free. At least the liberal attitude would seem to say so, and so far it is right. "Live and let live" seems a weary maxim; but what else can we do?

Nothing, on the workaday level, obviously. If people seem to us to choose error and destruction, we must defend to the death their right to do so, even if we write books (like this one), carry placards, and organize movements to try to dissuade them. But clearly this attitude, which you may call liberal if you wish, and which certainly seems to be required by simple civility, is very far from being the sort of thing that will nourish a man's soul. There is no life in the maxim "Live and let live." Mere liberalism is dead by itself. It is an ethic for people with certainties and goals, but it has no certainties and goals of its own. It might be compared to the yellow line down the middle of the road; it won't of itself get you anywhere, but it will warn you off violating the other fellow's right to drive in the opposite direction, even if he is headed wrong and you happen to know that. The liberal attitude is like the cautions that attend eating: Do have some vinegar on your salad, but don't try drinking a gallon; to do that is impolite, and besides it will make you sick. These cautions are there in the interest of civility and health, but they are not food. They help us to function, but they do not nourish us. They leave us cool and blasé, but they do not satisfy our imagination, nor touch the immortal longings of our souls.

This is all a way of pointing out a great hollow in our own century. If there is one point at which we would claim to have advanced over earlier generations, it would be on this point of open-mindedness. We do not like crusades, inquisitions, or uncouth, narrow, boorish prejudices (we say). Our spirits are liberal; we are for coolness and tolerance. This is all to the good. But we may have mistaken this liberality for the main thing. What do we feed on? You cannot feed on open-mindedness. Liberality is a fair safeguard, but like all safeguards it has no substance itself. We will starve if we tell ourselves that an open mind is enough. What is going into this open mind? What is escaping from it? It has been said that if you open your mind wide enough a lot of rubbish will get dumped into it; also the open-valve mind that lets out all the pressure has an uncomfortable flat-tire effect, slowing us down by making us feel that nothing matters much after all—making us, in fact, feel "punctured."

The human soul asks for more than this. No psalm of aspiration like the great *Quemadmodum desiderat cervus ad fontes aquarum*—"Like as the hart desireth the water brooks, so longeth my soul after thee, O God"—could be written about one's longing for liberality of mind. ". . . so longeth my soul for open-mindedness, O my God"? That is ashes! Even on the level of mere art, leaving aside religious exclamations like this psalm, you cannot get much out of liberality alone. What heroic figures do we know whose stature is to be attributed to mere open-mindedness? What frescoes, murals, statues, sonatas, or poems have we got that express and extol mere toleration? The desire for this open-mindedness in society has in the past called forth satire and invective against prejudice and ignorance; but it will not raise monuments like Dante's *Divina Commedia,* the Chartres Cathedral, or Beethoven's Ninth Symphony. It takes vision and passion to do that.

Christianity Speaks

It is hard to say what we human beings do long for. If there were only some magic key that would let us through the door in the wall! As we have seen already, any number of bidders offer us such keys: fascism, Marxism, mysticism, hedonism, existentialism, liberalism; the -isms that would bewitch us make a long line. But they are all beds that are too short for us and blankets that are too narrow. Like the dungeon called Little-ease, in which one could not lie down, they cramp and atrophy us in ways that are as painful as they are demeaning. Whatever their strengths and virtues at particular points, they end up selling us short. Whatever rides they took us for, whatever trips they gave us, whatever insights we feel we owe to them, the door in the wall remains shut. What, we ask, are we to make of ourselves? How shall we account for the fathomless hunger of the human spirit? For its serene dignity? For its contradictions—its cruelty and egoism, along with its capacity for good humor and its passion for freedom? What are these godlike aspirations that bedevil us? But why at the same time do we feel we should be diminished and disinherited if we were not cloaked in flesh and blood? What analysis, what story will account for our remorseless quest for identity, purity, peace, truth, beauty, joy, adoration, love, and meaning?

It is the argument of this book that in the Christian gospel we find the story that leaves nothing out. In the events of the Creation, Fall, Redemption, Law, Prophecy, Annunciation, Incarnation, Epiphany, Passion, Resurrection, Ascension, Pentecost, Judgment, and Final Glory, we have the whole drama of humanity brought to its proper fulfillment out of its present frustrations. We contend that, rightly understood, Christianity is the true humanism, since it has for its purpose the forming and freeing and exalting of our true humanness. The Christian story is ordinarily said to be about salvation from sin. But that means nothing different from what we are saying, for it is sin that dehumanizes, and it is only in the matrix of holiness that authentic humanness takes shape.

Ironically, all secular attempts to find a way by which we mortals may live fully and freely seem to end finally in inward desolation, or at best in a stoic refusal to succumb in face of what must horrify us beyond all else, namely the end of our own being. It is only outside of these little limits that we find a point to which we may trace all the random lines of our experience and for the first time begin to see a pattern where there seemed to be only a tangle.

Christianity brings news of that point into our small circumference. As one very early Christian writer put it: "God, who at sundry times and in divers manners spake in times past unto the fathers by the prophets, hath in these last days spoken unto us by his Son, . . . by whom also he made the worlds . . . the express image of his person . . ." (Hebrews 1:1–3; we cite the King James Version, which best preserves the dignity of the original). St. John tells of this same revelation in this way: "In the beginning was the Word, and the Word was with God, and the Word was God. . . . Through him all things were made. . . . The Word became flesh and lived for a while among us. We have seen his glory. . . ." (John 1:1,3,14, NIV).

These are very strange tidings. It becomes apparent at once that this "point" outside the circle is, on the Christian view, not so much a point as a Person. (Although it would certainly be the point at which all lines converge.)

This Person is God, the Creator, whose name is designated by the Hebrew letters YHWH.

That name began to be known to the Hebrews in the experience of the patriarchs and of Israel and their prophets and kings. And then, says Christianity, it appeared openly on the stage of our history, born as a man, of a Virgin mother, and given the human name Jesus. Since that time Jesus has been worshiped by Christians as the Lord, the Savior, the Holy One of God, the Word of God, the Son of God, Immanuel (God with us), and indeed as God himself. This same Jesus is also the Son of Man (his favorite designation for himself), which means, along with some other things, that he is the figure in whom we see all the potentialities and aspirations of our humanity in all of their freedom and full development. Morally and spiritually, intellectually and experientially, motivationally and relationally, the incarnate Son of God stands before us as perfect man, the one totally human being that history knows.

This acquaintance with the God-Man explains why Christians look on all attempts to define and arrange human life in merely "secular" terms as misbegotten, futile, and eventually blasphemous. Christ, by existing, has shown us that there is no authentically human life independent of its Source and End. We were made by God, for God, and it is we who have torn ourselves away, like rivulets trying to cut themselves off from the spring. The water may trickle on down the hill for a bit, giving the brief illusion that all is well. But presently what you have is a dry stream bed.

Some such bleak picture as this presents itself to the Christian imagination when "Man" is talked about with no reference to God. When you do that you are talking about an illusion. God is there even when you have your back to him, and it is he who gives you the breath with which you deny his reality. But the illusion that man can be human without God is one that our own era chases, says Christianity, like a fox-fire in a swamp. The "light" of our modern Enlightenment turns out to be a travesty of real light, like a glimmering and treacherous will-o'-the-wisp. In the name of humanism it has led us into subhuman life.

Commending the Christian Claim

Can we demonstrate the truth of what we have just said? Can we show infallibly from experience that while efforts to manage without the Christian God are always futile, the Christian ordering of life invariably yields conscious success and instant satisfaction? No; and we should not expect to, nor should we view our inability to do so as counting against the credibility of the Christian claim. There are two reasons for this. First, the earthly life of the One whom Christians follow was a life of apparent failure and bitter rejection, and the servant is not above his master. Second, the Bible writers, the prophets, psalmists, and apostles, along with the Lord whose words the evangelists record, have abundantly warned us that life will not be a bed of roses for those who serve God, and their biographical narratives amply bear this out.

Of certain of God's saints in the Old Testament period the writer to the Hebrews said: "Some faced jeers and flogging, while still others were chained and put in prison. They were stoned; they were sawed in two; they were put to death by the sword. They went about in sheepskins and goatskins, destitute, persecuted and mistreated—the world was not worthy of them. They . . . were all commended for their faith . . ." (Hebrews 11:36–39). Can we expect it to be different for New Testament Christians? No; we are told explicitly that it will not be. Says Paul in his last letter: "Everyone who wants to live a godly life in Christ Jesus will be persecuted" (2 Timothy 3:12). Constant pressure and pain may thus be confidently expected in the Christian life.

We are actually given the philosophy of this. Experiences of being opposed and crushed are God's fatherly discipline, whereby he licks us into moral shape and makes us sharers in his holiness (see Hebrews 12:5–11). Also, hardships provide occasion for supernatural life to show itself in us when natural life alone would have gone under (see 2 Corinthians 4:7–12). Also, they make Christians long the more earnestly for that future life that is their final goal, in which "God will wipe away every tear from their eyes" (Revelation 7:17; see Romans 8:16–25). All very clear in theory, you will agree; but as present confirmations of the truth of the claim that the Christian life is the truly human and fulfilled life, the thoughts clearly leave something to be desired. The only certainty seems to be that Christian confidence will itself again and again look like illusion, as the Christian pilgrimage unfolds in the form of trouble all the way.

But now look again. The oddest thing about the Christian vision is that, mad and unrealistic as it appears, it seems to have brought not only consolation but also joy and courage to hundreds of millions of people for two millennia now, and this despite the troubles of which, as expected, they have had what might seem to be more than their fair share. Unlike other religions, Christianity has leaped all boundaries of culture, race, intellect, sex, age, and preference, so that there are mumbling crones and urbane *ancien regime* cardinals, apple-cheeked Minnesota teenagers along with Zulu kings, Mississippi sharecroppers along with Oxford dons, Albanian Baptists along with Spanish Franciscans, and sobbing Appalachian zealots along with cool St. Albertus Magnus, all coming, awed and silent, to the stable where the Infant King lies and to the Cross on which the God-Man is nailed.

How shall we show that what they all claim to see—God incarnate, modeling the perfectly human life and then making it possible for sinful men and women to start living it—is not a massive illusion? How shall we prove to the satisfaction of all that the faith of this throng is not an elaborate piece of self-deception? As we said, there is no direct, knock-down way of doing it. There is a Cradle, a Cross, a Tomb that was found empty, and later an empty mountain top; these are historical facts which cannot reasonably be doubted or ignored; but a credibility gap at the level of the imagination still yawns when Christians begin to speak of the bearing of these facts on our humanness today. How do Christian claims hold up (it would be asked) over against the plain realities of life, especially of modern life? It looks for all the world (it would be said) as though all that ever came of those bygone concerns was superstition, religious war, and oppression of the human spirit. There is a whole new agenda now: science, and communications, and technology, and our knowledge of human behavior, and the shrinking global village, and computers, and the widening gap between affluence and poverty, and, most frightening of all, the thermonuclear cloud. These immensities do not leave us much leisure to dawdle in the precincts of those little Galilean shrines. We cannot imagine that the Christian story, whatever its basis in fact, has any direct significance for life in a world so different from the ancient world as ours is. So people feel, and so they often speak. What move can we make in response?

The best that we can do, perhaps, is look again at this great jumble that we call human experience and to listen to those who have believed that light has shined in our darkness and that the

Word has spoken—indeed, that our humanity was greeted with "Hail" by the Most High himself (as he prepared the body of the Virgin to bear him and his own body in which she was to bear him) when he came to redeem and glorify the humanity he had made and loved. That, therefore, is the course on which we now proceed.

4

Freedom

None of us wants to be bound. But of course everyone is bound one way or another. None of us is wholly free from responsibilities that hem us in: going out to work, getting there on time, doing the job, coming home to family, looking after taxes and bills, fixing leaky faucets, or mowing the lawn; there are a hundred items. Also, there are binding vows: the marriage covenant for example. These "bind" us in the sense that they limit our freedom to flit about in an unattached way. When you see a married man forever showing up alone at functions you know that something is awry. Some men and women have taken religious vows that would seem to destroy all freedom; poverty, chastity, and obedience hardly seem a recipe for liberty. Then, too, there are natural bonds: children, aging parents, and friends in need. These all stand between us and the scot-free ideal that our imaginations some-times conjure up.

Reaching for Freedom

That scot-free ideal looks for all the world like freedom. Think, for example, of what you are meant to feel about those lithe and languid creatures in *New Yorker* advertisements. There seem to be no restrictions on the money they have to put into clothes, for a start. And they never seem to eat dinner anywhere but at Maxim's, The Four Seasons, or in some chic little bistro. If they eat at home, it is always candles and firelight and silver and cognac, all of it leading up to something thrilling and probably illicit. What are you meant to feel about them? You are meant to feel *envious*, that's what. Fancy having all these gods and goddesses for your friends! You would spend your holidays draped on the deck of someone's yawl, with endless supplies of exotic foods and beverages aboard. You wouldn't even have a picnic without linen and wicker and cold poached salmon and champagne. You would have no worries about money or health. You would be *free*!

Most of us, of course, never approach this luxurious picture of things so glossily dangled in front of us, nor do we resent the fact that we cannot expect to. But we still find ourselves longing to be free from things as they are. It becomes very difficult for us to feel that our plain meat-and-potatoes routines are anything but a grind. This is no doubt one reason why so many people nowadays seek escape from flatness and tedium in cocaine, marijuana, or alcohol. That way you can have a brief experience of euphoria before the humdrum closes in once more. Whether that euphoria is really freedom is a question, but you feel that it is, and that feeling illustrates our point. We see ourselves as tied to a treadmill, and we want to be free.

The yearning for freedom in most of us must take simpler forms. Here is a woman, burdened with too much work and too much weight, with damp wisps of hair pasted to her sweat-beaded forehead; but it is Saturday afternoon in the park, and she has found a green bench, and she has kicked off her shoes and is wiggling her toes shyly in the grass. You could write a whole story from that one glimpse. The wiggling of those fat, white toes in that cool grass is an emblem of a soul crying out for the Elysian Fields. Or again: there is a ragtag of twelve-year-olds slouching and shuffling on the corner. What they want is *out*—out of dullness, out of households where they are brutalized, out of bondage of being under age. To be older, independent, able to go places and do things—that, to them, would be freedom, and for that they long. Or here is a weary man in a striped suit on the New York Central with just enough time to get a martini or two before the train stops at New Canaan. That glass is like a phial in a fairy tale: drink this elixir, and your troubles will recede a bit, and you will be that much more free. If it is Friday night, he is promising himself two days of freedom before the office routine starts again. ("I may be a wage slave on Monday / But I am a free man on Sunday.")

Or here is a woman in a tweed suit sitting in that same train with an attaché case open in her lap, glancing through a sheaf of high-level market analyses. She has come from the boardroom just now, and her vice-presidents have made their reports to her. No tiny jars of Gerber's strained apricots litter *her* kitchen; she has shucked off spouse and children for the boardroom and the condominium in Bronxville. She feels she has found freedom, and with it identity, self-respect, and a sense of power. Who, she asks herself, would go back to the strollers and potty-chairs from this? Lucky lady! But let multiple sclerosis be diagnosed, and her sense of freedom will be in jeopardy.

Ask the man with the martini why he did not order a glass of milk instead, and he will testify to the greater power of the gin to bring him a bit of relief. Relief from what? Oh, just from the general pressures and harryings of the day. Or ask the lads on the corner: "What are *you* doing?" "Nothing—what's it to you?" "Well I mean, are you more *comfortable* here than at home?" "Hey man—who's asking for comfort?" "We just want out. We can get things here." "What things?" Well, the usual commodities, it turns out, that promise an hour's escape from boredom. Even the sweaty lady on the park bench likes to get the old pumps off and feel something natural like grass stroking the white and pasty skin of her pinched feet. Not to be trussed in leather and nylon, just for five minutes—to her, it's a bit of freedom, and that's why she does it.

From the yawl to the martini to the street corner to the park bench, we all snatch at whatever tag ends of freedom we can get. We would go mad or die if we did not have at least some interludes when we can feel that we are calling our own shots, so to speak. If life is nothing at all but demands and obligations and deadlines and hopping to at others' beck and call, then we are no better off than galley slaves at their oars. And if we have only a limited span—say seventy years, give or take a few—then we had better see to it that we garner as much freedom as we can, right now.

The clever operators know how to do it, of course. They can parlay their money into huge increases in oil, real estate, securities, and so forth; and this gives them the power simply to purchase whatever freedom they want. By being clever and astute and hard-working, and by being at the right place at the right time, all sorts of people have "made it"—in journalism (at the time of this writing one television anchor man has a salary of over a million a year), or on the stage, or in films, or in management, or in academia, or government, or wherever. It is very exciting. Money is only part of the benefit. Prestige (which is the outside shell of self-esteem) is another. Power (still self-esteem, really) is another. But freedom is the real reward—now I can choose! No limitation need any longer dictate where I live, or in what sort of house, or who my circle of friends will be, or what "style of life" I shall opt for. Because of my success, I am now free to determine all these things for myself.

It all makes vast sense, and we admire those who "make the grade" in this way, and yet deep down we have our doubts. Almost everyone at some fleeting moment gasps out something about getting out of the rat race, or going off to some desert island, or whatever. In other words, there seems to be lodged deep inside us all some notion that something is wrong if we have to pay the sort of price exacted by the world for gaining the sort of freedom we have described. But only a rare few take any serious steps to think their way to the bottom of the problem.

Focusing Freedom

What we need to do at this point is to query our assumption that freedom is always and entirely a matter of externals. There is more to freedom than being free *from* particular conditions, limits, and pressures; though that is all we have talked about so far. But when you are free from everything that you feel is an unwelcome burden or restraint, you still may not be free in the deeper sense. The truth is that freedom at its heart relates to one's inner life. There is more to it than being off the treadmill and out of the rat race; more to it also than having a wide range of choices and being able to please oneself in making them. Freedom in essence is a matter of being free *for* the life that you recognize as the most gratifying and the most delightful. Freedom is thus the condition of the contented person, the person who chooses to continue as he is because he knows there is nothing better, who refuses to be shifted from what he is and where he is to something worse, and whose life is marked by enjoyment as a habitual experience.

Jesus as we meet him in the Gospels is the supreme example of freedom in this sense, as we shall see more fully in due course. For the moment it is enough to point out that his constant choice, and his lasting contentment, was to do his Father's will, and that, in his life of personal obedience, he was free, integrated, whole-hearted, and at peace, despite all the poverty, hostility, injustice, and degradation to which he was exposed. Inner freedom does not depend on external circumstances, as Aleksandr Solzhenitsyn found in Gulag; it depends, rather, on a degree of integrity and commitment to which many, it must be feared, never attain. From this point on in our argument, it is inner freedom that we talk about. For this, we believe, is what everyone is really after, no matter how unclear and unfocused their search. It's not the mere fact of not being pushed around or of being able to choose for oneself, but it's the inner contentment that a good choice, made and maintained with integrity, will bring. On this under-standing we proceed with our analysis.

Not all nonreligious people are selfish cynics. Some try to tem-per the claims of personal fulfillment with an awareness of the claims of others. All politeness, helpfulness, generosity, kind-ness, and unselfishness, spring from some such source as this. A man does not have to be religious to give some of his money for famine relief or cancer research, or to help his friend pack up a U-Haul, or to do volunteer work at the hospital. Common decency would seem to be all that is needed here. If we were to ask this generous man why he is carving out this slice of his time or his money for someone else, he would probably answer that this is what decent people do. We can't be wholly egocentric, or we'd all be at each other's throats and everything would bog down in suspicion, pushing, struggling, quarreling, screams, litigation, murder, and war. This, he might say, is just the way it is, and there is no need to fantasize it by topping it off with religious lore about rewards in the afterlife and so forth. Generosity needs no defense. This man might even toss it off with the old cliché about love making the world go 'round.

And if he did, he would have touched the central nerve of Christianity. What he thought was a cliché opens onto the gigantic vision that transfixed Dante when he spoke of "the love that moves the sun and other stars." Christianity teaches that in fact it is love that makes the world go 'round—the love of God the Creator for that which he has made.

So what? How does this link up with our problem of how to be free? Has the subject of discussion been changed? No, not at all. The divine love that makes the world go 'round, and that sets sinners on their feet again after each fall, is the archetypal demonstration of what freedom really means.

Up to this point we have gone along with everyone's first thoughts about freedom: namely, that it is the hard-won fruit of our assault on hampering circumstances, a matter of calling one's own shots as distinct from having them called for one. The only thing we have said to qualify this notion is that freedom from the pressure of hampering circumstances is only the shell of freedom and that the heart of the truly free life is the contentment that flows from tenacious integrity in holding to the best choice. But now we are to define that best choice, and it is as if we are watching a transformation scene in the theatre and suddenly finding ourselves looking at something which to our gaze was not previously there.

Here is the definition. The choice that spells freedom is choosing to love. True freedom for man is freedom to love—freedom to love others, even the unlovely, in and through God, and to love God himself. To be free is to have learned to love. No one who has not learned this lesson is free, and no one is more free than the one who loves. As God's freedom is precisely the freedom of love, so also is man's. When nothing and no one can stop you from loving, then you are free in the profoundest sense.

Christian life is not always testified to in terms of freedom, but freedom to love is its essence all the same. Ask Mother Teresa of Calcutta about her life, and she might say something about offering Christ to suffering humanity. The late Corrie ten Boom, having seen her father and sister die under Nazi cruelties, no doubt would have said something about the difference that it makes to know Jesus. A man who had been one of those Nazi guards and had then become a Christian might tell of making a 180-degree turn from that barking, booted, goose-stepping world of power and falling at the foot of the Cross in an agony of penitence and new resolve. A medieval doctor of divinity might say something about being perfected in charity. Ask any plain Christian about his life, and he will try to say something about being delivered from self-interest, about learning to share what he has, and about learning to receive with thanksgiving all that life serves up to him as coming from the Father in heaven. But all these are testimonies concerning freedom to love, when you look at them.

Love in the abstract is not something that fills Christian minds. When the saints talk of love they talk of God, and when they talk of God they talk of Jesus Christ, since it was in him that the God who is love showed himself to us and lived and died on earth on our behalf. The Christian gospel is the tale of love, we might say, showing us how it comes about that our freedom is bound up with love—not love as a generally diffused feeling of warmth and good will, but as a sharing in the very nature of God. The Christian position is not that love is God, but that God is love; and our sense of not being free, says the Christian gospel, is simply an index of our alienation from this God while we are in the state of self-centered nonlove that is, alas, natural to us all.

But here we can expect to be interrupted, and the interruption is in no way unreasonable. The world is full of outrages and horrors, starvation, cruelty, child abuse, exploitation, disease, misery. How do we square this with belief in a God who is love?

There is mystery here: this we frankly acknowledge. We hinted at it a moment ago when we spoke of the Christian thankfully receiving "all that life serves up to him as coming from the Father in heaven." To believe that there is a meaningful, providentially ordered relationship between life's riddles and God's love is a matter of faith, not of sight. It does not always look or feel like that. Logic, of course, offers three simple solutions to the perplexity: (a) One could conclude that God cannot be loving enough to want to stop the horrors; (b) one could infer that though God wants to, he lacks the power—the world is largely out of his control; (c) one could suppose that from the standpoint of his absolute sovereignty, the badness of such things as the cancerous agony of a small child somehow dissolves away. These suggestions can logically be made, but we cannot live with any of them; they leave us clutching our heads in horrified incredulity. No; God's love and power and lordship must be affirmed, and the badness of bad things must be affirmed also, and the problem of the horrors must be tackled another way, as the following discussion will show.

There is a dark place, says the gospel, that lies between the options of that intolerable logic; and it is here that we come upon the mystery of the love of God. It is a place where, as we shall see, obedience and freedom are found to be synonymous. The only thing visible in that darkness is the Cross. All formulas, equations, syllogisms, and slogans totter and collapse here. When we come to this place, only two postures are open to us. A man may stiffen in shock, disbelief, and loathing; in which case he will make his exit as quickly as he can. Or he may fall down and adore. For in this place we find the mystery that whatever is offered as a sacrifice and oblation to God will be received by him and transformed by the fire of his love into pure gold. This is stranger and more unnerving, as well as more unexpected, than any alchemy, but it is central to what Christianity really is.

How do we know this can be? we ask. The answer is: Because it actually was. It happened. The story that climaxes in Jesus' resurrection, an event once referred to by a top legal man as "the best attested fact in history," is a story of how gold did come out of the ashes. Life sprang from death. Glory burst from the pit. Victory leaped from defeat. It is more than this, actually. It is not so much that gold *arrived* where we saw only ashes a moment ago, or that life came frolicking in over death, or that victory was squeaked from near-defeat. The gold, the life, the victory *are* those ashes and death and defeat seen from the other side, as it were. The way down was the way up. The way to Easter ran straight through Good Friday—Passion Week was not a detour which might have been avoided in a more tightly planned itinerary. The freedom of Jesus' obedience in consenting to lay down his life for us turned the shame of his judicial murder into the glory of redemption accomplished. For, as Christians know, we were saved not by his pain as such, quantitatively measured, but by his pain sanctified through his free acceptance of it, and given its value by the love for us and the submission to the Father's will which it expressed.

So what about the horrors that we face? In brief, they are marks of a world out of joint through human sin; but the God who once used the horror of Calvary to rescue us from a destiny of unimaginable evil, and to start a process which will issue in a new world free from horrors, will also use our pains and griefs, accepted as from him and offered back to him, as means of unimaginable good. Mystery? Yes, but proven fact as well. Ask the saints, and they will tell you from their own experiences how God in this way redeems and revalues evil.

The cross that stands there in this darkness marks the place where these marvels of redemption occur and where the marvel of our passage from bondage to freedom also occurs. Christianity says that the way to real freedom has been opened and charted for us all by Jesus, in the course of doing his appointed work of dying for us. In him, the Son of Man, living as man was made to live, we see obedience leading to self-oblation. He offered himself to the Father, saying "not as I will, but as you will" (Matthew 26:39), and at the Father's direction he laid himself open for men to do as they liked with him. That, in our world, would seem to be a certain recipe for professional failure, horrific exploitation by others, and all sorts of tiresome neuroses and low, unhealthy self-concepts. But instead of this we find in Jesus a man who stands above the whole rack of history as the freest person ever to live. Concerns for such things as professional success and comfortable living blow away like dust when we confront him; and as for our suspicion that self-humbling is the fruit of a neurotically low self-concept, the words suddenly embarrass us. Jesus' *profession*, if we may use this wooden word here, was to hand over his life to God, as unprotesting as a lamb, and his *lifestyle* (a term even more wooden) of homelessness and poverty and of being endlessly at the disposal of sweating, desperate, and ignorant mobs, helping and teaching and healing them, may be described in just one word: *obedience.*

But what a conundrum. This free man obedient? Subservient? Completely at the disposal of his Father's will (for this is how he explained what he was doing)? It seems so. And not only this. Far from its having been a matter of his "knuckling under" to some tyrannical father-figure, Jesus said that his very "meat" was to do his Father's will. In other words, he *enjoyed* his obedience; it was food and drink to him; it brought him strength and contentment; it left him satisfied. It was the good choice, whole-heartedly made and sustained, in which he delighted and in which his freedom consisted. That is the inescapable impression which the four portraits of Jesus (those of Matthew, Mark, Luke, and John) leave on any thoughtful reader. In other emphases they vary, complementing each other; in this, they are solidly at one. Read them, and see.

We find ourselves presented, then, in the life of Jesus with the extreme oddity of complete obedience apparently issuing in complete freedom. And the will which was being obeyed asked, not just for decency and reasonableness and prudence but for this frightening self-oblation. It is hard to see this as freedom if we are still thinking about the topic in the way we have been taught to think about it, as escape from pressure and subservience and discomfort. But we know that we are on very different ground here. The more we watch and listen to Jesus, the more we know that we are hearing the clear peal of a true bell of liberty and the more we realize that the other bells clank dully, for indeed they are cracked.

Freedom and Subservience

Yet this peal of true liberty is a strange note—we must admit. At first it sounds simple: "Love God and your neighbor as yourself." This is Jesus' own summary of the whole thing. But when we look at him and see that he means for us to be utterly subservient to both, *obeying* God to the death and laying down our *life* for our neighbor, then we jib.

But that reaction of ours, however natural it seems at first blush, is actually stupid, unnatural, and perverse. To love God is to know once again that state of pure freedom for which we were made and which humans enjoyed briefly in Eden. The majesty and freedom which Scripture projects in the figures of Adam and Eve—who, as portrayed in the garden, strike us as much more royal and free than any tsar or khan tricked out in cloth of gold— was the other side of their obedience to God. For a brief while they loved and served him, as Jesus was later to do all his life long; and their dignity as his vassals, holding the fief of this world in trust, gives us a picture of a state of things where freedom, dignity, and obedience are not only not in conflict, but are synonymous.

This is difficult for us to grasp, accustomed as we are to thinking of freedom and obedience as being irreconcilable. But let us realize that we have examples of this paradox around us all the time. The lovely "freedom" of a gymnast, for example, is synonymous with his utter obedience to the exacting rules of his act; though what we see as the product of all his submission to discipline, far from looking like bondage, takes our breath away with its magnificence and power. We sit there wishing that our flabby bodies could enjoy that sort of freedom, but they cannot, just because we have never bowed to the iron rules of drill in muscle-culture and control. We see the same in a ballet dancer; all that austere choreography, far from being a grid in which he is being cramped and frustrated, is the very pattern of his freedom. In those situations not only is obedience synonymous with freedom, but freedom turns out to be synonymous with mastery, and with beauty and perfection and joy. We do not totter away from the display hall or theatre murmuring "Those poor gymnasts; those unhappy dancers; what slavery they suffer; somebody ought to set them *free!*" Our feelings are rather of envy: "How I would love to be able to do that!"

The examples could go on and on. We listen enthralled to a violinist whose fingers are moving in precise obedience to what Bach wrote, and we think of all the tedious afternoons, year after year, that lie behind the nimbleness and mastery in those fingers. We hear a soprano sing a piece by Verdi, and know that this wild ecstasy has nothing to do with spontaneity; it is the final fruit of singing scales for years under supervision. We see a race horse performing at the peak of his powers, and we notice there is a man on his back and a bit in his mouth. "Let him *go!*" we might shout; but the trainers and owner and jockey would look at us pityingly.

We come upon a bursting creative genius like Shakespeare, and we say, "Turn him loose on the language!"—but he would look at us blankly. His powers have already been set free by his attentive obedience to the genius of the language itself, and to the rigor of poetical rules. Sonnet form? fourteen lines, divided exactly thus and thus, rhymed exactly thus and thus, and each line with no more and no less than this number of up and down beats? Come, we say—no creative genius can function inside that cage. The trouble here is that Dante and Shakespeare and Milton and Wordsworth don't *agree* with us. They won't join our campaign for liberation. They found their freedom long ago, precisely in writing sonnets—sonnets that have lasted in a way that the "free-form" poetry of the twentieth century seems hardly likely to do.

And we find the same paradox closer to home than are the artists and athletes. Who is the child who is free? Is it not the one who has been taught what the limits for behavior are, and who is therefore at peace with himself and with others? The rules of courtesy, far from paralyzing him, set him free from the perils of his own resources when he has to greet older people. The plain conventions of shaking hands and saying "How do you do" deliver him from having to think of something of his own to say and hence from twisting his trousers and pouting. Or think of the yellow line down the middle of the road; far from hindering your progress and mine, it makes both possible at once, as long as we obey the rules and keep on our own side. Red and green lights, vexing as they may seem if I am in a hurry, set us all free from the clotted traffic, dented fenders, and fisticuffs that would mark our efforts to get through the city were we left to our own private preferences. Highway signs tell us that we must go *that* way if we want to get to Philadelphia. These things do not frustrate; they liberate.

The common factor in all these examples is some set pattern that arches over whatever is going on and calls forth success, beauty, and freedom, if it is observed. To learn the rules, in these situations, is to be set free from the fevered and perplexed indeterminateness of my own resources, inclinations, and uncertainties (think again of the gymnast, the dancer, the poet, the child, and the driver).

When we look at these things, we begin to see that the strange paradoxes we find in the Christian gospel are rooted in the same reality in which we must all live our lives anyway—in which, indeed, the whole universe seems to function. Scientists use the word "laws" to refer to the predictable way things behave: the stars are found in their same "locations" age after age; springtime follows winter; an oak tree grows from an acorn put into the ground, and a stalk of corn from a kernel of corn; lions congregate with lions and gnus with gnus; red collects at one end of the spectrum and violet at the other; water turns to ice at thirty-two degrees Fahrenheit; a human fetus results when the sperm and ovum of human parents combine. On and on it goes, like the choreography of a dance, where the "rules" are the very pattern of beauty.

Now the rule, or pattern, for our human life and hence for human freedom, says Christianity, is the rule of love. This is the will of God who called us into being. The point is, God is love, and we are made in his image; which means, we have been made to live as he lives, doing at our level what he does at his. There is the axis of the whole pattern. We don't really know just how all the other creatures in the universe find their fulfillment, if we may speak thus. They seem to glorify God simply by being them-selves—stars, waves, winds, dragonflies, snowflakes. But for us men the stakes are higher. We are made like God, we are told, and we can find our fulfillment and joy only by loving as he loves, thus becoming increasingly like him in personal moral practice. There is no contentment and therefore no freedom for human creatures if we try to live any other way. And, says the gospel, that is exactly what has gone wrong with us. In solidarity with Adam, our God-likeness was blighted when we tried to assert our auton-omy in Eden by claiming our life as our own. By trying to grab hold of freedom (that is, by grabbing the autonomy which we mistook for freedom) we actually lost freedom. We tried to stand alone, and in so doing, we fell.

For to stand alone is to forsake the image in which we were made. That image is worshiped by Christians, not as a solitude, but as "God in Three Persons." We will never understand the promise of freedom that Christianity holds out to us, as over against what we are told by the received wisdom of our own era, unless we do pursue things all the way back to this fountainhead. God is love, says Christianity. But love is not a mere abstraction, nor does it operate in a vacuum. Before the Creation ever ap-peared, God, who is both singular and plural, unique and triune, solitary and social, existed and rejoiced in love—the love of the Father for the Son and the Son for the Father, love in which the Holy Spirit was and is somehow the agent, the issue, and the sharer, all in one. (We are obliged to say "somehow" since all language and analytical competence dies away in the precincts of the Holy Trinity.) This divine life of love and joy was one of the eternal realities, so Christianity holds, which the words and deeds of the incarnate Son revealed; when Christians claim that Jesus made God known, the abiding interrelations of the triune Godhead are included in their meaning. It is in the moral image of this God that we mortals were created. We have been made to love him, to be loved by him, and to love each other. Our true freedom is found in doing this.

Now we see how utterly the Adamic grab for freedom negates and destroys the freedom in which, and for which, our race was brought into being. For love is always outgoing, always serving, always seeking someone else's joy. It is the stark opposite of all egocentrism, self-interest, avarice, pride, and self-assertion—

the very things, so we thought, that are necessary if we are ever to wrest any freedom from this struggling, overcrowded, and oppressive world of ours.

No, says Christianity. Not so. This jockeying fight for freedom will never bring freedom. We will find our life, and hence our freedom, by "laying it down"—the opposite of the strategy that Adam tried in Eden, and that which, at the behest of our Adamic instincts, we have all been trying ever since in this now spoiled world. Remember the grain of wheat? The crop begins when the kernel dies. Where Adam and Eve stumbled, ironically, into bondage in the very attempt to assert their independence, the "Second Adam" (one of the Christian designations for Jesus) restored that freedom by his obedience. Where we all have said, "Be it unto me according to *my* word," and have thus lost our dignity and freedom, ages ago a woman said, "Be it unto me according to *thy* Word," and thus was hailed as highly exalted. The figure whom we find crowned with glory in Christian painting as the very model and type of redeemed and restored humanity is not our mother Eve, awesome as she may be. It is the Virgin Mary, the poor provincial Jewish girl, now glorified in heaven. In this she pictures what St. Paul teaches when he says that Christians "sit with him [Christ, their Savior] in the heavenly places" (see Ephesians 2:6, RSV). This majesty and dignity is the direct result of our embracing Christ's humiliation and obedience and of following him on this track of love, right through the grave (the death of all our obstinate self-assertion and calculated self-interest), into the freedom that lies on the far side of that death.

That is why the Cross is the focal point for Christians and, instrument of death though it is, the very badge of freedom. It is the sign of that love which has set us free from bondage to ourselves.

We do not seek to spell out here the full meaning of the Cross, any more than we have tried to spell out the full truth about our oneness with and in Adam. There is, in fact, mystery—that is, reality beyond our grasp—at both points. With respect to Adam, what is essential is for us to recognize that, though Adam was a historical person and in that sense is not every man, every one of us is an embodiment of Adam in terms of his motivation, his folly, his guilt, and his corrupted nature. With respect to the Cross, what matters is for us to understand that, though no one can spell out with exhaustive precision the "transaction" that occurred for us at the Cross, yet it was there that through God's mercy we were saved. "God demonstrates his own love for us in this: While we were still sinners, Christ died for us" (Romans 5:8). "This is how God showed his love among us: He sent his one and only Son into the world that we might live through him. This is love: not that we loved God, but that he loved us and sent his Son as an atoning sacrifice for our sins" (1 John 4:9–10). "For God so loved the world that he gave his one and only Son, that whoever believes in him shall not perish, but have eternal life" (John 3:16). "To him who loves us and has freed us from our sins by his blood" (Revelation 1:5). The gospel rings with this theme. Somehow our *rescue* depends on the love of God, with its mysterious fountainhead in the Trinity, flowing out to us in the figure of Jesus Christ and in his sacrificial death. Our salvation was won, says the gospel, when Jesus Christ, who had taught us about the love of God, and who had enacted it for us day after day, made the perfect offering of love, laying down his own life in our behalf so that we who were "lost" and "bound" and "dead" and "unclean" might be restored and freed and made alive and purified.

And there, says Christianity, is the pattern for the only true freedom. Those whom Christ has thus rescued are called to live by that same self-giving love that he showed when he embraced the Cross. Self-assertion and self-aggrandizement must go; giving and serving must take their place. Is this new life folly? No, not really, whatever the casual and cynical may think. It is humanness; it is integrity, dignity, equanimity; it is the freedom that we were looking for all along.

How may we enter into it? We shall come back to this. For the moment, it is enough to say that only in personal commitment to the risen Christ shall we find it. Freedom is not our achievement, but his gift.

Finding Freedom

Take a survey. Who professes to have found freedom? Not those who had the money and the connections and the lucky breaks; not those who have "made it" in this world. There is, indeed, a deafening silence when such a profession is asked for. Let us therefore pose a different question. Who appears to have found freedom? Folk of a rather different sort, folk who impress us as go-givers rather than go-getters. Here are one or two of them.

Meet first Mother Teresa of Calcutta. She does not feel awkward about whether she will be properly dressed for such and such a splashy occasion. She does not thumb anxiously through the pages of *Women's Wear Daily, Harper's Bazaar,* and *Vogue,* to find out what is in fashion these days. She is quite free on that front. And that face of hers breaks into a great and kind smile, whether she is greeting a dying pauper from the gutter or the President and Fellows of Harvard. She is not agitated socially. She is not afraid of silence, trying to fill in awkward gaps in conversation with knowledgeable comments about this and that. She is inwardly at liberty in either din or quiet. She does not watch the real-estate pages, hawk-like, to see if a chic address is opening up. She is at home with the One who made do without even so predictable a house as a fox's hole or a bird's nest. She is not embarrassed to tell us all that freedom for her is blazoned when she makes the sign of the Cross on herself.

Oh yes, but she is a *nun,* we protest. We can't all do *that.*

No. But if we can learn nothing else from people like Mother Teresa, or St. Francis of Assisi, or the rural Cornish saint Billy Bray for that matter, we may at least see that it is possible in the inner man to be healthy and merry and fulfilled—to be free, in other words—quite apart from everything that is dinned at us by the world as being indispensable to the good life.

But let us ask a lay person. Consider the late Corrie ten Boom. She had no nun's habit. She had to buy and wear clothes that were acceptable and looked normal in day-to-day situations. But was she hagridden with anguish as to whether everyone would see that what she wore had just the right label on it? When she sat on the platform, visible to hundreds, would that sharp mind behind those peaceful and merry eyes be wondering whether everyone knows that "Balenciaga" or "Lily Pulitzer" are stitched in her clothes? Would we have found her sitting across the table from her investment counselor, purple in the face and with the veins standing out in her neck, shrilly wondering why he had bungled things yet again and missed the chance of a lifetime for a windfall? Would we have overheard her on the telephone snapping out, "My dear, I'm *sorry*. But that is just too much to ask of *anyone*. I have things to do, and I simply can't be bothered with *that*, and you may tell them so"? Would we have come upon her dickering with her agent as to whether the publicity for her forthcoming visit to Buenos Aires or San Francisco had been touted with at least as much splash and color and noise as was the visit of some other Christian celebrity who had taken the place by storm the previous month?

Anyone who ever heard what this woman had to say about the lessons life had taught her would have had great difficulty fitting her into any of the above scenes. For she seemed to radiate a tranquillity, a lack of cynicism, and a good humor, that stands at a polar extreme from all the strife and scuffle implied in those imagined episodes. She seemed to be free from all that; and this freedom of hers, like Mother Teresa's, seemed to be synonymous with love. It had nothing to do with her having won the right to assert her independence and dignity. She, of course, when asked for her secret would give some brief answer like "Jesus." Perhaps by now we can see something of what that answer meant.

But we are still too far afield from the world where most of us must slog along. Mother Teresa is a nun, and Corrie ten Boom was a celebrity who was met at airports and moved from red carpet to banquet table to guest room complete with fresh flowers. What about the rest of us? We live down in the middle of things where it does seem to matter how you look and what everyone thinks of you and what sort of an impression your style of life is making and whether you know so-and-so, or have a Ph.D., or went to an Ivy League school, or wrote so many books, and so forth. But leave all that sort of thing out if you wish. How about the plain, routine grind? What about the clutter of fitting what one has to get done into the space of any given twenty-four hours? What about the demands on one's time that jostle each other so mercilessly? What about traffic jams, committee meetings, crying infants, deadlines, quarrels, missed connections, the telephone, the doorbell, irritating colleagues, demeaning tasks, and people's insensitivity and ingratitude? How is a person supposed to be free in all of *this*?

The answer, as we keep trying to say, lies in the direction indicated by the gospel. The call to true liberation comes to us, not from the yelling caucus with their fists in the air, but from the silence and defeat of the Cross. Jesus Christ, with the sweating and frantic mobs pushing at him, and with the soldiers jeering and hitting him, testifies that freedom is possible even there. And his followers bear this out in their plain mortal flesh. There were many years of clutter, filth, bedpans, and cries of despair surrounding Mother Teresa in the school of charity (that is to say, of freedom) to which God sent her. For Corrie ten Boom there were years of grim struggle with hatred and resentment and even the "righteous" desire for revenge, before she learned the lesson which we saw written on her peaceful face in the last phase of her life.

Just what form the lessons will take for me, no one else can dictate. Consider, for example, the person who finds that very searching lessons in charity are set before him every single day on the roads of Massachusetts, where the drivers outstrip the Parisians, the New Yorkers, and the Arabs for sheer, murderous cynicism. Rage and competition boil up in this man when he is victimized on these roads; but he knows that until he learns to say, "The Lord be with you!" and give way with a chuckle, he will never know freedom on this front. It might seem too pompous and solemn to talk of the Cross in stupid situations like this when any remotely amiable person ought to be able to take it all with a shrug. But if the person is as we described him, the Cross of Christ is in truth his only source of help. If ruthless and inconsiderate drivers really do bother him, then the way out of his irritation is going to lie in the direction of learning that a free man does not have to assert himself, even on Route 128, much less beat the other guy out. It's a sort of kindergarten lesson in the same sort of non-self-interest which was supremely exhibited at the Cross.

For some people, lessons like this are harder than for others. For all of us, they are harder at some points than at others. No one can dictate what the lessons will be. Someone else may find the simultaneous ringing of the telephone and the crying of the baby too much to cope with. And the chances are that no slogan or formula ("I must accept the Cross here") will bring much instant serenity. But if the situations are looked upon as slow, long, hard lessons in that school of charity—where we seem to be taught, not by the Master's waving a wand and magically conferring freedom or patience or peace, but by his assuring us that this way is the way which he and all the long train of his good servants have gone—then we may at least begin to see that the Cross is not merely a glimmering artifact to be gazed at with brimming eyes by souls who have the leisure to steal away to quiet shrines, but that it is here, now, today, in this wretched situation, inviting me to that same painful laying down of life which was pioneered for me by Jesus.

Worth and Freedom

This view of the Cross raises a troublesome question, especially for us moderns who believe so passionately (and perhaps correctly) that, for us to be set free from our bondage, we need to know that we are esteemed. We need to know that others see in us dignity. We need to know that we are loved. What we need, says our current jargon, is "affirmation" and a sense of "self-worth." How do we fit this, that seems so crucial, into our formula of living according to the Cross, which would seem to have as its program, when you get right down to it, the wrecking and spoiling of all that could possibly be called Me? Doesn't this gospel come out, after all, as a recipe for masochism and self-destruction?

For the answer we must look again at the people in whom we see the principle at work. Jesus laid down his life for others, not only at the Cross but every day of his ministry. And yet he was free. Was his freedom the ghastly self-delusion of the poor soul who says to himself, "Little me. It's just poor little me. Oh do trample on me. I'm nothing"? No, it was not. One of the things that maddened his enemies, even up to the high priests and Roman officialdom, was his serene majesty. Which one of them, all mantled in the dignity of religion or empire, was as calmly at home with himself, and as sure of his "self-worth," as this naked wretch who stood so quietly on the floor of the judgment hall?

And what was the source of the serenity and freedom that we see in Jesus? Was it not his sure knowledge of who he was? He was the Son of God, and it was in perfect oneness with his Father's will that he lived. He knew he was loved. "The Father loveth the Son, and hath given all things into his hand," he said. His obedience to his Father in laying down his life for the sake of others was his free response to the love that the Father had for him.

The Christian gospel says that we mortals are brought into that same relationship with the Father: "sonship," as it is called. We are "adopted," says St. Paul. We have a Father who loves us. That we are made by him in his image is the ground of our dignity; and that we are loved by him is the well-spring of our freedom. The world advises us to strive for a sense of "self-worth." That is perhaps the best that the world can advise, and it has a certain tang of truth in it. But if it means that I must concentrate on making sure that my dignity is recognized by everyone, and that my rights are not tampered with, and that everyone knows that I am in fact somebody, then we are back in the dismaying struggle for a place in the sun, with everyone around me being a threat and a competitor. If, however, I draw my sense of dignity and worth from the much deeper mysteries of having been created, loved, and redeemed by God, then I will have been set free.

The terrible difficulty that many of us have with this is that our past human experience may have made it hard for us to *feel* thus loved. We may have had thoughtless parents, or foolish parents, or no parents; or our own lack of beauty, prowess, or intelligence may have made us the butt of jokes and snubs all our life; so that we have long since concluded that we are "no good." Counselors, psychiatrists, and pastors spend long, difficult hours with people who are thus trapped. Often it happens that our ability to respond to the word of God's love in Christ will have to be propped up and encouraged by our meeting some human being who will be able to *show* us this love, which hitherto we have never seen at work, not at any rate directed toward ourselves.

This "human" way whereby God's love seeps into our inner-most being is very much in keeping with the gospel itself, for every single incident in that gospel was "mediated," so to speak, by human flesh—from the annunciation to the baptism of Jesus; through his ministry, passion, death, resurrection, and ascension; and then on to Pentecost, when the treasure of heavenly glory was put into the earthen vessels of the apostles and the rest of the Church. The whole thing was enacted in human flesh—the flesh of Mary, of the Incarnate Word himself, of the apostles, and then of the whole train of Christian people, martyrs and otherwise, who, says St. Paul, are the "Body" of Christ here on earth.

So it does no violence to this apparently high-flown talk of our having to come to the point of knowing ourselves to be loved by God to say that we may need to be led, halting and hesitating, toward this by some plain mortal who will simply show us that love by loving us. This is what Christian parents know their real role to be; their love to their children will introduce those children to the whole web of mysteries, as it were, preparing them in ordinary family life to receive the gospel which, like family life itself, is full of riddles like authority being synonymous with love, and obedience being the route to freedom, and the laying down of life ("sharing" and so forth, even in the sandbox) being the very condition of joy.

And here, surely, is the answer to the charge that the gospel is a recipe for masochistic self-destruction. The freedom to serve others, even to the point of laying down one's life, rises from the noblest source of all, namely the mystery of the Son's obedience to the Father. From that source we learn that true human dignity displays itself most exquisitely in qualities of mercy, generosity, self-forgetfulness, and going to any lengths to make others good, and great, and happy. This, as we have seen, is fulfillment and freedom for us creatures, just as it was freedom and fulfillment for the great Pioneer of our salvation and Liberator of our lives. He said himself: "If the Son sets you free, you will be free indeed" (John 8:36). He lives, says the gospel, to do just that for us; and this is where our real humanness begins.

A Lost World

In Sir Arthur Conan Doyle's adventure tale for boys from nine to ninety, *The Lost World,* Professor Challenger and his explorer friends climb to a plateau previously thought inaccessible. There they find prehistoric creatures and a hitherto unknown pattern of human life. This chapter has sought to lead its readers on a comparable journey to a comparable discovery. We began by climbing out of the everyday world of thought, where freedom is conceived in external terms as a matter of overcoming restrictions and getting rid of what weighs one down. We reached the point where we saw freedom as essentially an inward quality, that of contentment in the conscious maintaining of a good choice. It was plain then that the removing of outward constraints like poverty, overwork, exploitation, injustice, bad health, destructive relationships, deprivation of rights, or torture of body and mind cannot guarantee freedom; yet true freedom can coexist with all these things. Exploring the plateau we had reached, we perceived in Jesus Christ and his followers a pattern of inner contentment in the negating of egoism and the offering of oneself with steady and sustained goodwill to love and serve God and others at all costs, and it became clear that this is human freedom at its height. We also learned that it is God who through Christ enables those who want this freedom to find it, and that he ennobles those whom he thus enables by giving them inalienable worth with Christ as his own beloved children. Thus we mapped the territory of the lost world of freedom, the only world that truly merits the name of *free*. This freedom, which is basic to fulfilled humanness, now stands revealed as one of the open secrets of the Christian faith.

But will anyone believe that this lost world really exists? Will anyone recognize the life we have described as freedom in its fullness? *The Lost World* ends with Challenger battling frozen scepticism among his scientific peers as to what he had discovered, and similarly our readers may be finding it hard to adjust to the idea that human freedom in essence is not the independence that the world hankers after, nor the power to indulge any whim, lust, or fancy one may have in one's heart, but the disposition of selfless goodwill that we have described. Can such an antique, premodern idea possibly be right? Can this way of living, so old and unfamiliar as to sound new and revolutionary when expounded, possibly be the liberty which Westerners have been seeking through the fine arts since the Renaissance, and through politics since the French Revolution, and through psychology since Freud, and through education and technology since H. G. Wells? The rest of this book offers parallel and corroborative lines of reasoning which may help to confirm conviction on this point. We ask our readers to follow along with us and see.

5

Hope

"Hope springs eternal," may be one of those platitudes that leave us more or less cold, but, like all platitudes, it is true. The only thing wrong is that, though true, it has gone flat on us because we are too familiar with it—or at least with its words. But platitudes leap into renewed vitality when we run into the kind of experiences which gave them birth. So if the statement that "hope springs eternal" strikes us as dull or barren, the chances are that we are showing ourselves not so much insightful as impoverished in the areas of life to which it refers.

Granted, we often toss out this remark in a very casual way. We say it with a chuckle as we watch an ardent young wooer whose chances look dim. We say it with a wry shake of the head when we see a dog leaping and barking at the bottom of a tree trunk with his eyes on the squirrel that has scampered up out of his reach. We say it with a knowing lift of the eyebrow as the picnic party sets out with heavy gray clouds gathering overhead. None of these situations seems to us too serious, and the fact that hope springs eternal may not at that moment present itself to us as a very significant insight into life either. But in this we are wrong. These words touch a central nerve of human experience.

Hope Is the Spur

What keeps a young athlete working with such titanic determination month after month? The answer is, hope; he hopes to excel, and become a winner. There may, of course, be a few rare spirits who do the whole thing out of sheer zest; but if they exist, they are certainly not typical. Stop a man at his punching bag or a boy on the track and convince either that he will never win anything, and his vigor and zeal with start to peter out. Or consider what keeps a pianist drumming so earnestly at the keys for so many hours each day. Maybe he simply likes doing this more than anything else; he would rather sit playing forever than be out capering with his friends. But even he will probably tell us that he hopes all this work will reward him, if not with the prize at the Moscow competition and celebrity recitals in Carnegie Hall, then at least with some recognition from his peers, and perhaps some sort of a career in music. At the very minimum, he hopes to give pleasure to others by his playing. But if he knew he would be contracting rheumatoid arthritis and would not be able to keep his fingers moving, or if his teacher had to tell him one bleak morning that he would never succeed in playing well, one could expect his passion for the keyboard to diminish at once.

Look now at students. Why do they sit at their desks so diligently? They will tell you, if you ask, that it is because they hope to pass. And why does this one sit there longer, studying harder? "Because I hope to get into Harvard Business School, and I need a 4.0 grade-point average for that." Why Harvard Business School? "Because I am shooting for the top, and you have to have been to Harvard to get there." Hope of this sort hovers over all the laden library tables, carrels, cluttered desks, and midnight cramming sessions. Those with no such hope, however, make lesser efforts.

Everywhere we look we see hope spurring effort on. A child hopping along in a potato-bag race at a Sunday school picnic hopes to be first. Presumably the spider that swings between the fencepost and the bush to build his web hopes for some fat flies. The small boy gathering dandelions hopes that his mother will like them.

Hope rewarded is sweet. The lover may now possess the divine creature whom he wooed. The athlete may run to the podium to collect the trophy while the crowd cheers. The Harvard Business School graduate may wheel his Mercedes into the parking slot marked "Reserved for Chairman." The boy may hear his mother say, "Lovely! Thank you, darling, you've made my day"; and by saying it, she makes his.

Hope dashed, however, is another story. We did not pass the course. We did not get into Harvard. The Australian beat us into second place in the 440. Our mother sniffed and brushed the dandelions aside. We are disappointed; we are hurt; we feel anger, perhaps, and grief and shame; our self-esteem is ruined; and we've lost the will to try again. Next time our hopes will probably be less high, and our anxieties greater.

Hope snuffed out can be killingly destructive. Think of the boy whose present was spurned. What wound has buried itself in his inner being? If it was only a passing moment of impatience of his mother's part, and he knows from all his five years' worth of experience that she loves him and delights in him, there will be enough confidence inside him to help him through this setback. But if the rejected bouquet is one of a thousand such rejections, which finally extinguish all the natural hopes he ever had of pleasing his mother, soon there is going to be a youth, and then an adult, with a seared and bitter heart. His soul was made to be warmed by his parents' love as a buttercup seems shaped to catch the sun and be filled by it. Buttercups wilt, however, in the cold and dark. Human souls, alas, may do the same when hope is extinguished.

Hope and Hopelessness

We need to note here that there are two elements in hope. The first is imagination, whereby we think ahead to envisage something delightful. The more delightful this prospect is, the more we dwell on it, and the more of our passion and desire we invest in it. The second element is expectation, whereby we actually look forward to the reward and anticipate it, and so make ourselves vulnerable to disappointment if things do not go as we had hoped. Levels of expectation vary, of course, from situation to situation. One may enter a race for fun, or for the experience, not expecting to win—pleasant though winning would be; one does not spend time dreaming of being the winner, because one is sure one will not be; and in that case, since expectation is low, losing will not be a major trauma. But if a man hopes for, say, a promotion, and feels confident that he is entitled to it and will get it, and is already imagining what it will feel like to have received it, his level of expectation has become high; and if he is then passed over, the shock and discouragement will be sickening. The higher the level of expectation, the worse the let-down when hopes fail to materialize.

All disappointments tend to dry up the springs of inner energy, and the greater the disappointment, the more paralyzing the experience of it will be. For hope is a basic human need. We live. very much in our hopes and invest much of ourselves in them, and it would be soul-destroying in the most literal sense to have all hopes taken away. We say, "While there's life, there's hope"; equally true, and equally basic, is the reverse statement, "While there's hope, there's life." To have nothing to hope for is to be robbed of energy and sucked down into apathy and misery. A brilliant classical scholar, poet, and school head, now in his eighties and a widower, was visited by a one-time colleague. Later, a former student of the scholar asked the visitor how the old man was doing. "Terribly gloomy," was the answer; "I asked him how he spent his time, and all he would say was: 'Waiting for the end.'" The scholar in question had long since exchanged the faith of his clergyman father for a quiet mixture of Buddhism and Marxism. It was heartbreaking to learn of the intense and paralyzing hopelessness in which he was now sunk at the close of his days. But what else can happen to a thoughtful, sensitive person who grows old without senility sapping his mind and who has no hope that extends beyond the day of his own last heartbeat? Is there any way of growing old—noting in oneself the irreversible loss of energy and the decay of one's faculties, moving toward death and finally into it—without loss of hope? In a world that, as a result of modern medicine, is increasingly populated by the elderly, this question bears down on us heavily and urgently.

Perhaps the grimmest form in which we mortals encounter the drama of hope is when disease strikes, with death threatening to be the outcome. In the fourteenth century, if you showed up with buboes welling up under your skin, everyone fled from you, and you were left to shriek vainly at heaven in your last agony. For centuries the first spot of leprosy spelled the death of hope for anyone thus blighted. Nowadays the drama is in some ways more piquant since modern medicine is gaining ground hitherto left wholly to the sway of disease. We hardly need raise the question of hope with erstwhile killers like diphtheria, smallpox, measles, influenza, meningitis and polio; for we have learned how to counter them.

But then there is cancer. None of us feels very plucky when the malignancy is first diagnosed. "Oh, tremendous strides have been made in the last two years!" they tell us desperately. But we know that we must now gird up our loins to do battle with a monster, and no assurances will close the dread abyss that has suddenly opened in our hearts. Hope? Is it even worth mustering? Of course it is; so into the breach we go: surgery, radiation, chemotherapy, and all. Up goes hope, and thousands of us are vouchsafed what appears to be the return of health—but not without the nagging question, "Will it come back?" For other thousands, however, hope rises only to be mocked. Up and down it oscillates, wildly, until we lose all track of whether we are hanging onto genuine hope or vainly indulging a hysterical refusal to face the grisly truth.

If our cancer is terminal, do we want to be told? The question could well be idle, for our medical attendants may not in any case be willing to tell us; they see us as always needing hope, even if it is illusory, in order to keep us fighting our diseases. So dare we believe them when they say to us that we are going to be all right? We can't be sure.

Will this uncertainty worry us? Each must speak to that for himself. Ought it to worry us? On that the present writers express no opinion at this time. All we do here is underline the difference that hope, as distinct from hopelessness, actually makes in human lives. What we are seeing is that the presence of hope makes all the difference in the world.

Hope and Death

And now, to press home one final sample of how hope girds our experience like a sea-wall, what do you say to the man in Death Row? After the Supreme Court, the Governor, and the President have turned down all the lawyers' appeals, so that no hope may be summoned from any legal quarter, what will your word to him be? Tomorrow is the day. An old story has it that prisons will give a man whatever he wants for breakfast on the morning of his execution. Heaven help us all. Filet mignon would be a macabre farce on an occasion like this. What possible difference can it make? So what do you say to the man?

At this point we come to a watershed. If you are a nonreligious person with the courage of your convictions, then you will not demean yourself by mumbling insincerities about God being very loving and everybody entering into rest. Hope in this world has now gone for good. Is there anything encouraging you can still say? Indeed, the extremity of the situation will shine a terrible light back across the whole of experience, and force on you the question: Are all hopes, finally, illusionary? Is every hope a mere rearranging of the deck chairs on the *Titanic* while she sinks? If the point of view called secular humanism is true, then indeed this is the case. We as individuals are going, quite simply, nowhere.

An implacable honesty on this front could quickly lead to a consuming cynicism that throws up its hands and says, "Fine! Now we know! Nothing is worth anything eventually, so nothing is ever worth anything at all. How do your medals and cups and Maseratis and dignities and loves and pleasures look now? Can't you *see*, you fools? The ship is going down. Poor, pathetic idiots! You are dancing the Dance of Death."

Such jeering pessimism is mercifully rare. Most of us, religious or not, manage to make our way along fairly reasonably, and even pleasantly, putting aside thoughts about death as long as possible. "When it comes it comes," we say, "but I won't let that ruin everything for me now. A man has to live."

Well, yes; but does that make our unrealism a virtue? Should we not face facts? Is it worthy behavior on the part of human beings to act like ostriches? Was not the cynic's outburst to us a moment of truth for us? Can we find it in us now to eat, drink, and be merry, knowing that tomorrow we die? Or if we can, is not that the most unpardonable escapism—an escapism of which thoughtful, intelligent, and imaginative folk would not be capable? Escapism argues childishness; realism is the mark of maturity. So we ought to face squarely the fact that if death is the end, the prospect of having to die will destroy for alert people now, and for everyone eventually, the joy of life.

If hope is essential to sustain the effort and enterprise which turns bodily continuance into human living, then we shall have to admit that what we call our "life"—personal existence, with all that it entails—is indeed ultimately a cheat, because sooner or later death destroys all the hopes that life raises. This is inescapably so unless, in fact, personal life reaches beyond this awful abyss we call death and continues with enrichment on the far side.

There is the rub, though! As Hamlet says in his somber way, no traveler has ever returned from the borders of that country with any news. To be sure, the attempt to see across that border has gone on for aeons; all mediums and soothsayers and necromancers and sibyls have made their living from our frantic wish to learn something about what goes on beyond the curtain that hangs between our little life here and whatever immensities encircle it. The most ironic and touching of all attempts to pierce that curtain is our own modern one. We are a nonreligious generation, we say briskly. We have gone beyond priests, dogma, and religion itself. We will live our life as secular, down-to-earth, matter-of-fact, this-worldly people and leave it at that. So we say.

But then, like Nathaniel Hawthorne's villagers who led respectable and commonplace lives all day long only to creep off at nightfall for their obscenities, we sneak away to find teachers of mystical transcendence who will show us the path to peace and confidence by weaning us away from this very secularity that we insist on so earnestly in our school textbooks and public forums. "Separation of Church and State!" we cry in our zeal to immunize everyone from the threat of being touched by religion—but "Teach me to transcend myself," we whisper to the Oriental guru as he beams on us out of knowing eyes or sits rapt and still in the lotus position. Or, more pitiably yet, we come from our classroom where we have learned that mankind's gods may all be explained by what anthropologists and psychologists have discovered about man and his civilizations, and at once we pop into the nearest newsstand to buy the paper with the daily horoscope.

Tarot cards, incense, lotus positions, the endless repeating of "om," and all the flea-market tackle of occultism and the satanist trade—what pathetic ironies there are in the efflorescence of all of this in the midst of our technology and secularism. But, as we know, if you drive nature out through the front door, she will find her way in again at the back, and that is what is happening here.

For, whatever we may say to the contrary (and bravado leads many modern sophisticates to claim the contrary), we cannot stop hoping that there is something more to life than the merely physical, and in particular we cannot stop hoping that meaningful personal survival is included in that "something more." That is why our murky mix of mysticism and superstition is so constantly pervaded by thoughts and dreams of reincarnation, spirit-guides, and contacting the dead. Wishful thinking? Yes, beyond any shadow of doubt. Our human nature dictates it, and the blasé worldliness of our cultural pose cannot stop it.

One poignant modern attempt to get some news from across the border is our scrutiny of what we call "life after life." There is a busy market in books and articles on this topic, all taking their cue from Raymond A. Moody's book with that title. The method is to quiz people who have been in a smashup or on an operating table and who have "returned" after having taken leave of their bodies. We say they have died. They themselves may or may not wish to use this word (some do), but we get from them reports of themselves, for instance, hovering, disembodied, above the highway, looking down on the grisly scene with its stopped traffic, screaming sirens, police cars flashing blue and ambulances flashing red, crumpled metal, and gore spread over the roadway; or of how they saw from ceiling level anxious surgeons working to restart the heart of a corpse on the operating table. "That's my body down there," they said to themselves from their airy vantage point.

Who will jeer at this? None of us, religious or secularist, has any very firm vantage point from which to affirm or deny what those with this kind of experience say. Some of us are sure we know the answer. They weren't *dead*, we say; what they report may be true enough, but it was all a form of deep coma with some hitherto uncharted form of hallucination attached to it; perhaps they were "medically dead," in the sense of their heart having stopped, but the very fact that they have come "back" to tell the tale means, by definition, that they were not *dead* in the full sense, since that word must be reserved for the state in which either we are blotted out entirely (the secularist view) or we have really gone on into another realm, not to return (the religious view). We will have to reach for some label like "temporarily suspended animation" for classifying the reports.

What we are to make of the widespread accounts of these souls seeing a very bright light drawing them no one knows. Some will dismiss it as wishful thinking, or imagining—the ultimate, we might say, in daydreams. People who urge, with dogmatic optimism, that all will turn out for the best in the end will add to their store of bright hopes: "You see—we are all journeying into light; we shall all get there eventually." Skeptics will say it's no use getting agitated about this light since it could mean anything or nothing. (Still others will want to know if any souls have reported having run into *darkness*. It appears, in fact, that some have, though this is not a matter for us to pursue here.)

What then shall we conclude? Certainly that the human race shows an endless, unquenchable interest in the question of final hope beyond death, and that thoughtful folk, spurred by a nagging sense of the incompleteness of this life and its achievements, will continue to feel this interest as long as the race survives. And it is at least arguable that, just as our interest in food and our desire (often passionate) for it corresponds to the objective reality of food present in the universe for our nourishment, so our desire for fulfillment through continuance of life may correspond to a real possibility for us in the cosmos.

At this point, however, we should perhaps backtrack a little.

Cynicism, Anybody?

Some people, we know, are unable to conceive that our hopes of fulfillment in any form might be an index of reality, because cynicism possesses their souls. Cynicism—first cousin of that death-dealing disease of the spirit which the medievals called *sloth* and *accidie*—may be described as the disposition to believe that truth-claims cannot ever be trusted; that virtue, however apparent, is never real; and that hopelessness is the only real wisdom that there is. Cynicism, as a state of mind, is the child of specific disappointments. When hopes and achievements, longings and realities, expectations and experiences have been "out of sync" with each other for a sufficient period of time, an individual's capacity to go on hoping, longing, and expecting gets eaten away. Then he will externalize his inner hurt—for hopelessness does hurt; make no mistake about that—by becoming a bitter critic of his more sanguine associates, in the confidence that his urge to debunk their hopes argues superior insight on his part rather than sickness of soul.

But cynicism really is a sickness, whether or not one recognizes it as such; it is a defense mechanism whereby one who has been disillusioned and hurt once too often tries to guard against ever being disillusioned and hurt again. Self-protective cynicism, with all its brash claims to "see through" idealism and hopefulness as so much immature naiveté, is in truth a form of spiritual blindness—a sour and festering inward condition that prompts apathetic refusal of, irritated resentment at, and aggressive hostility toward anything that sounds like a formula for fulfillment and joy put forward by anyone anywhere. In the country of the blind anyone who claims to see will not be honored, for he will be felt as a threat, and it will become important to the rest to put his eyes out. Accordingly, any cynic who has read our book thus far is bound by now to be wanting to silence us (which he could do by putting the book down). But if we have been right to claim that hope is essential for fully human living, then cynicism must be judged to have something intrinsically dehumanizing and antihuman about it.

Just to say that, and then move on, is not, however, enough. Diagnosis alone does not stop disease, and the modern West has on its hands an incipient epidemic of cynicism that could spread like wildfire in our time. For secular humanism, the ideology that has animated our technological culture for the past century, is currently demonstrating itself to be very much a broken reed and a light that fails. Humanism, having trumpeted abroad its conviction that religion everywhere obstructs human fulfillment, has promised in broad and general utopian terms to effect that fulfillment by means of education, technology, and wise handling of natural resources. Being sure that this is the only life there is, humanists have no antidote to hopelessness in old age, nor can they do anything about lack of brains, balance, physical well-being, or chutzpa in less favored members of the human race.

All humanism can do is what it has done—that is, put all its eggs into the one basket of environmental management as the crucial means of bettering everyone's condition, making life for all of us less bad even where it cannot be made good in any substantial sense. But now we find that its ventures in this direction have opened a veritable Pandora's box of new troubles—the nuclear arms race, the rape of nonreplaceable resources, huge and irreversible ecological disruptions, endless instability in the global economic system, not to mention more. The humanist assumptions (1) that our supply of natural and technical resources is for practical purposes infinite, (2) that we can rely on a person-ified abstraction called "nature" to be always on our side, (3) that acceptable alternatives to everything in "nature" are always in principle available, and (4) that therefore clever leaders and man-agers can in principle remove all obstacles to endless ecstasy for everyone, if only we give them room to work, are starting to look distinctly threadbare. Specific solutions to environmental prob-lems, by altering the balance of the natural order, regularly raise other problems greater than were there before, and there is no reason to expect this pattern of things to change. (For evidence and argument to confirm this overwhelming point, see David Ehrenfeld, *The Arrogance of Humanism,* New York: Oxford Uni-versity Press, 1978.)

So a landslide into cynicism over the next few decades (assum-ing that the world lasts that long) seems inevitable; and while that landslide is unlikely to cure our materialist mentality, it is certain to bring to an end the hundred years of what may be called scientific-humanist hope. That hope went up like a rocket in the days of H. G. Wells and John Dewey; it is now coming down like a stick as the twentieth century prepares to limp offstage. Our Western culture is fast sinking, even now, into bitterness and savagery as our hopes of happiness through material advance vanish. The frenetically optimistic voices which still sound, like phonograph records stuck in the same groove, are heeded less and less; behind the ballyhoo, despair, strident or quiet, is taking over. Facing this onrush of cynicism, this universal and seeming-ly unstoppable epidemic that is creeping through Western culture as rabies is creeping through Western Europe, we may well ask: Have Christians anything useful to say?

Yes, we think they do; and the first thing to be said is that our problem—the problem of disillusionment, producing the va-cuum of hope in which the cancers of cynicism, apathy, irrespon-sibility, and disgust all grow so fast—is not new. It is as old as the Old Testament, where it is tackled head-on in one of the most poignant writings of all time, the Book of Ecclesiastes. In that book the anonymous author, personating Solomon—the wealthi-

est, wisest, and most widely experienced man in Israel's history—formulates in an intricate prose poem his own deeply tragic
sense of life. In the age of shallow optimism that is now ending,
Ecclesiastes ("the Preacher," as his name means in both Hebrew
and Greek) was pooh-poohed as a life-cheapening pessimist and
sneered at as being himself a cynic, an exponent of bitter scepticism for whom human existence was fundamentally brutish and
nasty. In the age of cynical pessimism into which we are now
moving, perhaps this ancient wisdom-writer will be better understood. Far from being a cynical pessimist himself, the writer of
Ecclesiastes answers cynical pessimism; and instead of spreading
gloom and despair, as many commentators and critics have taken
him to be doing, his concern is to teach joy and hope to those who
live on the edge of tragedy and, indeed, get engulfed in it. Writing, it seems, at late middle age, with most of his life behind him
and the doddering senility described in 12:1–7 quite close to him,
and having closely observed, partly in personal experience, how
self-indulgence, self-assertion, and self-expression work out in
the worlds of politics, public and private life, religion, labor, the
law, the family, and relations between the sexes—he piles on the
agony of hope frustrated and builds up his picture of life's let-
downs with a somber artistry that makes that heart ache. Do not
kid yourself, he says, that life is a bed of roses for anyone; it is
more like a bed of nails. Yet he is not a cynic; on the contrary, his
whole aim is to make clear three things which, when grasped and
understood, become a permanent bulwark against cynicism in
the human heart. Here they are.

The Bulwark against Cynicism

First, we must *get clear about our lot in this world*.

The human condition, as the writer of Ecclesiastes, theist and
realist, views it, is one of not being able to see moral rhyme or
reason in most of the things that happen. We would like to watch
virtue being rewarded, crime not paying, and wisdom bringing
happiness, but that is not what we observe. "Under the sun" in
God's world—that is, from our present, this-worldly point of
view—the whole range of human life and action appears as "vanity"—that is, a fruitless, unfulfilling, unsatisfying, frustrating outlay of energy. No one can plan or work for happiness with any

assurance of success; the law of divine providence is, in effect, Murphy's law, that anything that can go wrong will go wrong, and at the most awkward time too. God the invisible king is inscrutable. The only thing clear about his present providential government is that he will not as yet establish the correspondences between aim and achievement, or expectation and event, or merit and outcome that we with our innate sense of fitness want to see.

Why does God act thus? "So men will revere him" (Ecclesiastes 3:14), acknowledging that all actual good comes from him as his own free gift and not falling into the folly of trying to be the source of their own joy. We were made, not for self-sufficiency, but for a life of worship and dependence; and the discipline of providence is meant to drill us and keep us in such a life. The Book of Job shows us that unexplained pain and grief may come to anyone, even the best of men, for special reasons. Ecclesiastes, picking up where Job stops, assures us that unexplained pain and grief will come to everyone, as part of God's ordinary dealing with a race that has to be weaned from the sin of self-reliance. This, then, under God, is how things are, and they will not change. So one of our first steps in wisdom is realistically to face this reality and to crucify all our self-sufficient, self-indulgent, self-deifying hopes accordingly. Did we think we could build heaven on earth, for ourselves or for others? We were wrong. Frustration, injustice, and random troubles, rather than any form of self-made contentment, are the appointed lot of all human beings. But if we are prepared in advance to find this true, we shall not be emotionally shattered nor pitchforked into cynicism by the impact of the blows when they come.

Second, we must *get clear about our joy in this world.*

Life is tragic, says our author. Tragedy is in essence the frustration of nobility and the waste of good, and much of everyone's life is tragedy in relation to their hopes, plans, powers, and deserts. "The race is not to the swift or the battle to the strong, nor does food come to the wise or wealth to the brilliant or favor to the learned; but time and chance happen to them all. Moreover, no man knows when his hour will come: As fish are caught in a cruel net, or birds are taken in a snare, so men are trapped by evil times that fall unexpectedly upon them" (Ecclesiastes 9:11–12).

But tragedy is not the whole story. God gives joy too. Joy,

which is deeper than pleasure just as grief is deeper than pain, is a sense of well-being and contentment, plus (more or less, according to its intensity) a sense of significance in what one is doing and of insight into some aspect of life's real meaning. Those whose arrogance makes them spend their time resenting the way things are and planning egoistically for their own pleasure miss these joys entirely; humble folk, however, who live in the present moment and allow things around them to make their proper impression on them, find sweetness in life's simplicities, however much sourness may flow to them from more ambitious schemes. Central to the message of Ecclesiastes is the writer's insistence that this is so, and that these joys should be acknowledged as God's gift. Inscrutable providence, as he describes it, has its generous side.

> I commend the enjoyment of life, because nothing is better for a man under the sun than to eat and drink and be glad. Then joy will accompany him in his work. . . (8:15).

> A man can do nothing better than to eat and drink and find satisfaction in his work. This too, I see, is from the hand of God, for without him, who can eat or find enjoyment? (2:24–25; see also 3:12–13; 5:19).

> Light is sweet, and it pleases the eyes to see the sun. However many years a man may live, let him enjoy them all (11:7–8).

> Enjoy life with your wife, whom you love, all the days of this meaningless life that God has given you under the sun (9:9).

Ecclesiastes here directs us not to a calculating hedonism, as has sometimes been thought, but to a humble openness to the many simple joys with which our path is strewn, and which genuine cynics are, alas, too proud, too hurt, or simply too complicated to notice and accept.

So life under the sun is not universal tragedy, which excludes joy, but rather tragicomedy, in which, through divine action, joy and happiness are constantly winning out in the heart over tragic external circumstances. And no one who is alive in this world will miss God's gifts of joy at this level save those who shut their hearts against them. Joy will keep breaking in; God will see to that.

Third, we must *get clear about our hope in this world.*

Ecclesiastes is an Old Testament writer. He does not know much about the hope beyond this world that was brought to light by the resurrection and ascension of Jesus. But he knows that because God is just, somehow, somewhere, at some point in the future, there will be a judgment—that is, a final transmuting of our desert and direction in this life into our destiny forever. On this note he ends. "Now all has been heard; here is the conclusion of the matter: Fear God and keep his commandments, for this is the whole duty of man. For God will bring every deed into judgment, including every hidden thing, whether it is good or evil" (12:13–14; see also 3:17, 11:9). Which is as much as to say: Man's hope in this world is precisely his hope of divine judgment.

What's that? you say. *Hope* of divine *judgment?* Yes. The word *judgment* may suggest to us condemnation only, but in the Old Testament it regularly points to God's vindication too. The Book of Ecclesiastes is so somber and low-key that it would be easy to hear its last words only as a grim warning, which indeed from our standpoint they are. But they are more than that. They are words of encouragement to the harassed, bewildered, and frustrated victims of the "vanity" that we experience when we invest ourselves in trying to shape things to our own will. They are a plea to us to give up trying to play God to ourselves and to concentrate on worshiping and working for the real God instead. They are a reminder that God knows and notes all honest attempts to do this, and that he will not forget any genuine effort after reverence and righteousness, however little appreciation it may win from our fellow-humans and however pathetic the circumstantial background out of which it comes.

The pre-Christian sage is here like a solo bassoon hinting *sotto voce* at the truth that blazes so triumphantly (full orchestra!) in the words of the apostle Paul: "Therefore, my dear brothers, stand firm. Let nothing move you. Always give yourselves fully to the work of the Lord, because you know that your labor in the Lord is not in vain" (1 Corinthians 15:58). In the knowledge that God through Christ will one day reward, beyond this world, every "good deed"—that is, every bit of service truly rendered to him and to others for his sake—lies the hope by which today's cynical mood, brought on as it is by disappointment and disillusionment, may be finally vanquished.

"Anyone who comes to [God] must believe that he exists and that he rewards those who earnestly seek him," we are told (Hebrews 11:6). Cynicism takes over through disbelief of this. Clearly, from the thoughts that filled his mind, the man we know as Ecclesiastes lived on the very edge of the abyss of sceptical cynicism—but his knowledge of joy and his hope of judgment, in the sense explained, acted as guardrails which kept him from falling, however dizzy his head might grow as he looked down. And his hope remains the answer—the only answer—to the more secular and nihilistic cynicism that is flooding the West today.

But we are running ahead of ourselves. Let us once more backtrack, and state things in order.

Christian Hope

The Christian gospel speaks unabashedly about hope. On the surface of things this might not seem to call for much comment. Of course Christianity speaks of hope. What else? Isn't Christianity the best of all forms of optimism, teaching faith and hope and love as the only sound attitudes to life? If we have faith we can prevail, we hear. If we have hope, all sorts of possibilities will open up for us like morning glories. If we love, serenity will be our lot. But is that the essence of the message?

Well, Christians must say yes and no to this blithe description of what they believe; and their demurral is echoed by, or rather springs from, the Scriptures. All we need do is turn to the prophets, the evangelists, the apostles, and our Lord himself to find that the above description, familiar as it is from the gushings of a certain type of popular pulpit, has papered over almost everything that matters.

Christian hope, like Christian faith and Christian love, is a hard, bright, keen-edged thing. In fact, this hope, like this faith and love, is not a feeling or mood or disposition that can be described subjectively in terms of itself. Christians do not speak of "hope" by itself, any more than they speak of faith by itself, or love by itself. These words, as Christians use them, all point beyond themselves. They denote relational realities which in each case spring from God himself and return to him. They signify, in other words, a precise relationship to God based on what God himself has revealed, and where this specific reference is absent they are not being used in a Christian sense. There are quasi-religious sentiments aplenty abroad in our own time which encourage us in general terms to have hope. Such have every right to be heard in a pluralistic society like our own; but they are not Christianity.

Christian hope arises in response to what God has told us about himself. Like every other detail of the gospel, it is focused on Jesus Christ. "He is our hope," affirms the New Testament (see 1 Timothy 1:1; Colossians 1:27). This is, so says St. Paul, because in him all the promises of God find their fulfillment (Romans 15:8; 2 Corinthians 1:20).

Christ and God's Promises

By referring to God's promises, the gospel reaches back to the very beginning of human history. There in that strange and dim story of Eden we find the ultimate explanation of our need for hope. We were made for God, says the story, and our whole environment was to be the scene of our communion with him. There is a blissful harmony depicted in this story, a harmony which is recalled in pagan myths of the original Golden Age. But sin, we are told, now bars us from Eden; and our exile from that perfect realm in and with Adam is the root cause of our present despair, which is the state we are left in when hope is gone. Humanist hopes, as we saw earlier, are currently failing as man-made hopes have always failed, and despair now stares all thoughtful persons in the face.

Yet right at the outset, says the story, as soon as sin had come, God arrived with hope, so that we would not be obliged to live out our lives in despair. However, the hope he offered to mankind was mingled with dreadful pain. In his divine tact he began by finding coverings for human nakedness, the awful irony being that this very nakedness had been the very mantle of our majesty here-tofore. But since we could no longer bear the weight of that mantle, we had to be wrapped in coverings. The first such cover-ings were the skins of animals, so much more adequate than the fig leaves which Adam and Eve had snatched in their shame. (And we all have our own pathetic equivalents.) The first thing that God did for the first sinners, after pronouncing sentence on them, was to clothe them in skin garments (Genesis 3:21). (The first thing you do with any shivering, naked waif is to wrap him in a coat or a blanket.) But as any hunter with a hall full of trophies will tell you, the business of getting a pelt is a bloody one, with all the disemboweling and tearing of tissue that must go on before the fur piece is ready. So we are to note that the first killing ever, according to the story, was God's own killing, followed by his skinning of animals to cover the nakedness of Adam and Eve.

Here, then, at the beginning of hope, when God acts to rescue mankind from despair, we have blood and death. Hope does not arrive on Peter Pan wings and beckon us to a magic flight into instant bliss. We, who have torn the fabric of our whole existence, nay, of the whole world, by ripping ourselves free from God, are required to appreciate the pain entailed in the knitting back up of the fabric. But aeons and aeons must pass before that knitting up is complete, and until that day it is our lot not only to discover the pain of this rebellion in ourselves, but also to witness the suffering and groaning of the whole creation, which is itself paying the price for the perfidy of us, its stewards. Every fieldmouse torn by the hawk's talons, and every peccary squeezed to death by a constrictor, is being taxed, so to speak, for our crime.

Does someone protest that this is unthinkable? The Christian gospel, that lovely story of peace, good will, and love, says that it is so. "The whole creation has been groaning as in the pains of childbirth right up to the present time," wrote Paul. Before ever man started abusing the environment God cursed the ground for man's sake, marring his own work so that there could be no heaven on earth for us sinners (see Romans 8:19–22; Genesis 3:17–19). So the gospel is not entirely a tale of sweetness and light—or rather it is; but the sweetness and light must be bought at fearsome cost.

That cost is in fact far greater than the blood of fieldmice and peccaries, or even of lambs brought to altars. God spoke some strange and cryptic words in his sad encounter with Adam and Eve, about the seed of the woman who would "bruise" the villainous serpent's head (Genesis 3:15). Aha, so there is some glimmer of hope, then? Some destiny of triumph for mankind? That sounds like good news. But what exactly does it mean?

As Scripture shows, aeons had to pass before we could find out just what was meant. The way must be prepared for the event: altars must be built, and numberless animals slaughtered in sacrifice, and the Law must be obeyed on pain of death, and the prophets must cry out with their enigmatic visions of doom and salvation. But it is all a matter of preparing the way.

Whose way? we might ask. There is the crucial question; and the gospel furnishes the answer. The victorious seed of the woman promised in Eden, turns out to be the same person as the prophesied king, the son of David, and the prophesied man of sorrows who would be "wounded for our transgressions," and the child announced by the angel to Mary. It is Jesus. All these holocausts, century after century, and all this rigor of the Mosaic Law, and all these prophecies, strain forward toward the single event that brings them all to a point and unfurls their deepest meaning. The sacrifices won't save; the Law won't save; the prophecies won't save. These are all the shapes that hope takes during the long centuries between the ruin and the rescue of our race.

The great awe that falls on one person after another as the event emerges indicates the immensity of what is happening. Mary; Zechariah; Joseph; Elisabeth; the shepherds; the Magi; Simeon; Anna; Peter, James, and John at the transfiguration; even the troops arresting Jesus; and Pontius Pilate in his craven timeserving—all are dumbstruck (not to mention Paul on his busy way to Damascus). What prompts the awe, whether it goes with worship or with refusal to worship, is the dawning, electrifying suspicion that this might be *it*. This? The Messiah? In *our* time? Is this the one the prophets spoke about? Is this the Christ? Is this Israel's hope?

Yes, says the gospel, it is; and therein lies all hope, on the Christian view. For hope is not a mere refusal to accept defeat, a heroic virtue to be mustered and maintained by noble souls in the face of suffering, disaster, despair, or even of life's mere drudgery. Much less is it an attitude of general optimism to be cultivated from, by, and for itself. It is the response of joy that flashes to life in anyone who sees what Christ's coming means, like the thrill that comes to haggard clumps of war prisoners who see the camp gates suddenly crashing inward and their own troops arriving.

For what happened? As the Apostles' Creed puts it, Jesus was crucified, dead, and buried; then the third day he rose again from the dead and ascended into heaven. Jesus' resurrection, the most stupendous reversal of expectations in all history, has the status not of myth but of event, not of fancy but of fact, not of fiction but of reality. As has often been shown, it is wholly unreasonable to doubt that it happened, for the evidence available to us is compelling. Apostolic Christianity started as a resurrection faith, a supremely confident proclamation that Jesus, lately crucified, was risen, alive and enthroned over the world, and nothing can account for that save the supposition that the rock tomb really was empty, so that Jesus' corpse could not be found, and that Jesus really showed himself alive to his disciples, thus convincing them that so far from being a ghost he was now enjoying the power of a new kind of bodily life, over which death had no control.

It is not possible to suppose that the emptying of the tomb and the preaching of the resurrection were two stages in an apostolic deception of the public, a put-up job planned to save Jesus' reputation; for, first, the apostles had been as sure as everyone else that they would never see Jesus alive again, and were as bewildered as the women when the tomb was first found empty (see John 20:1–9); and, second, the apostles were prepared to die for their faith, which surely argues sincerity rather than duplicity. Nor is it possible to suppose that the dozen or so resurrection appearances which the New Testament records, involving more than five hundred witnesses (see 1 Corinthians 15:6), were all hallucinations. Such an idea is too wild to take seriously. But, as Sherlock Holmes said, when all the impossibilities have been eliminated what remains, however improbable, must be the truth; and so it appears in this instance. Dogmatic *a priori* denials of the possibility of resurrection fall to the ground in face of the fact that Christianity actually started, and could not conceivably have started had Jesus not risen. St. Paul, for one, thought the evidence cogent (he himself, of course, was part of it) and told the Athenian intelligentsia that God "has set a day when he will judge the world with justice by the man he has appointed. *He has given proof of this to all men by raising him from the dead*" (Acts 17:31). Even on the limited amount of evidence provided in the New Testament, it has to be admitted that Paul's claim is not at all too strong.

Christian hope is pinned on Jesus. Indeed, the title by which he is known in Christendom, Jesus Christ the Lord, spells out the nature of that hope. For if this man Jesus, who said what he said and lived as he lived and died as he died, is indeed the Christ, that is, the One chosen and anointed by God to be Messiah to his own people Israel and also the Savior of the whole world; and if he did rise from the dead to reign as Lord—then we may hope. For in that case all of history, and all the groaning creation, and all the tangled skein of your life and mine are in his hands. Here is no gang of Furies waiting with their shears to snip the poor thread of my life, as the Greeks taught. Here is no noble doom when we all go down fighting everything against the giants as the Norsemen taught. Here is no bright hazy blur suffusing everything at the end as some optimists teach. Here is no absorption into the oblivion of the One, nor any return to the treadmill of endless lives repeated in this world, as some Orientals teach. Here rather is the expectation of Israel and the hope of all Christian souls— namely the promise of a new life in a renewed world.

The Christian gospel declares that the great enemy of all hope, namely death, was destroyed by Christ. Death itself is apparently the "child" of evil, and made its entry into our world when sin came. Christ's overcoming of death following his achievement of redemption on the cross was a comprehensive defeat of the devil, which constituted the bruising of the serpent's head hinted at in Eden. Or at least, it was the vicarious, archetypal, representative, and decisive bruising of his head; for it guaranteed, among other things, that Christians (who are also the woman's seed, and are now in Christ) would themselves have victory over the tempter, hammering his head as he strikes at their heels till in due time they pass out of his reach altogether through sharing Jesus' new life of bodily resurrection.

No one has ever been able to give an exhaustive account of all that happened when Christ died. The event was unique and the New Testament accounts of it leave many questions unanswered. But the gospel teaches clearly and emphatically that he died "for us." In other words, he died so that he would not have to die. Or, to put it another way, by taking on himself the evil that we had introduced into the world (our sin, and hence our guilt), he set us free from the doom attached to our crime. In that sense he was our sin-bearing substitute. Put yet another way, Christ was our Champion who fought our enemy and beat him, thus securing our release from his clutches. Put still another way, he "paid the price" demanded by God's justice for our transgressions; or again, he offered the atoning sacrifice of himself on God's altar, and thus made "propitiation" before God for our sins—in other words, averted God's punitive wrath by wiping away our sins from his sight. And yet again, by dying and rising he broke our bondage to sin so that he would not have to live all chained up in our pride and fear and egoism and cruelty and ungodliness and greed, in other words, in what is at present our natural state, the state into which Adam brought us.

Does this sound complicated? It is the great achievement that is regularly celebrated in Christian worship, lauded in Christian hymns, and adored by Christians in their hearts. The biggest help in understanding the Cross is to see our need of it; then all these truths about it open up to us and become clear and precious in our sight. Mentally we cannot get beyond the realm of mystery (divine fact that passes our understanding), but we can realize what it is that we should thank the Lord Jesus for, and that is what really matters. In spirit we may come to the Manger, the Cross, the Empty Tomb, Nazareth, Galilee, Bethany, Nain, Caesarea Philippi, and all the other places where Jesus showed that he is the Christ, man's Savior and Lord, and learn to hope in him there as the people who met him in those places themselves learned to do. Some of the associated theology may defeat us, but it is Jesus himself who is our life and our hope, and the first purpose of the theology is to lead us to his feet. So then, if we hear and explore the theology from that standpoint, we will not go far wrong.

Hope of Glory

But how does the good news that we have been set free from guilt and bondage and punishment shape our hope for the future? To what, in positive terms, have we now to look forward?

The New Testament boils down its answer to one word: *glory*. Christ in you, says Paul, is your hope of glory (Colossians 1:27).

What is *glory*? One meaning which the New Testament word carries is "praise," and when we talk about glory in ordinary speech it is usually the state of being honored and praised that we have in mind—fame, money, limousines stopping at important doorways, flashbulbs and chanting crowds and klieg lights; or, as in an older era, crowns and ermine and trumpets. Christians would say that all those dazzling forms of glory are thin and shadowy hints of what is in store for those who receive the gospel. But when Christians say this, their minds are still centered on Jesus Christ. For the Christian "hope of glory" is grounded firmly on the life, death, resurrection, ascension, and second coming of Christ. It is in this sequence that we may see our own destiny blazoned; it is in terms of Jesus' glory that our own coming glory must be understood. For our hope is precisely to be glorified *with him* (see Romans 8:17).

Jesus took our flesh and lived as one of us enduring all the routine demands, the fatigue, the pressure, and the suffering that mark our mortal lives. He died as one of us, in weakness, grief, pain, and apparent defeat. But thereby he defeated death in his own death, and rose again, bringing our mortal flesh with him to immortality. This is the reason for all the Christian hilarity at Easter: Death, our worst enemy, has been conquered, and with that enemy, all our despair. Hope therefore rises. And when Jesus ascended, so the gospel teaches, he took human flesh with him into the impenetrable glory and mystery of the Holy Trinity itself. This guarantees that he will do the same for our flesh, yours and mine, one day. The New Testament simply tells us that he did thus ascend, returning to his Father, and is now enthroned at the Father's right hand (the place of active government) in his official role as our High Priest, wearing the vestment of our flesh, constantly intervening with his Father to ask and act on our behalf. Christian hope grasps hold of this fact every time a Christian prays. We do not need to paw the arm of some remote and capricious deity as the priests of Baal did in Elijah's day; our prayer is already being offered before we can get it said, and more than this, St. Paul teaches that when we do not know what to pray for, as is very often the case, the Holy Spirit is making intercession for us "with groans that words cannot express" (Romans 8:26). This knowledge is a lifeline of hope for any Christian struggling to wring some sort of prayer from his sluggish and often blank heart.

But the story does not end here. The gospel teaches that Christ will come again. Indeed, our Lord said those very words: "I will come back and take you to be with me that you also may be where I am" (John 14:3). In similar vein the angel said to the apostles who stood goggling at the Ascension: "This same Jesus, who has been taken from you into heaven, will come back in the same way you have seen him go into heaven" (Acts 1:11). The whole New Testament rings with this expectation: Christ will come again!

For Christian hope this means that history is going somewhere, as distinct from nowhere. It is not an endless treadmill, nor an enormous cycle, nor a downhill curve trailing off into oblivion. However we may wish to chart the course of history itself (and historians quarrel about this: Are we going up, down, forward, or round and round?). One thing is sure, says the gospel: It is all going to be "consummated" in the return of Christ. All the dangling threads will be gathered up and knit back together. All cruelty and unfairness will be sorted out. All that is lost will be found. Everything will be brought into a form that will commend itself to us as *right*.

But here again, Christian hope does not envisage a mere waving of Peter Pan's wand to make everything and everyone magically happy. All this straightening out and squaring up, as the prophets and apostles and Jesus himself picture it, is part of the process of *judgment*. We spoke of judgment earlier; it is a matter of discerning the worth of our works, which in turn reveal the worth of us the workers, and of determining our destiny accordingly. (Paul spells out the principle with great precision in Romans 2:5–16.) Judgment is "based on truth" (Romans 2:2); it means acknowledgment and vindication for the godly, just as it means exposure and condemnation for the ungodly. Christ is coming to judgment; and if we cannot face that judgment, our hope of glory becomes a pipe-dream, an illusion, a bubble destined to burst.

The Way to Glory

The question now becomes personal and poignant, both for us who write this book and for you who read it. We are bad inside, double-minded, morally unstable in our motives, self-absorbed, and self-seeking, not lovers of God nor of men as we should be. Our track record is of failures and shortcomings, as it seems, all along the line. How can we face that final judgment? If we get what we deserve, we shall be cut off from God forever. Well may we fear death, not only because dying means leaving behind all the good and pleasant aspects of life in this world, but also because "man is destined to die once, *and after that to face judgment*" (Hebrews 9:27). What hope have we? The hope of glory, of which we spoke so blithely a few paragraphs back, seems to have vanished away. How can we possibly be accepted at the judgment-throne on the basis of our own performance?

Have we forgotten? Or did we not understand what was said of Christ's death just now? We are never to rest our hope in our own performance, but only in what Jesus has done and suffered for us. "God made him who had no sin to be sin for us, so that in him we might become the righteousness of God" (2 Corinthians 5:21). Righteousness—that is, a right relationship, a righteous man's standing, a state of noncondemnation, a verdict of forgiveness and acceptance with God—is God's own gift. It is given in virtue of Christ's atonement and obedience and is bestowed by the risen Lord himself upon all who center their faith and hope upon him. "Those who receive God's abundant provision of grace and of the gift of righteousness [will] reign in life through the one man, Jesus Christ" (Romans 5:17). This is the deepest meaning of the cross; this is the precious truth of justification by faith.

Good gracious, you say. That does not make any sense. Righteousness *transferred,* as by a legal fiction, from Jesus to me? Righteousness *accounted* to sinners, as if God juggles his own books? If you are not joking, you must be blaspheming.

But there is no mistake. Scandalous as it sounds, this is the true gospel, the source book of peace in the present and hope for the future. It is, in fact, the best news ever. It amounts to this: that Jesus, the crucified, risen, and reigning Savior, has taken full responsibility to all eternity for each one of those who trust him. Salvation is therefore everlasting; it reaches to the end of one's mortal existence and past it, through the day of judgment into that ultimate happiness which lies beyond for those who are Christ's. And this salvation is ours for the asking. You and I may know at this moment that when we stand before God and the books are opened, stamped across the debit account will be the momentous word "JUSTIFIED"—if we would like it that way.

If we would like it that way? Silly question! Or is it? Perhaps not. For not everyone who hears the gospel offer is pleased to receive it. Some would prefer, it seems, to stand before God as they are and be judged accordingly. Why is that? There seems to be a double cause: partly self-righteous pride, taking the form of reluctance to receive favors and thus become dependent, and partly a strange unawareness of the problem of one's own sin— the fruit, perhaps, of not facing the fact that the God revealed in Scripture is holy. But how heartbreakingly sad! For the gospel is God's last word to mankind before judgment comes, and to reject God's last word is to reject one's own last hope.

There is here another mystery that we must acknowledge, namely our freedom (free agency, some would call it) with regard to receiving or repelling God's approaches to us in grace. We see this freedom in action, both ways, in the gospel stories of different people who crossed Jesus' path during his ministry—frantic beggars and lepers, and busy fishermen, and individual householders who received him and in some cases sought him out and proud, wealthy pillars of the community who watched him critically from afar but would have nothing directly to do with him. We all have both options. Free agency, or moral self-determination, is a power that God sustains in each one of us. (How it relates to his universal sovereignty is a mystery which need not be discussed here.) What we have to face is that the Most High will not force himself on anyone who wishes and chooses to repel him. We are not robots; we have permission to say no to God, to choose death, to reject hope, and to ruin our souls. We have permission also, and encouragement with it, to ask God so to change our hearts that we shall not do this. "God so loved the world" says the best-known and best-loved verse in the Bible "that he gave his one and only Son, that whoever believes in him shall not perish but have eternal life" (John 3:16). *Whoever* expresses an inclusive invitation; none are excluded save those who exclude themselves, refusing faith and so negating hope forever. To ourselves, as to our readers, we say, with all the weight and passion we can command: For God's sake don't refuse. *Choose life*—and if you are uncertain at present whether you have a clear enough grasp of what is involved to make that choice, then *choose to choose life*, and ask God so to work in your mind and heart that you will soon have the light and strength you need to rest your faith and hope in Christ as Christians do.

Commitment to Jesus Christ, then, is the path to glory; and being with Jesus Christ will in some unimaginable way be the essence of glory for every believer. As every Christian is already, in this world, the object of the divine Savior's undivided love and attention, so it will be to all eternity. (Do not think that *undivided* love and attention are impossible because of the numbers involved; remember, Jesus Christ is *God!*) And as the Savior's self-giving to the saints is already their *life*, so in that consummated love-relationship it will be their *reward*.

Two points must be made if we are to understand what the New Testament means when it promises rewards, as it often does, to servants of God. The first point is that the reward is always a gift of love to one who tried rather than payment of earnings to one who succeeded; it is loyal faithfulness rather than dazzling fruitfulness that is being rewarded, as when parents reward clumsy children for honest attempts, however incompetent, to give pleasure by doing household jobs. The second point is that the reward consists, not of something different from the activity that qualified for it (as when academic achievement is rewarded by a money prize), but of that same activity in its perfected form. As when the wooer wins his lady his reward is just that life of fully expressing and receiving love to which their marriage opens the door, so the reward which the Father and the Son through the Spirit bestow on Christians is just more of their love and fellowship and generosity—in short, more of themselves—than those Christians ever knew on this earth. That is what the gorgeous New Testament pictures of crowns and robes and thrones and feasts and seeing God in new Jerusalem are really saying. This is the reward to which believers go—the dignity, we might say, to which they are promoted—when heartstop day arrives.

Here is a man who some years ago moved from England to Vancouver, Canada. Ask him, and he will tell you that he has fallen in love with the place, and the honeymoon is not yet over and is never likely to be; he hopes to spend the rest of his life there, and cannot imagine ever getting tired of having the city as his home. So, too, Christianity is a love affair with the God of love, and whether "here" or "there," as modern Christians like to put it, believers cannot imagine themselves ever growing weary of love's exchanges between themselves and their Lord. They know, indeed, that heaven includes the end of bodily pain and spiritual convalescence, and the start of a kind of health that they never before experienced; they know that in heaven all the values they could ever conceive are present, all the good goals that they ever sought are some way realized, and the company of the redeemed is an endless riot of mutual affection and delight, free from all the inhibitions, insensitivities, and stupidities that mar Christian fellowship in this world. But for all that, the heart of the hope of heaven for Christians is the prospect of being "with the Lord forever" (1 Thessalonians 4:17). It is the presence and the friendship of their beloved Savior that will make heaven for them. As it is expressed in a much-loved hymn, whose sugariness we can forgive as we contemplate the sweetness of its theme:

O Christ, He is the fountain,
  The deep sweet well of love!
The streams on earth I've tasted,
  More deep I'll drink above!
There, to an ocean fullness,
  His mercy doth expand,
And glory, glory dwelleth
  in Immanuel's land.

The bride eyes not her garment,
  But her dear Bridegroom's face;
I will not gaze at glory,
  But on my King of grace—
Not at the crown He giveth,
  But on His pierced hand:
The Lamb is all the glory
  of Immanuel's land.

Anne R. Cousins

So the Christian's personal hope of glory may be focused thus:

Forever with the Lord!
  Amen, so let it be!
Life from the dead is in that word;
  'Tis immortality.
Here in the body pent,
  Absent from Him I roam,
Yet nightly pitch my moving tent
  A day's march nearer home.

So when my latest breath
  Shall rend the veil in twain,
By death I shall escape from death,
  And life eternal gain.
Knowing as I am known,
  How shall I love that word!
And oft repeat before the throne,
  For ever with the Lord!

James Montgomery

Hope of Righteousness

In exploring the Christian's personal hope, we took our eyes off the prospect of all things being retrieved, restored, knit up, and fulfilled with Christ's coming at the end of history. We must now get back to that, for this is where New Testament teaching about the future centers.

The first thing to say is that Christ's personal reappearance will have enormous *cosmic* consequences. It will literally put an end to our world. "The day of the Lord will come like a thief. The heavens will disappear with a roar; the elements will be destroyed by fire, and the earth and everything in it will be laid bare [or: burned up]. . . . But in keeping with his promise we are looking forward to a new heaven and a new earth, the home of right-eousness" (2 Peter 3:10, 13). Peter pictures the cosmos as being re-created through entering the fire, in the manner of the mythical phoenix. What this will mean in experience is unimaginable, and we shall not waste our time trying to imagine the unimaginable; there are better things to do! We would only say that for the individual the significance of Christ's public coming is the same as the significance of one's personal death, which will also put an end to one's world; and since the latter may come as suddenly and catastrophically as the former will (see, on that point, Luke 17:26–35; Matthew 24:36–44, 25:13; 1 Thessalonians 5:1–3), the wise man will school himself to see this present life as temporary, to keep short accounts with God, and to live, as it were, packed up and ready to go. If one is not ready for death, viewing life in the manner of those old healthy-minded medievals and Puritans as a preparation for dying, and living each day *sub specie aeternitatis* (in the light, and the sight, of eternity), one is not ready for the Lord's return, whatever one may think and say to the contrary. It is to be feared that many Christians have slipped at this point.

The second thing to say is that Christ's personal reappearance will have enormous *moral* consequences. The new cosmic order that will be created will be, as Peter said, "the home of right-eousness." This means not only that stable and confirmed holiness will mark all its inhabitants but also that there it will be made plain that all the evil, pain, and grief that God permitted in this world was justified by the superabundant good that came out of it, and that would not have existed apart from it. In that sense we shall see evil, pain, and grief as having been *redeemed*, and all our perplexities and uncertainties about the rightness of God's ways with us will then be banished forever. But what an audacious thing to envisage! As Ecclesiastes reminded us earlier, evil, pain, and grief are all around us on the grand scale, and mere Pollyannaism is so inadequate to the facts as to be odious. To point this up, let us, as good disciples of Ecclesiastes, mention some specifics.

What of all the millions whose lives have been snuffed out like that of so many gnats under the boots of tyrants and conquerors? What of the victims of the Holocaust and the Cambodian genocide? What of the widows and orphans left desolate by war, murder, and the miscarriage of justice? What of women immured for decades behind convent walls against their will because there was no place for them in Peter the Great's Russia or Louis XIV's Versailles? What of Huguenot fugitives and Catholic men who tried to help them escape, all chained in galleys for the rest of their lives? What of the victims of the eighteenth-century slave trade? What of the perfidious and lecherous sultans, kings, plutocrats, and politicians who have feasted on all life's dainties and whose hands are smeared with the blood of the innocents from whom they wrung their sumptuous fare? What of the Victorian gentlemen who made a specialty of deflowering teenage virgins, and of the rapists and child abusers of our own day? What of the Prisoner of Chillon who walked back and forth in his dungeon till the stone floor was worn down, or the anonymous Man in the Iron Mask, both incarcerated for no fault of their own, simply for reasons of state? What of the golden eagle who sits in his cage year after year, unable even to spread his wings, while visitors to the zoo drift by licking their ice cream cones? What of the finches which Algerian boys torment till some passing tourist pays money to have the bird set free? For that matter, what about all the mice batted about and teased to death by our cats? What of children run down and fellow motorists killed, maimed, and paralyzed by drunken drivers? What of wives battered by their husbands, and what of the eight-figure tally of modern Western mothers-to-be who elected to have their children put to death while still inside their bodies? What of . . . .

Oh Christ! you cry. *Stop it.*

And in that cry, whether you intend it this way or not, you are joining in a prayer which has been made in the church for nearly two thousand years—*Kyrie eleison! Christe eleison!* (Lord, have mercy! Christ, have mercy!). And that prayer is the Christian voicing of a plea that runs all through Israel's psalms and prayers. *O Lord, how long? Help, Lord!* Hope in God! comes the answer, time and time again. But no help came, as it seems, at least no help of the kind that the psalmist hoped for. His enemies went on flourishing and making fun of him; the heathen prospered; widows died without redress, and orphans starved; finally Israel was carried off into exile, and ruin was everywhere. Christians pray today in terms similar to the psalmists, and externally nothing seems to change for them either. (The gift of strength to endure is of course a real answer to prayers for help in time of trouble, but it is not relevant to the point we are making.) We ask the Lord to stop the evil, and the evil goes on.

So what should we say? Is the whole faith a tissue of fantasy? Is religion, after all, no more than an opiate, as Marx thought? Is the hope of Israel and Christendom a mockery? What about the countless suffering souls who have gone into the oblivion of death down the centuries, indeed the millennia, prior to our own day? Surely they, and the many vile situations that entrapped them, are beyond help now? It is no doubt easy, and very fine, to talk of our own salvation; but what of the sheer pain of things? Have we a right, even, to rejoice in our personal hope of heaven when the world is in agony? How, in any case, could one retrieve and redress evils that belong to the past? We can't re-do history. Should we then curse God for his unwillingness to take action, or pity him for his inability to do so, or resolve to destroy him by a defiantly willed atheism, as so many in our era have done since Karl Marx, Sigmund Freud, Jean Paul Sartre, Bertrand Russell, and secular humanists as a body pointed the way? What should our next thoughts be?

We should keep on hoping in God. That is the answer. His power, as revealed in creation and providence—omnipotence backed by omniscience and omnipresence, in short omnicompetence—and his character, as revealed supremely in Christ—love, goodness, mercy, wisdom, long-suffering, truthfulness, faithfulness, justice, holiness—guarantee that he knows, cares, works to a plan, and is resolved to triumph finally over evil in his own appointed way and at his own appointed time. Indeed, the triumph has already begun. God took decisive responsibility for the presence of evil in his world, undertaking to bring out of that evil such good as would make the creating of a world into which evil could enter appear in retrospect as a glorious thing; and through the agony of Calvary, which was the cost to God of his redemptive enterprise, he has in principle accomplished his purpose.

In the death, resurrection, and ascension of the incarnate Son, we see God's victory over badness of all sorts—sin, death, outrage, loss, pain, satanic malice, tragic waste. All these evil things were redeemed—that is, made the means of good which would not otherwise have existed, in this case salvation for us sinners—through Jesus' dying and rising. Nor is that all. Through "the redemption that is in Christ Jesus," as Paul calls it (Romans 3:24, KJV), all evils in the life of redeemed persons have themselves been similarly redeemed, as those redeemed persons are sometimes able to see already in particular matters, and as they expect to be enabled to perceive comprehensively when Christ comes again.

An example of what we mean by this is the case of the man who, because of a head injury as a child which blighted his schooldays, was rejected for military service in the second World War and thus could go straight from school to university, where he became a Christian under influences which he would not have met in the army. He now sees the injury as redeemed, since it was made a means of his being saved through Christ, and he expects that he will one day see similar divine sense in all the many Murphy's-law experiences that have scattered themselves through his life.

And there is more yet to be said. Redemption through Christ is to touch the whole created order. In its reconstitution it will be set free from all the evil, decay, and unfulfillment that have marked and marred it since God cursed it in Eden. Paul speaks of the creation as *waiting* and *groaning* till the day when heaven and earth are made new. His words are so intriguing and arresting (not to say enigmatic and mysterious!) that we had better quote the passage in full.

> The creation waits in eager expectation for the sons of God to be revealed. For the creation was subjected to frustration, not by its own choice, but by the will of the one who subjected it, in hope that the creation itself will be liberated from its bondage to decay and brought into the glorious freedom of the children of God. We know that the whole creation has been groaning as in the pains of childbirth right up to the present time (Romans 8:19–22).

How precisely will the evils that we listed above, and the myriad more that we did not list, be redressed when creation is renewed? We do not know; God has not told us, and it is beyond us to guess. But the picture of the new order which we find in the

Gospels, and in the teaching of the apostles, and most exquisitely in the Revelation given to John is of joy, hilarity, triumph, gratitude, fullness, light, and splendor. Our hope is that one day we the redeemed will find ourselves part of that scene, and we may be sure that then we shall be able to see in each case the answer to the question with which this paragraph started; for the redressing will then have been done. The new cosmos will thus be "the home of righteousness" indeed.

Hope and Humanness

It is a paradox of Christian hope that we await something which (we are told) has already been accomplished, though at present we do not see it. (Paul notes in Romans 8:24 that sight and hope are exclusive of each other.) Believing that Christ has set us free from sin's dominion, we sin nonetheless. Believing that we are sanctified by the Holy Spirit, we find little enough sanctity in our actual behavior. We hope for full redemption from sin and death; we believe that in a real sense redemption is ours already; yet in another sense it is clearly not ours yet, at least not fully, and sometimes hope falters and we wonder if it ever will be. How should we handle this hiatus between what we believe about ourselves and what we observe in ourselves?

It may help us to recall that nature, too, has her optical illusions. The whole of an oak tree is in a real sense in the acorn hidden in the earth—but who would know? It does not look like it. Or again, when we see the last of a sunset, the sun appears to have sunk and there is nothing in the immediate situation to arouse hope of our ever seeing it again. But next day up it comes, all the same. Appearance is not always a sure index of reality. "You *died*," writes Paul to Christians, "and your life is now *hidden* with Christ in God." Does it look like it, or feel like it? Doubtless not; but—"When Christ, who is your life, *appears*, then you also will *appear* with him in glory" (Colossians 3:3, 4). The truth about us will be made evident when Christ comes, says Paul; till then, it is hidden, and in relation to it we walk by faith, not by sight. We need to grasp this, and to grasp with it our obligation to live out with all our powers the new, invisible Christ-life that God has wrought in all Christians; and then we shall find ourselves able to cope with this tension between faith and sight, knowing that even though we are not yet what we should be, and one day will be, yet by God's grace we are not what we were, and there is no question which way we are heading. The new life is becoming manifest, even if the process is incomplete and slow; Christian believers really are being changed. Which brings us to our final point.

Christian hope has ethical effects. It is sometimes accused of being madness and delusion, but its consequences in human conduct do not look in the least like the fruit of those conditions. For Christian hope nourishes, not a rash, fevered, glittery-eyed defiance of reality, but fortitude, patience, and gladness. It sets one free from egocentric frenzy, for it means that one entrusts one's own future well-being and the future well-being of all that might be called one's interests (family, property, career, health, and so forth) to God. It sets one free for sober realism, for one whose treasure is in heaven can afford to face the facts about earth, however grim, in a way that others (secular humanists, for instance, as we saw) can scarcely do. It thus makes for sensitivity, objectivity, wisdom, and sanity—qualities of which today's world seems to stand in acute need.

Also, hope sets one free for compassion. It is true, we know, that in the name of Christian hope some have taken a thoroughly callous attitude toward the agonies of our modern world. (Famine? Disaster? War? Hurrah—it means that Christ's coming is drawing nearer.) But this is to misconceive utterly the nature of Christian hope, which is the near sister of sympathy and charity. One whose hope is in God has ceased to be self-seeking, so his mind is free to care whole heartedly for others, and it is the distress of others more than any other motive that will make him cry *How long, O Lord? how long?* Christian hope is, after all, *Christian*—that is, it centers upon, draws sustenance from, and invokes the mercy of the One who died on behalf of this suffering world. It can never be callous or cavalier about the suffering of so much as a sparrow.

Also, Christian hope sustains resolution and gives strength to resist pressure. Hope sustained Jesus himself, "who for the joy set before him endured the cross, scorning its shame, and sat down at the right hand of the throne of God" (Hebrews 12:2). Hope, as we said at the start of this chapter, is a spur to effort, and the brighter the hope, the spunkier the effort will be. It is hope that keeps at bay both weariness in well-doing and paralyzing fears of opposition and hostility. "Prepare your minds for action," wrote Peter to churches entering persecution; "be self-controlled; *set your hope fully on the grace to be given you when Jesus Christ is revealed*" (1 Peter 1:13). Firm hope leads to a firm stand.

Finally—and here again we return to an earlier point—Christian hope enables one to face death: to watch it creeping up as the cancer tightens its grip, or as one's physical frame wastes away, and finally to meet it and go down into it with calm confidence and joy, in the knowledge that Christ is there and one goes to be with him. It was in this spirit that early martyrs met the lions and latter-day martyrs, the Mau Mau knives and the gunmen of Idi Amin. Christians die, as the Anglican burial service puts it, "in sure and certain hope of the Resurrection to eternal life, through our Lord Jesus Christ"; death is thus something they can *handle*. "Our people die well," said John Wesley. It was a good testimony to his Methodists; it remains a good testimony to the power of Christian hope.

Would it be too much, do you think, to say that Christian hope *humanizes*? You have read our discussion; now it is for you to judge. We rest our case.

6

Health and Virtue

Two reasons could be given for not titling this chapter "Health and Virtue." First, it looks like a confusion, health being one thing and virtue being another. We shall see, however, that from the Christian point of view not only is there not a very wide gap between them, but that to speak of one involves speaking of the other. They almost come to the same thing. The second reason would be the obvious one, namely that this title will put people off. For the word *virtue* nowadays seems to us both comic and hollow, conjuring up pictures of twittering Victorian spinsters with teacups, or stern-faced nuns scolding schoolgirls for their naughty minds, or smiling humbugs softly parading moral superiority in order to put us down. Furthermore, to link the two words is to invite notions of bright-eyed dietary rectitude and strident, back-slapping camaraderie—the sort of thing offered by vegetarian communal farms and mind-cure spas, where inmates are encouraged to pile their hair in loose buns on top of their heads, put on sensible walking shoes, drink carrot juice, and start doing breathing exercises. Such notions are unlikely to appeal.

But the plan of our book requires us to take the risk of tackling these themes, and tackling them together. For to speak of health and of virtue is to touch on two topics that everyone will agree are central to any properly human life. It is easier to see this, of course, in the case of health, since there is not much room for disagreement as to what constitutes health. Also, ours is an age that is very conscious of what a misery lack of health is. So we shall discuss health first.

Health of Body

Athletes furnish most of us with our ideal of physical health. Every few years we see the Olympic games on television. We watch the parades of young men and women filing with springy and agile steps into the arena for the starting ceremonies, each one of them with bodies brought to a poised, lithe pitch of perfection—clear skin, keen eyes, jawlines that show years of discipline and determination, flat stomachs, taut thighs. We slump in our chairs with our bag of potato chips and try not to look down at our own bulgy flabbiness. This is *health*, we feel. Oh, to be able to enjoy that cheetah-like suppleness. We watch them on the giant slalom or pounding the track or thrashing through the water or straining at the pole vault, and we know that we are looking at a level of health and fitness that very few people enjoy.

Most of us settle for a great deal less, by choice. The food we eat is of our own choosing, and we know that potato chips, cola, peanuts and popcorn, Big Macs and six-packs are not going to help us in the struggle to stay "in shape." "Very well then," we say, "we'll just eat and drink what we enjoy, and settle for carrying about with us as much duty as our metabolism levies on these pleasures." It may be more weight, trouble with our teeth or our circulation or our respiration, or any of a thousand other plagues. But one way or another we are ready to risk our health (within limits, of course) for what we enjoy doing. If the doctor puts his foot down, however, and rules out all salt or oils or milk products as the price of physical well-being for the future, then we shift over, to live as best we can with these abstinences. Why do we thus put our health ahead of our enjoyment? Because it has now become more important. It is no longer a matter of flab and short-windedness; the doctor is assuring us that serious illness threatens. In a flippant moment we might have said that we would rather have sugar, whatever ills it brings. But when the danger signal goes up, we do not dilly-dally. Out goes the sugar.

What we are showing is that not one of us will deliberately

choose sickness over health. Health, no less than freedom and hope, is a basic human requirement. To have our health taken away is to suffer a major misfortune. It is to have lost something that we valued enormously. To be in the category of the sick, we feel, is not nearly as good as being well.

Most of us, of course, come in that category at some point. Migraines, asthma, hay fever, allergies, myopia, tennis elbow, low back pain, flat feet, corns, boils, acne, nervous tics, soft teeth, moles, pimples, gray hair—all of us lug about some such signs of mortality. But we can function more or less "normally," even if it means carrying insulin or aspirin or Valium or nitro-glycerin around in our pocket, or wearing an elastic sleeve or corset.

Sometimes, however, we cannot function so, and then we have to be hospitalized. Suddenly the tools of our trade are replaced with tubes and bottles and machines that crank out graph paper. Suddenly all our responsibilities are lifted right out of our hands and set on one side without the slightest consideration of how important they (or we) are. I may be the President of France or the father of five children or the linchpin in some delicate enterprise, but this all blows away like chaff at the breath of sickness. Now there is nothing in all the world left for me to do but to be sick. I am helpless, and this is not a state of affairs that I would choose. It does violence to my notion of what I am—an adult with some measure of free choice and self-determination, and certainly with duties that I must carry out. I don't *like* this interloper—this tumor, this occlusion, this malfunction. Oh, to be sure, there is expert help here with all these specialists and surgeons and technicians. But perhaps they cannot stop the intruder, perhaps they can only slow him down, and in that case I have to face the fact that I shall get slowly worse and never be fully healthy again. That leaves me with a great sense of being diminished. Permanent loss of health is a very grievous loss indeed.

Often we pause at the doorway before stepping into someone's hospital room. Why? Because we do not know what we are going to see. What will he (or she) look like? Will the face that we have known in its healthy state now be gray and shrunken? Will there be visible tokens of the rampage of the disease? The point is, we do not like the signs left by the departure of health. And if they are hard for us to bear when we see them on the face of an old or middle-aged person, they are intolerable on the face of a child.

There is almost an obscenity here, we think, in the defacing of this little creature. Whether we are religious or nonreligious, our feelings at this point are the same. We want to scream and shake our fist at a universe in which such horrors can happen. No doubt familiarity with these sights will deaden our sensitivity to them, but the first time, at any rate, will leave us quite unnerved. As well as being a harbinger of mortality, disease affronts us by its very ugliness. It is, we feel, a cosmic monstrosity—and our feeling here is right, as we shall see.

Health of Mind

We have spoken so far only of physical health, which is what we immediately think of when health is mentioned. Mental health, however, is actually more important. A healthy mind can achieve a calm and radiant triumph over the waste of bodily sickness, but no amount of bodily health can relieve or restore a sick mind. What a dark vista stretches away in front of us, however, when we turn to all the plagues that bedevil our mental and emotional health. Who can chart these? From the smallest routine anxieties to the most ravaging psychoses we find the assault of irrationality threatening our humanness. Whether it is a fear of spiders, stage-fright, social awkwardness, nightmares, dark desires which we would rather not name, obsessive loves and hates, monomania, or paranoia most of us have known one form or another of debility on this front. And once again, if we stand far enough from it to get any sort of perspective on it, we know that whatever it is, no matter how small, it is violating something important in our identity as human beings. Somehow we ought to be in charge of ourselves better than this, we tell ourselves. I mean—it's only a spider. The audience is on my side. That *grande dame* is nobody to be afraid of. It was only a dream. I'm silly to feel so strongly about him. And so on, and so forth. But we find that it's no good. The whole edifice of our dignity and self-command goes down in a heap before maggots in the mind.

All this is true, says someone, but has it any place in a discussion of secular humanism and Christianity? Surely the only question that arises is how to cure these diseased conditions, and questions of religion or irreligion do not enter into that.

Not at surface level—granted. For in the treatment of physical sickness, the only possible sorts of division between religious and nonreligious people would arise from patients whose religious views led them to seek divine healing without medical help, or to refuse, say, blood transfusions or particular forms of diet, or else from physicians whose antireligious views made them insist that the presence of a chaplain on a hospital staff is undesirable, since it introduces God into the agenda of poor people whose recovery depends on having minds free from the traumas and tensions which God-thoughts cause. (Here the humanist dogma that religion is bad for you surfaces again.) But these are rare extremes. Ordinarily a Baptist surgeon and an atheist anesthesiologist can work quite harmoniously over a human thorax.

In treating mental and emotional disturbance it is less easy to keep religion out of the picture, for both patient and therapist have basic convictions which shape their thoughts about the disturbance itself, above and beyond what the narrow clinical facts may indicate. If the patient feels unable to trust the therapist because of religious differences, the latter's healing strategy will be badly disrupted. Nonetheless, in functional terms it is ordinarily possible for psychiatrists and psychological counselors, using the same basic skills, to help their patients irrespective of how much or how little religious rapport may exist between them, and the prejudice of some Christians against any form of secular psychiatry does not seem to be well founded.

Humanists and Christians on Ill Health

But huge differences appear between religious and non-religious people, particularly between Christians and humanists, as soon as one asks why we have to face ill health, physical degeneration in its many forms, and ultimately death. For here the basic frames of references are involved.

The secularist is usually an evolutionist, and as such he sees human life in primarily physical and developmental terms. He thinks of human individuals as structurally and functionally a little higher than the apes from which we came, and he thinks structurally and functionally about every phenomenon and problem in human life. His explanations of human sickness and death will therefore be descriptive rather than evaluative and genetic rather than interpretive; that is to say, assuming as he does that there is no knowable point outside the circle of our experience from which we may take our bearings, he will use language that simply tells us what is going on (such and such cells are doing so and so, or whatever). Thus he will reduce the question *Why?* to a form of the question, *For what physical reason?* or *From what physical cause?* He will avoid and, indeed, object to any attempt to answer the question *Why?* in terms of personal purpose or value. Sickness is just a fact, he will say, and sometimes it is possible to do something about it; death is just a fact, and often it is not possible to do anything about it; that's all there is to know. He may be a pessimist, guessing that it will always be so, or an optimist who dreams of producing disease-free human organisms by selective breeding and genetic engineering, whereby the evolutionary process may be hurried up. But in either case he will not look for any explanation deeper than the physical, and will dismiss as fanciful and trivial any goal- or value-oriented answer to *Why?* which metaphysics or theology might suggest.

At this point, however, the Christian is on an altogether different wavelength. He is already committed. Like Jews, Hindus, and Moslems, he has accepted an outlook on life which does in fact take its bearings from a point outside our present experience. Unlike Hindus, he believes in a God who is as personal as we are; unlike Jews, he acknowledges Jesus Christ as the divine Son who definitively revealed God; unlike Moslems, he believes that God is actively and empathetically involved in the world he has made. As a recipient of revelation from his Creator, who is working out a personal cosmic purpose in literally everything that happens, the Christian believes himself to have access to a picture which includes in principle the whole of our experience, leaving nothing out, and which shows that it all has meaning in terms of God's own goals. This is not to say that the Christian thinks he can explain each event in specific terms, interpreting what God was up to in each case; he knows that he cannot do that, and he has settled for living in ignorance of God's specific purpose in a thousand ontological riddles and ten thousand cosmic outrages.

Two things, however, he does know and labors never to lose sight of. The first is that this world is out of joint because of sin (we spoke of that conviction in the last chapter); all our race shares in the Adamic curse of which disease is a part. The second is that redemption is afoot and has, indeed, already been in principle achieved, just as a war is in principle won when the decisive battle has taken place. Putting it more concretely, the Christian knows that the blackest holes of Calcutta, that the worst inhumanities and degradations of the Dachaus and the Buchenwalds of Nazi Germany, and that all the most malicious cruelties and the most destructive agonies that are ever seen are somehow subsumed under the archetypal atrocity, which is also the best thing that has ever taken place—namely, the Cross and passion of God incarnate, our Lord and Savior Jesus Christ. And it is at the Cross and through the Cross, claims the Christian, that we finally learn what to make of sickness, and what to do about it.

But wait a minute, the humanist interrupts. You are wandering off our subject. We were talking of sickness and health, and now you bring in this religious symbol, the Cross. That is the trouble with religion; it is always bustling in with amulets and wands and spells and cloudy verbiage about what looks and feels all wrong really being all right. None of that ever advanced the human cause very far; beakers and charts and scalpels and drips and medication are much more to the point if you want to see sickness cured.

To which we reply:

First, we certainly want to see sickness cured, and the quest for a religious understanding of it in no way runs counter to the quest for medical means of alleviating it. There is nothing anti-Christian in seeking to counter disease; Jesus' own healing ministry (to look no further) shows that; and where God in his providence provides the physician's skills and the surgeon's expertise, we should avail ourselves gratefully of their help.

Second, the humanist's impatience with us reflects the fact that for him our *Why?* is, as we saw, a nonquestion, since for him there is no God and no transcendent purpose in anything. But if, as Christians believe, God exists, and is good, and rules, and in some sense works out his will in all that happens, then there is a question here, and a major one, to which we need to give our minds. It breaks down, in fact, into five questions, as follows:

1. Does full humanness require health?

2. If so, why is there, in God's world, ill health, disease, and death?

3. What should we think of the God who in his providential overruling permits, and does not abolish, these things?

4. How, on the Christian view, can the Cross of Christ affect the invalid's situation?

5. How should Christians cope with ill health when it comes their way?

We continue exploring these matters, and it seems that to deal with them properly there are seven things that we need to say. The rest of this chapter is devoted to spelling them out.

In God We Trust

The first thing we want to say is that *Christianity is an invitation to trust God's love at all times and in all situations because of the Cross*. Christianity does not answer all our questions by any means; instead, it introduces us to the God in whom the answer to all questions lies, and teaches us to trust him, which means (among other things) placing our confidence in him *before* we have the answers to all our questions from him.

Those answers, we are told, will mostly be given in heaven, where faith becomes sight and we know as we are known; Christians look forward to that day and live trustfully meanwhile. The New Testament points to the cross of Christ as the decisive proof of God's love—that is, his redemptive good will and purpose of blessing to all who trust him. "God so loved the world that he gave his one and only Son, that whoever believes in him shall not perish but have eternal life" (John 3:16). "God demonstrates his own love for us in this: While we were still sinners, Christ died for us" (Romans 5:8). "God is love. This is how God showed his love among us: He sent his one and only Son into the world that we might live through him . . . he loved us and sent his Son as an atoning sacrifice for our sins" (1 John 4:8–10).

On this basis we are required to trust God in all things as a child trusts his parents when they are leading him through strange and rough country—"My father is taking me, and he knows the way"; "My mother is here with me—I'll be all right." New Testament Christians were told that "We must go through many hardships to enter the kingdom of God" (Acts 14:22), and they accepted this because they trusted their heavenly Father who had proved his love to them by paying such a staggering price at Calvary for their redemption. Latter-day Christians are called similarly to trust God's love, whatever hardships may come our way, and however little we understand the specific purpose of the Father, who in his providence ordained them for us.

The second thing we want to say is that *health questions test and challenge our faith in God's love to the utmost.* This is because, as we have already said, they are so acutely painful. To be seriously ill oneself is a bad experience, but to stand by and watch the sufferings of one's spouse or one's children, or indeed of any children, or any friend—or to contemplate the maiming of both soldiers and bystanders in war or through terrorism, or to look at the wasted limbs and swollen stomachs of the starving—is really much worse. Why so much pain? we ask, and we have to admit that in truth we don't know. When faithful Job, having lost his wealth and his progeny, was also deprived of his health, breaking out in sores, boils, and skin ulcers, or perhaps leprosy, all over his body, his wife said to him, "Curse God and die!" (Job 2:9)—and though he resisted the temptation to blaspheme at that time, he very nearly fell victim to it on more than one occasion before his ordeal was over. We can sympathize! Constant physical discomfort and aching, with the attendant messes (Job sat on a rubbish-heap scraping discharged matter off himself, 2:7–8), would leave anyone feeling demoralized and indeed dehumanized; nothing more depressing can be imagined. Maintaining faith in God's love in such a condition can be as difficult as anything in this world. The letter to the Hebrews has a formula which covers it: Such experience is discipline, and "No discipline seems pleasant at the time, but painful. Later on, however, it produces a harvest of righteousness and peace for those who have been trained by it" (Hebrews 12:11). But to say this will not make it any less painful to endure when one is in the thick of it, or when one's loved ones are.

The third thing we want to say—and it is a hard thing to say—is that *the physical evils of sickness, pain, and unproductive suffering are bound up with the moral evil of sin:* Adam's sin, communal sin, and our own sin, three realities which Scripture binds together and historic Christian wisdom holds together. All human experience which involves suffering is a retributive consequence of mankind's rejection of God's rule, a rejection in which we are all implicated. We speak of suffering that is innocent and undeserved, but in the full and absolute sense of those words there is no such thing.

For saying this we shall no doubt be howled at from all sides. Secular-minded followers of the man in Hilaire Belloc's poem who "didn't believe in Adam and Eve / And laughed at original sin" will find our assertion incredible. Those for whom God is too much like Santa Claus, or one's favorite uncle, to be a just and holy judge or to build a principle of communal guilt and retribution into his world, will find our idea near-blasphemous. Sick folk and those who tend them, especially those who care for sick children, will find our thought morally offensive and unreal. We therefore have need to beg patience from our readers while we explain ourselves.

First let us make clear what we do not mean. We are not suggesting that illness, injury, congenital weakness or deformity, and premature death are always God's direct judgment for past sin committed or that these things can always be correlated with present sinning by the patient or his relatives or friends or dependents. To suggest this was the mistake of Job's comforters, who helped more when they sat silent with Job (Job 2:13) than when they lectured him, and whose theology made God angry (42:7). Scripture shows that though pain and suffering may be a direct judgment (see, for example, Numbers 12:9–15, 21:4–9; Acts 12:21–23) it also may not be; often God's immediate reason for including it in his plan lies in the sufferer's future rather than his past or his present (look, for instance, at Job 42:10–15; Psalm 119:67, 71; John 9:1–3; Romans 8:17; 2 Corinthians 1:3–6; Philippians 3:10; Hebrews 12:5–11; 1 Peter 1:6–7, 2:18–23, 5:10).

Nor, at the opposite extreme, do we suggest that we who share the racial experience of sinning and suffering should see ourselves as hapless victims of Adam's lapse in the same way that passengers on the *Titanic* were hapless victims of the captain's lapse. The will that is expressed in our sinning is our own, not Adam's, and so is the guilt that results. To blame Adam for it, therefore, and excuse ourselves, would be as much an evasion of moral reality as was Adam's blaming Eve and Eve's blaming the serpent (Genesis 3:12–13). So it is with suffering; all of us have so sinned as to deserve much more of it than we get. Rather than see ourselves as robbed of our natural rights, therefore, when we are sick or troubled, we should regard each healthy, trouble-free day as an undeserved mercy and see the fallacy of being angry with God when trouble comes, for whatever it is, we deserve worse.

What, then, are we saying? We are following Paul in Romans, where he *first* shows that all mankind, corporately and individually, is under the power of sin and guilt before God the judge (1:18–3:21); *then* he points to Adam as the one through whom sin, guilt, and death entered the world to involve us all in this way (5:12–21); *then* he goes on to tell us how he first learned that he himself was a guilty sinner through finding sinful urges in his heart (7:7–13); and *then* he speaks of all created reality as cursed with corruption but destined for redemption (8:19–23). We are stating that sickness, infection, viruses, genetic defects, and degenerative conditions leading to death, no less than (for instance) callousness, cruelty, and self-seeking, will be with us as long as this world lasts. We are thus affirming racial solidarity in the penal deprivations of good that have resulted from sin, as well as in sinfulness itself.

Where does Adam, mankind's progenitor according to Genesis, come into all this? Paul speaks of him as the representative of our race before God—as Christ was also our representative before God. A President or Prime Minister or chief or hereditary monarch represents his nation or tribe; if he declares war, then his people are all at war; that is what the representative relationship means. Solidarity operated, Paul tells us, in a comparable sense when Adam turned from God, and when Christ lived and died to redeem us. In neither case did we share personally in our representative's action, but in both cases we share in its consequences as though we had performed it ourselves. Adam sinned, and we suffer penal loss; Christ was obedient to death, and we are forgiven and accepted as righteous. Paul states the parallel thus: "If, by the trespass of the one man, death reigned through that one man, how much more will those who receive God's abundant provision of grace and of the gift of righteousness reign in life through the one man, Jesus Christ. Consequently, just as the result of one trespass was condemnation for all men, so also the result of one act of righteousness was justification that brings life for all men. For just as through the disobedience of the one man the many were made sinners, so also through the obedience of the one man the many will be made righteous" (Romans 5:17–19).

There is a mystery here which theologians have discussed for centuries, namely the full dimensions of the two solidarity-relationships that are being affirmed. Is there, for instance, some sense in which we were "in Adam" personally, as well as being represented by him? Our guess is that exactly what it means to be "in Adam" and "in Christ" will go on being debated till kingdom come. But there is no mystery about the idea of involvement by representation, nor about the fruits for us of our representative's action in each of these cases. From Christ we receive the gift of righteousness, which means pardon and a sharing in his own acceptance with the Father—in other words, the bestowal of a righteous person's status on us sinners. From Adam, by contrast, mankind in every generation inherits what was detailed in Genesis 3:16–19 as his and Eve's punishment: the soil is recalcitrant; childbirth is painful; marriage is vulnerable; no utopian Eden is open to us; and in due course we die. There is no denying that this is how things are, and no good reason for denying Paul's account of why they are so. Sickness, of course, belongs with death, since sickness in its own nature is death's first stage.

Basic to what we are saying is the insight to which the Hindu and Buddhist ideas of *karma*, the Greek notion of nemesis (plus any amount of pagan mythology, as well as Scripture and the honest conscience) all testify—namely, that for each individual moral retribution is a reality. This in turn points to the reality of the divine holiness. It is well to remember that, however robustly we believe the Bible, and Genesis 3 as part of the Bible, there is a deep sense in which we do not and cannot know what happened when Adam sinned. This is partly because we do not know from the inside what the state of unfallenness was like. Partly this is because we do not know how to measure the unfathomable holiness of God which Adam's transgression affronted, nor, therefore, how to assess the gravity of that initial act of sin. We have no way of knowing what cosmic fabric was ripped, what measure of presumption was mounted, what degree of sacrilege was committed. All we see in the story is the outside face of the event. Here was perfection and harmony and bliss; then suddenly sin; then measureless loss. The great God declared his judgment, and we are in no position to be judges of God's judgment. We are to trust the God of redeeming love as having done right in penalizing our entire race for Adam's one transgression. We are not to demand explanations, as if God were answerable to us. Rather we are to settle for the certainty that his action was morally appropriate and would appear glorious to us if we know, as he already knows, how much good will have resulted from it by the time history ends. In this, as in all else, God's justice and wisdom are not to be queried, but to be adored.

Objections may be raised to what we have said.

It may be objected that it was morally improper for God to make Adam our representative head, so that we were involved in his downfall. But in that case it was morally improper for God to make Jesus our representative head, so that we might receive the benefit of his substitutionary death on our behalf. No one who thanks God for salvation through Christ as head has any grounds for objecting to the principle of headship in the case of Adam.

It may be objected that babies and young children who are sick are genuinely innocent sufferers and that it is monstrous to suggest otherwise. But God looks on the heart, where the dispositions that will later produce acts of sin are present in embryo from the beginning of every life.

It may be objected that the call to cultivate trust, obedience, and adoration as the fitting response to the love, sovereignty, and holiness which God has made known to us is childish and primitive and negates human maturity. But the paradoxical truth, which shows up not only in Israel and in Christianity but in all human history, is that the noblest notions and celebrations of human dignity come from the ages most conscious of the watchfulness of God, or the gods. These ages have known that we must one day answer to a divine tribunal, and already our circumstances may be revealing divine displeasure. One would anticipate the opposite effect: eras of such faith, called superstitious by some (Marxists and secular humanists in particular tend to speak so), might be expected to produce mortals who creep about fawning, groveling, hiding, dithering, running scared, and generally living mean and cheapened lives. But lordly creatures like Achilles, Antigone, Oedipus, Aeneas, Roland, Arthur, Beowulf, Lear, and Hamlet (to look no further) come from religious centuries. All these great and noble literary figures knew they were accountable to the gods they acknowledged. Not one of them thought himself or herself free to declare independence of divine sanctions and controls. When, however, that independence is declared, as in the fiction, poetry, painting, sculpture, and drama of the twentieth century, the image of man which the artists project dwindles and shrivels into inanity, impotence, ennui, and fatuousness. The misadventures of the pathetic puppets of modern literature do not even qualify as tragedy, since to have tragedy you must have a person of great stature in the toils. A worm cannot be a tragic hero, for he does not have far enough to fall; no one cares much as he goes down, whereas when Achilles or Lear fall, we are stunned.

How revealing this perspective is! Art is the most vivid clue to how an age sees itself, and in contemporary art we do not seem to have come up with a single heroic figure. We proclaim ourselves liberated, autonomous, independent; but our novels, films, and songs tell us that we are lonely, confused, weak, and pitiable. "Help!" said one of the famous rock songs of this century.

But back to our theme. The Christian view of ill health and pain may be summed up as follows. Now that the moral evil of sin has come into the world and divine judgment on sin has disrupted the advancing perfection of the world's order, all of us must live with the loss of the thing that would seem to be our birthright, namely health, both in ourselves, sooner or later, and in a thousand creatures around us here and now, human and animal. But we cannot settle for this suffering as "normal." If we call it normal, we mean only that it is normal to this state of our sad exile, the way the men in Gulag might say it is normal to have to shiver all day. It is not what we were made for. Both Christians and secularists will agree that poor health and suffering always represent some breakdown of usual function—of cells or of nature or of human decency. Cancer, earthquakes, and torture chambers all rob us of our health and comfort. The secularist will place these functional breakdowns in categories like "natural causes" or "political expediency" and will look to technology and politics for relief. The Christian, while he may share the secularist's hope that medical technology will find a cure for cancer and that politics will hold off war (though who in San Francisco knows what to do with the earthquake?), will think further. Looking back he will believe that in some awful sense, through Adam, we humans under God are ourselves the cause of all suffering, even, alas, the suffering of those we call innocents; and looking forward, he will place his ultimate hope not in technology and diplomacy, least of all in dreams of some slowly growing amiability in the human race but rather in Redemption—the release of all things from this bondage of suffering at the end of time when Christ returns.

The Forward Look

The fourth thing we want to say is that *this life is not the only life*. It never was. Life on earth was always, at best, preparation for a larger, richer, more important, and endless life beyond. Had Adam not fallen, he would still no doubt have passed into that larger life in due course, though by a less ominous and painful process than death as we know it today. For Christians, death ceases to be a gateway into ultimate darkness and becomes a place of meeting with Christ, who takes us through final physical dissolution into closer fellowship with him than ever before. Christians know that it is for God to decide how long or short their time in this world should be before they are taken to their final glory, and they can be content to leave that matter in his hands. To humanists, the shortening and terminating of life in this world seems the ultimate tragedy, because they see this as the only life there is. But to Christians early death, however traumatic for those left behind, is not a major disaster in itself, for it may validly be viewed as rapid promotion. Scripture specifies seventy years as an ordinary life span (Psalm 90:10), yet by that standard Jesus himself lived less than half a life, for he died at thirty-three. The length of a life is no real index of its value, one way or the other.

A minister and his wife had a "miracle baby" years after they had been told that pregnancy was impossible; but the child was internally malformed and despite intensive care and surgery lived only a week. Many had hoped and prayed for another miracle, this time a miracle of healing, but the minister himself, preaching the following Sunday on "The Sovereignty of God in the Death of Our Daughter," was surely on target when he said, "God healed Joy Anne by taking her to heaven." It was in that way that prayer for healing was answered. The two-world view of life, according to which joy in heaven is the fruit of all earth's painful disciplines, is integral to Christianity; and much of the so-called problem of suffering dissolves when this view is kept at the forefront of one's mind.

The fifth thing we want to say is that *Christianity was from the first announced as the way of the cross.* "If anyone would come after me" said Jesus, "he must deny himself and take up his cross daily and follow me. For whoever wants to save his life will lose it, but whoever loses his life for me will save it. . . . Anyone who does not carry his cross and follow me cannot be my disciple" (Luke 9:23–24, 14:27). It was condemned criminals going out to execution who carried their cross in ancient Palestine; Jesus himself was to do it at the end of his ministry. His meaning clearly was that anyone who resolves to follow him must realize that he is choosing a life in which he must expect to suffer the pain and grief of rejection and humiliation without human sympathy—a life which would constantly feel like a crushing out and draining away of energy, and an entering into death.

Why would this be? The answer: partly because of the radical antipathy between different kinds of fallen men, and between secularists and believers in particular, which exposes Christians to active human opposition; partly because, as the visions of the Book of Revelation show (especially the seals and trumpets of chapters 6–11) God's plan for history includes large-scale inflictions of his wrath (judicial repudiation and sentence) on the arrogant self-sufficiency and godlessness of human groups. Christians will be caught in these calamities just as Israel's godly remnant was caught in the Babylonian sack of Jersualem. Plagues, epidemics, starvation, and wholesale community ill health are among the forms which God's wrath may take. But Christ is explicit about these ordeals, so that they become part of the cost that must be counted by would-be disciples, and the fact that they are chosen voluntarily and with open eyes as part of the discipleship package should mean that when they come, they are only what was expected and so present no problem of adjustment to the sufferer, however shocking and scandalous his or her relatives and friends may feel them to be. The victim, however, will take these things in stride, as did for instance, the seventeenth century English Puritans (great sufferers, every one).

A contemporary tract tells us that the Puritan saw his whole life as a warfare, in which his arms were prayers and tears, and his motto *Vincit qui patitur* (he who suffers conquers). When the source of Puritan suffering was not pressure from the authorities or poverty, it was regularly ill health. For example, Richard Baxter, the apostle of Kidderminster and the most prolific English theologian of all time, was for half a century tubercular and a walking museum of other diseases—incessant dyspepsia, kidney stones, headaches, toothaches, swollen limbs, intermittent bleeding from various parts of his body, and all in the days before painkilling drugs—yet he remained equable, energetic, uncomplaining, and outgoing to the very end. "Why should I complain of want or distress,/Temptation or pain? He told me no less," wrote John Newton. "The heirs of salvation, I know from his word,/Through much tribulation must follow their Lord." That is a very Puritan sentiment. In their frank awareness that Christianity is the way of the cross—a life of "losses and crosses," to use their regular phrase—the Puritans stand as a model for us all.

Humanness through Pain

The sixth thing we want to say is that *trust in God through the experience of ill health and suffering humanizes*. It does so by ripening us spiritually, for humanness and godliness are correlative concepts in the Christian view of things. In the process whereby those who are biologically human become human in personal and spiritual terms—become, in other words, Christlike—pain and suffering regularly play a major part. Christ himself, "although he was a son, . . . learned obedience from what he suffered" (Hebrews 5:8), and Christians do the same. Those who never suffer are likely to remain intellectually superficial and emotionally immature; character is formed in the furnace. Granted, pain and ill health diminish and embitter some, breaking their spirit by thwarting plans in which they had heavily invested themselves; but even outside the circle of faith, realistic acceptance of the helplessness that major and long-continued illness brings has amazingly ennobling effects, as every nurse knows, and among believers the sanctifying effects of sickness and suffering are a constant marvel.

What happens? Well, in the first place *suffering prompts prayer*. Those who have been touched by pain, whether their own or that of the child in bed in the next ward or of the dying dog that accidentally ate rat poison, even that of the mouse tormented by the cat, pray with a poignancy and passion to which all of us are ordinarily strangers, and to which they themselves are strangers at other times. They pray as the psalmists did, out of the depths of their distressed hearts, bringing their grief and frenzy and agony to the altar of God, or rather to that which now corresponds to Israel's altars, namely the cross of Jesus Christ, where God in person suffered in our own flesh. One movement of true prayer is to give back to God as an offering that which he sends us as a discipline, and so we learn to do here. By bringing us to the fountainhead from which all health flows, namely God, and by bringing us to the altar where our mortality meets his holiness, namely Christ's cross, the Christian gospel leads us to see that through making our suffering and that of others an offering to God in union with Christ's self-offering—that is, through giving it to God to make of it what he in his sovereign love and wisdom can— we may come to bear it, not just bravely and patiently as the stoics did (though let us hope that courage and patience will be seen in us), but with hope too. For the New Testament teaches that "our present sufferings are not worth comparing with the glory that will be revealed in us" (Romans 8:18), and furthermore that our present sufferings work in us the beginnings of that glory (see 2 Corinthians 4:17). Knowing that this is true both of ourselves and of others, we can offer even sufferings to God with good will and in gratitude for the holy purpose which suffering furthers.

Then, second, *suffering brings humility*. It makes the self-reliant self-assertion which spoils so many lives, even Christian lives, impossible, and the sufferer has to depend on others and most of all on God. Through being helpless we learn to resign ourselves into God's hands, to settle for the fact that he is in charge, and to find peace in that fact.

Joni Eareckson Tada, who became a quadriplegic through an accident in her teens, and who now lives by day in a wheelchair, learned this lesson agonizingly but well, as she shows us in her two books, *Joni* and *A Step Further* (Grand Rapids: Zondervan, 1976, 1978). On public platforms, where she often appears, she is radiant; dignity, gaiety, goodwill, naturalness, and inner ease are the qualities which mark her. She was once introduced to a large audience with the prediction that she would leave them feeling that she was the only really healthy person in the place, and the prediction appeared to be fulfilled. We do not suggest that the only persons to attain fortitude and peace in the midst of suffering are Christians; we know that all sorts of good people, of all faiths and none, have achieved it; but Joni's testimony is that her present humble, cheerful acceptance of lifelong paralysis came after bitter suicidal broodings when she finally acknowledged the love and lordship of God the Redeemer in Christ, and we would wish that testimony to be properly heard and weighed. Humanized through suffering? Yes, decidedly.

Health and Holiness

This leads to our seventh point, which is a turning-point in our argument, namely that *ill health of the person is more than ill health of the body.* From a Christian standpoint, ill health of the person means the deforming of the image of God in him or her so that the image of Satan comes to replace it—in other words, it means moral and spiritual deficiency. Thus a person can be in desperately bad health while his body is in good health. When we speak of health today, we usually have in mind the body only. But Scripture teaches that, just as we are more than our bodies, so our health is more than efficient physical functioning. In short, health and virtue coincide; health is wholeness, and wholeness is integration in the practice of love and righteousness. At this point biblical Christianity parts company completely with those who measure health by how the body works. Biblical Christianity will call no one healthy who is not good. Once more, Christian humanism and secular humanism are found at opposite extremes.

What, then, is the connection between bodily health and virtue? It is not the easy equation, that good people are going to be freed from headaches, toothaches, misery, poverty, and adversity. That is made clear in the psalms, where godly men are found on the rack while practitioners of vice grow fat and happy. The connection is, rather, that to set about being good is the sure path to real personal wholeness. Wholeness comes wholly through holiness.

This may be put in a score of ways. To follow Chirst and obey him is to be raised from spiritual death (unresponsiveness to and separation from God) and to be healed in the inner man. It is to be "born again," that is, to begin to live a new kind of life called *eternal,* and hence to be ultimately invulnerable to debility, misfortune, and death. It is to begin to be set free from the egoism that lies at the root of every single form of emotional and psychological disorder that the behavioral sciences ever charted. To be "in Christ" is to be like a branch on a vine whose roots are right down in the source of all vitality and fruitfulness. To be "sanctified" is to be restored to that place lost by Adam of belonging wholly to God, and thus to be enjoying the very thing that human life was made for in the first place. It is to be clean, alive, free, strong, and glad—even, says Christianity, on my death bed or in Belsen or Gulag or in the Black Hole of Calcutta.

Some will call this madness; but it is the same madness that sees the King of Glory in that poor convict pinned to the cross, and the same madness that sang songs in the arena while the lions mumbled and gnashed. It is always tempting from the outside to equate faith with lunacy, just because it is strange. That which is strange, however, may yet be true, and we claim this as a case in point. All this biblical and evangelical talk of being "in Christ," and of "the vine and the branch," and of being "sanctified" and "free" and "born again," and so forth may be unfamiliar to your modern ears. And you may be asking if there is any way we can translate it out of our own "insider's" jargon.

In a sense, no. Every field has its own special vocabulary. We don't talk to a man in his sloop about ropes; there are lines and sheets and halyards, but not ropes. We learn the language as we sail with him. Likewise we don't talk to the Master of the Hunt about the dogs wagging their tails; the hounds are feathering their sterns. The same is true everywhere; mountaineers, printers, lawyers, accountants, chefs, nurses—all have some special argot they talk, and one learns it by being around them. So it is with Christians. When they speak of being "in Christ," or being "born again," or of "sanctification," they are talking of realities by which they live. These words and phrases name real events and stages in the Christian life, just as the words "infancy" and "adolescence" name stages in our physical life. The only way to understand the vocabulary is by sharing the experience. The language of vision will always present a problem to folk who cannot see.

To a Christian, then, real health means being in Christ, that is, knowing and obeying him, and being known by him. He actually comes and lives in a Christian, says the gospel; that is what is celebrated at the Feast of Pentecost, when the Holy Spirit was sent from heaven to implant in all believers the eternal life of which Jesus spoke so much when he was here. "Eternal" in that phrase does not refer merely to a length of life. It signifies, rather, a kind of life—the Christ-life, the life of God. It is the life experienced by the citizens in the City of God, where charity is the rule. As God loves, so we (says the gospel) are to learn to love.

And here we see the connection between health and virtue. Health in Christian thought is the state of well-being and wholeness and power and freedom that we mortals were made to enjoy when God created us, and that is returned to us in salvation. If we think of it that way, we can see that virtue comes to about the same thing. To be virtuous is to be living life as God intended it to be lived, and to be enjoying all the benefits of that kind of life. To be full of love, in other words, is to be truly exhibiting that image of God in which we were made. It is to be healthy. Being healthy is essentially a matter of being good.

To know God, then, is to be back in touch with the source of true life; and that life, pure and holy as it is, will show itself in what we mortals call virtue. The Vine will bear fruit in all sorts of good things, not only actions but attitudes too. Love will become visible in an increasing gentleness, generosity, good-humor, self-control, helpfulness, quickness to sense others' discomfort and pain and embarrassment, and so forth. And these qualities that show up on the outside will flow from the good health that is being formed inside: the increasing freedom from self-centeredness; the quietness that comes from trust replacing agitation and anxiety; the patience that comes from learning little by little to give thanks in all sorts of awkward and vexing situations; the strength that results, as it does in the physical life, from one's being exercised over and over in all kinds of demanding experiences; and above all, surely, the thing that we can only call holiness. It is this last quality that begins to be visible in the man or woman who, by learning to lift every single experience up to God as an oblation, has learned once more the thing we refused in Eden, namely, that all things come from God and that all life belongs to God and that our chief calling as human beings is to offer him everything— ourselves and our goods and talents as well as our pains and defeats—in grateful adoration.

This is part of what it means to be priests, which may seem a long way from the themes of health and virtue. But the New Testament teaches us that we whom Christ restores to human health through new creation are called to be priests, that is, those who join Christ in his ministry of self-offering and intercession for the whole world. To have begun in this apprenticeship is to have begun to experience a kind of freedom and wholeness and goodness that the secularist cannot even conceive.

Who Is Healthy?

Now once again we must turn from generalization to find the people in whom this process of health, as we may call it, is at work. Who, we ask, are the truly healthy human beings? Whom shall we pick as our paragons of that exuberant vitality, ripeness, and wholeness, inside and out, that we all dream wistfully about? The decathlon champions would surely be someone's candidates. And here are the fashion models, male and female, from the covers of *Gentlemen's Quarterly* and *Vogue*—such perfect specimens. Very strong candidates, surely. And here are the people who have emerged from years and years of psychoanalysis; they must by this time have got their problems all resolved and know how to live fully. Front-running candidates, then, beyond a doubt! So whom shall we choose as our emblems of health today? To whom shall we give the laurel crown?

It is not easy. But whomever we pick, we will want, not primarily physical beauty (although heaven knows that is a gift most gratefully to be prized) nor muscle tone and agility and youth and freedom from allergies and malfunctions (although once more, who would not give half his kingdom for these?). Good as those things are, they are not on their own good enough. No; the more we think of what we mortals really are, and of what is implied in this word "human," the more clearly we shall know that we want someone in whom we see love, joy, peace, longsuffering, gentleness, goodness, meekness, temperance, and fidelity. We will want generosity and courage and honesty. We will want good-humor and selflessness. We will want purity of heart and sympathy and stamina and kindness. These, surely, are the qualities that crown us with glory. The man or woman in whom all this is visible may truly be said to be whole. We may see in this person all that we mean when we use the terms health and virtue. And we may, furthermore, see that there is no separating out of which qualities contribute to health and which to virtue. It all seems to be one seamless whole. Here is a complete man or woman. Here is what God envisaged when he thought of Adam and Eve, and made them.

Two pictures will assist us here. On the one hand, imagine a ruddy specimen of the body beautiful who turns out to be eaten up with egoism or lust or rapacity. Of him we will say that his lovely physical prowess is all very well, but one fine day he is going to wake up with his agenda full of troubles. Something is badly wrong with him. In any case, we know how fragile his bodily well-being is; a cancer cell or a careless driver is all that is needed to overthrow the whole edifice, and his place on the cover of *Sports Illustrated* or *Gentlemen's Quarterly* will go to someone else very suddenly.

On the other hand, think of the man or woman who, having identified with Christ's self-offering, has been set free from egoism and has begun to learn charity. This "priestly" task to which he has been called, of presenting to God himself, his powers, and his prayers in behalf of others, has turned out to be the school in which he has begun to learn love, joy, peace, longsuffering, purity, kindness, generosity, fortitude, and so forth—all of which are *virtues*. And these virtues themselves turn out to be precisely the things which the rest of us who seek real health need. Everything that our counselors and therapists and experts want to nudge us along toward as the way out of the trap of our fears and self-loathing and anger—everything is here. To be good really is to be healthy and free.

Somehow this remains true, even in the extremes of terminal illness. For a weak, crippled, or dying Christian, there is not only the hope of future release and vitality; there can be a present fortitude, patience, and joy that somehow overflows his own cup and becomes a health-giving elixir to the "healthy" bystanders. And this is something that cannot be shaken. Diocletian's lions, cancer, war, bankruptcy, bereavement—these assail us as human beings, and most of us, Christian or not, do not make a brave showing. But the quality of life which Christ exhibits in himself, and which he offers to us through his own self-giving for us, is truly everlasting, and nothing in heaven, earth, or hell can take it away from us. It is pure goodness and, as such, pure good health, too.

7

Dignity

There are some things that we never learn to value till we face the prospect of losing them or, even worse, wake up to the fact that they have already gone. Health is one. Peace of mind is another. Dignity is a third.

Dignity, False and True

To many, no doubt, the thought of dignity will seem somewhat remote and alien. We are, after all, an informal generation, in the throes of reaction against what strikes us as the excessive stiffness of an earlier day. Speak of dignity, and you conjure up thoughts of white-whiskered old gentlemen glaring over the tops of their glasses, or duchesses with lorgnettes drawing themselves up to their full height in the presence of some ghastly social blunder. "Standing on one's dignity" is not something we often think of doing ourselves nor find impressive when others do it. Our clothes reveal us as a thoroughly "laid-back" lot. No stiff wing collars, waistcoats with watchchains, stick-pins, and gold-headed canes for the men. No corsets, gloves, heavy taffeta, and swishing skirts for the women. The sartorial rectitude and reticence of the Victorians is not for us. In fact, it began to be dropped about the time of World War I. Women then started to appear in floppy draperies that changed the Western world's whole picture of what a woman was. Men's clothes got lighter and looser, simpler and softer. Posture changed, especially for women; a lithe, languid slinkiness supplanted the ramrod image with its severely piled-up ringlets, tiny waist, and thinly rolled parasol. Today we see open-necked shirts at dinner, blue jeans in trains and airplanes, acres of flesh exposed at beaches and by shoppers and workmen on hot days, pant-suits and even shorts allowed on Fifth Avenue and in Saks . . . dignity, it seems, is at a discount, and casual comfort is the only thing that anyone cares about any more.

But that is not quite the way to put it. What we have consciously turned our backs on is *false* dignity, the pompous putting on of airs, the urge to act in a superior manner when you are not really superior at all. One thing that unites the human race is delight at seeing pompous people tread on banana skins, or otherwise receive their comeuppance; this is a universal trait, and a very healthy one. But it would be wrong to say that we have lost all concern for human dignity in its deeper and truer sense. On the contrary, it is precisely our sense that the rest of us have dignity, too, that makes us resent pomposity and feel a sense of outrage when people at the top do not treat the ordinary person—the "little man," as we say—with proper respect.

One of the things that horrifies us about the photographs captured from the Nazis recording the pogroms in Poland and other countries is how men, women, and children were handled by those who collected them for disposal. They treated them like cattle! we say, appalled. But what is the trouble here? Ordinarily cattle are treated fairly decently. They are fed and moved about from one place to another and generally tended with much more care than we would give to sacks of potatoes or scrap metal. Granted, the killing was awful, but what was the matter with those slatted freight cars and naked line-ups? we might ask. But if we did, everyone would turn away from the question in disbelief and disgust. What do you mean, what was the matter? Can't you see? These were *people,* not cattle!

The point of course is that, long before any actual torture or killing had started, human dignity had been desecrated. You don't stuff people into cattle cars. Besides being uncomfortable, it is demeaning. And you don't forcibly strip crowds of people and make them line up naked. The most brisk nudist would protest here. But why? we ask. Do we have to have clothes? And at this point the whole question opens out, and we find ourselves obliged to admit that, unlike the animals who may go about with nothing more than their natural covering, we human beings demand a whole regalia to adorn us in public. Nor is this simply a matter of clothes, though clothes are part of it. (In tribes that go naked the chiefs regularly wear something to mark and guard their dignity.) But the wider truth is that human dignity must be recognized and protected by a series of defenses and approaches, as we might call them, like a shrine or a great house.

The analogy is apt. There is something quite literally "unapproachable" about us, and those who would come near to us must do so cautiously, reticently, even reverently. The rules must be obeyed. Every courtesy shown to someone else and every restraint in ordinary human contact says the same thing. Why don't I muss up the hair of my friend's mother? I certainly tousle her dog and scratch its ears. Why don't I start right in pulling the clothes off a person who looks so tempting? Why, indeed, do I hesitate a bit before I even say hello or hi to someone, and then presently give my name and ask his or hers? I can start right in with a cat or dog, rumpling and patting and burbling; why not with my adult human peers?

Somehow or other there seem to be *precincts* around people, and the most barefooted commune in Arizona will be found recognizing these precincts sooner or later. The people who have tried to set up households and communities with no reference at all to the various reticences and taboos that have surrounded men and women and children in all tribes and civilizations tell us that it does not work. Nakedness becomes drab and offensive. Spontaneity runs dry. Structurelessness slumps. Informality palls. Ennui sets in. One's soul cries out for some clothes, and some tact, and some routine. Even some restraints, and some rules.

The correct conclusion seems to be that our humanness needs to be fenced and hedged and draped. For there is some quality about us that simply is not there in the animals. Surely there are few things nobler than the profile of a great golden retriever, or of a bald eagle, and few things more exquisite than the shape of a doe or a filly. And what could be more impressive than the bulk of an African bull elephant coming straight on, trunk waving and ears fanning? And for sheer grace, where shall we find anything to excel the dolphin or the swallow? But none of these creatures even approaches in dignity the meanest human being. We do not like to see any living creature violated; but if we must choose between this eagle and this derelict in the gutter, we do not hesitate. Dribbling senility must take precedence over the king of birds or of beasts. A baby screaming and fouling his diapers has more dignity than the elk on the crag.

From the secular point of view it is hard to explain why we feel as we do about this, since on secular principles it is impossible, finally, to isolate anything about us that should entitle us to such precedence and privilege over all other living creatures on our planet. Anatomy throws no light at all on the question. And if we talk of man's self-consciousness or intelligence or creativity, we are still left with the question as to why those qualities should be preferred above swiftness or strength or suppleness, in all of which the animals outstrip us.

It would be absurd, no doubt, to drive a secularist to the wall insisting that he tell us what makes human beings unique in relation to the animals, or (as he might prefer to say) to the rest of the animals. The uniqueness is self-evident, and he could fairly retort that we might as well insist on knowing why our lungs need oxygen rather than helium. It's just the way things happen to be. It is a waste of time, he might add, to worry at questions that do not need to be answered. If you want to imagine a planet where they breathe helium, or where men and women are on the same footing with lobsters and ocelots, by all means do so. But meanwhile the rest of us must get on with the world we do live in. Humanity is at the top of the pecking order, and there we are.

A secular humanist talking thus sounds as if he is affirming in positive practical terms the same unique dignity that Christians ascribe to human beings, what Francis Schaeffer termed the "mannishness" of man. But if he is a consistent humanist he is not really doing that. He is looking on man as *relatively* unique, being the most highly developed organism to date on the evolutionary scale, rather than as *absolutely* unique, having an inalienable worth that does not depend on his development in any sense at all. And by making dignity depend on development, the humanist is opening the door to the idea that less favored, less well-developed human beings have less dignity than others and consequently less claim to be protected and kept from violation than others. So humanist ethics will justify, and humanist spokesmen have repeatedly risen up to defend, the weak going to the wall for the convenience of the strong. For instance, many humanists will justify the killing by abortion of a new person forming in its mother's womb, and the killing by starvation of handicapped new-borns and by euthanasia, the killing of old persons who can no longer function skillfully and productively in society or in their own families. The same thinking was invoked to justify the killing, in Nazi Germany, of six million Jews lest their genes and influence should somehow corrupt the master race. The principle is the same in each case; some human beings are to be eliminated (a gruesome euphemism, suggesting excretion) from the social system for the convenience of other human beings who are strong enough to maintain a claim to be better developed than their victims. Ideological might thus becomes right, and cool clinical murder, a recognized social convention. Familiarity, as we know, dulls the moral sense, and we are now-adays so familiar with this immoral pagan reasoning that we do not feel outraged and defiled by its obscenity in the way that truly good and clear-headed people would. Surely, however, it is plain that by locating people's dignity in their versatility and social usefulness, humanism denies, rather than affirms, the dignity which we instinctively acknowledge in members of our own race, however limited or handicapped.

Man in God's Image

On the Christian view, the secret of our dignity is no secret. Every human being is made in the image of God. No other creature has this dignity, not even the angels. The climax of the creation story is that "God said, 'Let us make man in our image, in our likeness . . .' So God created man in his own image, in the image of God he created him; male and female he created them" (Genesis 1:26–27). The repetition is, of course, for emphasis, as in all human language; the story is drumming into us that our dignity as bearers of God's image is the first thing about ourselves that we need to grasp.

But what does it involve? The truth, strange as it sounds, is that nobody fully knows! The declaration of Genesis 1:26–27 means at least that man is personal, purposive, creative, and conscious of value, for so God appears in verses 1–25. Just to say this, however, does not get us very close to the real problem, which is to relate the image-idea to the truth of God's uniqueness. Theologians insist that God is unimaginable and that we must not think of him in our own image, as if he were an enlarged man, a celestial giant, having body and organs, hands and feet, intellectual problems and emotional vulnerabilities, and differing from us only in his size and resourcefulness and freedom from certain limitations of time and space. God is ineffable and impassible, say the theologians, meaning that he is not open to being described or affected by us. He is, they continue, incomprehensible, that is, beyond our grasp, so that we can only ever be clear on what he is not, never on what he is.

As against the fantasies of God in man's image that come natural to us and run all through pagan myths, the theologian's point is true and must be taken. Yet there is hardly a page in the Bible that does not speak of God in some unabashedly pictorial way—as king, captain, shepherd, father, archer, husbandman, or ancient. We read of his arm, right hand, feet, loins, eye, heart, even his nostrils. He smites, he presses grapes, he holds a scepter, he rides in a chariot, he laughs, he repents, he turns his face away, he rejoices, he breaks the teeth of the wicked. He wears a crown, he wears a robe, he puts on armor, he has a footstool.

What does this mean? One thing it means is that we are not only permitted but actually required to think of God in these terms, for there is no other way, really, in which we can think of him without demeaning him. Because man bears God's image in a way that other creatures do not, thinking of him in human terms is less inadequate than thinking of him in subhuman terms (which is what all nonhuman categories prove in one way or another to be). Therefore we must think of him in a quasi-human way.

Oh, to be sure, Scripture also pictures God as a rock and a hen and a shield and a sun. But no one has ever painted a hen on the sapphire throne, and no liturgy has ever addressed God as a boulder. These less-than-personal concepts are to be "cashed" in terms of the personal ones. Moral personhood is the real center of our likeness to God, and his to us. And the biblical way to think of God is, not indeed as a man, but as an analogy of man—in other words, as having in him, alongside that which transcends us, that which corresponds to everything in us that is properly human.

The God who is said to dwell in darkness too thick to penetrate or in light too bright to look at (two Bible pictures of divine transcendence) is also said to hear, see, smell, perceive, think, touch, and speak. In other words, he is pictured in Scripture as if he were a man. Why? Not to teach us that God is manlike, but rather to convince us that man is Godlike. The reason why the language of humanness is more adequate to describe God than any other is because human beings were made in his image. To put it technically, the created theomorphism of man is the basis of the linguistic anthropomorphism of biblical thought.

Does the consistently masculine presentation of God in Scripture mean that men bear more of God's image than women do? No; the declaration that God made humanity, male and female, in his own image shows that just as all authentically masculine characteristics find their source in God, so do all authentically feminine characteristics. Women bear God's image as truly and fully as men do. What we should learn, as it seems, from the fact that God is "he" in Scripture and that the Word was incarnated as a human male is not that men are more like God than women, but that we are all, men and women alike, feminine (so to speak) in relation to our Maker and Redeemer.

Some recent theology has asked whether we may not properly call God "she" as well as, or rather than, "he." But this would mean conceiving the Father as the Mother, the Son of God as the Daughter, and the King of heaven as the Queen; it would oblige us to think of the Triune God as what Scripture and every mythology in the world would require us to call our Triune Goddess. And that will not do! Those for whom Scripture is revelation will not feel free thus to change the way of conceiving God which informs all biblical narratives, teachings, and prayers. Those for whom Jesus Christ is God incarnate will regard this change as forbidden by the very fact that God's definitive self-revelation was made in male humanity. Furthermore, thoughtful Christians everywhere will see that the very fact of being made in God's image confers the highest dignity on women, just as it does on men, and there is no need to recast biblical ways of thought to stress the point.

So all human beings are made in God's image, says Christianity. We share with the animals our creaturehood, the elements of our physical makeup, many feelings and needs such as hunger and fear and the impulse of self-defense, and the cycle of birth, growth, aging, and death; but here is a unique fact about us that sets our race apart. However, the Bible does not delimit for us exactly what constitutes the image, and questions still arise.

Is our upright posture, for instance, anything to do with the image? Maybe so, though the apes come close to us here—yet with a difference. They stoop naturally, whereas when we find ourselves having to stoop, whether from lumbago or old age or any other cause, we know that things have gone wrong; we feel we should not have to go along with our knuckles on the ground like an orangutan.

Is it, perhaps, moral self-consciousness that makes us uniquely Godlike? This, in its degree, is a quality that seems distinctively human. Domestic pets exhibit traces of something like it; they act guilty and embarrassed when they are caught in a forbidden chair and proud when they bring us a stick or a mouse. But we cannot ascribe to them moral aims and self-discipline of the kind we see in good men and women.

Is the essence of the image of God in which we are created our power of analysis and the creativity that goes with it? These capacities certainly set us apart from the animal kingdom. Though spiders and ants figure out difficult engineering problems, and orioles and mud daubers and paper wasps and silkworms produce staggeringly complex artifacts, they are all programed by what we call instinct. And instinct, whatever it is, is no more innovative than the computer. No oriole, therefore, ever comes up with a new style of nest, Greek Revival or rococo or Regency. And though birds sing constantly their song does not change. No white-throat sparrow or winter wren has ever opened a new musical epoch; there is no history of wren music in which plain chant, polyphony, sonata form, and program music succeeded one another as they did in the music of Western man. If Methuselah heard a wren, he heard what we hear now. But human beings are innovators and developers, and the history of every human activity is a narrative of change from one era to another.

Is our capacity for love the essence of the divine image within us? This too, it seems, we share with the animals to some extent, if we may judge by the nuzzling and cooing and romping and mating rituals that go on, and by the manifest distress when nests are robbed or cubs shot or calves taken away. Yet the rational, moral love of human spouses, parents, and friends who seek constantly the goodness and welfare of their loved ones is not matched, so far as we can tell, by any robin or bear or cow.

Do angels bear God's image as men and women do? We know almost nothing of the angels, but it is natural to suppose that their intelligence and power and glory leaves ours looking paltry. If "God-consciousness" is a distinctive badge of humanity, surely the angels have more of it than we. Yet they are never said to be like God, to be made in his image and to be central in his plans for this world, in the way that we humans are.

Perhaps our unique dignity lies in our excelling the animals in posture; in moral self-awareness; in our ability to analyze, abstract, and create; and in our capacity for righteous, rational love, all together; plus our excelling the angels (if indeed this is so) in our emotional capacities within relationships—capacities which have something to do with our being physically embodied. Perhaps we should expound the image of God in terms of all these qualities put together. It may be, however, that it is beyond us to conceive the full essence of the image, not only because we cannot grasp all that God is, but also because we are so largely mysterious to ourselves, being ignorant of the depths of our own fallen and disordered natures. Perhaps, therefore, we should limit ourselves to saying that the dignity of humanity lies in a God-likeness which doubtless has more to it than we can know in any single case, least of all our own.

Dignity and Worship

Human dignity has been felt and celebrated since the beginning of time. We see it in art, for example, in every human figure painted or drawn or worked in marble, bronze, mosaic, tapestry, or porcelain. Perhaps the most striking witness to this sense of our dignity appears in Greek sculpture. Here we find, not necessarily a famous man immortalized in marble serenity but just a *man*. But to say "just" a man is to miss the whole point. It is *a man*. This is the noblest creature of them all.

It is to the Greeks' credit that they did not worship these statues. They brought incense and libations and sacrifices to the statues of Zeus and Athena and Apollo to be sure, but there was no cult of man-worship. Our very nobility, for them, lay in keeping man's role distinct. It was *hubris* (the sin of overweening pride) to try to mimic the gods. To that extent at least a witness to spiritual truth is found in Athens.

But in the monuments of Egypt and Babylon we find not only human figures, but bulls, birds, and dogs, or worse, men with the heads of bulls, birds, and dogs; and these were depictions of gods. Somehow "bull-ness" (strength?) and "bird-ness" (speed?) had come to be seen as divine. As a result, human beings were set to worship something less and lower than themselves. This was topsy-turvy, and its effect was not ennobling but dehumanizing. Some of its more obvious fruits to which the records testify are fear of divine caprice, sacrifice (including human sacrifice) practiced as celestial bribery, cult prostitution, ritual debauchery, tyrannical priestcraft, the divorcing of religion and morality, and the glorifying of cruelty if it furthered the national cause.

The truth is that our supreme fulfillment, as moral beings made in God's image, is found and expressed in actively worshiping our holy Creator. When the object of homage is noble, the rendering of homage is ennobling; but when the objects of homage are not noble, the rendering of it is degrading. The idea that man's dignity is most fully realized when he acknowledges no dependence and worships nothing is as false as is the idea that it does not matter what he worships, provided he worships something. In fact, it is impossible to worship nothing: we humans are worshiping creatures, and if we do not worship the God who made us, we shall inevitably worship someone or something else, however far from being worthy of our worship he, she, or it may be.

Some of us, for instance, worship our investment portfolios: not, indeed, by burning incense before the bank vaults where they lie, but by giving the stocks and shares our devoted and undivided attention. Day and night, year in and year out, we tend our financial interests, watching over them and propitiating them with fully as much anxiety and punctilio as was ever brought to the temple of Dagon. We plan, worry, calculate, scrutinize, risk, and gamble, maybe for the whole of our adult lives, in the service of mammon. But thus to spend and be spent in the worship of wealth is demeaning, whatever the greedy and envious world may think of those who do it successfully and profit by it. It is *beneath our dignity*, in the most precise sense of that phrase.

Not that money-making is an intrinsically unworthy activity, or that the present writers want their readers to think that it is! No honest work is of itself unworthy, and no one may tell another that his work is unworthy when that work is being done with modesty, integrity, and generosity. However, there are some occupations such as pimping, piracy, counterfeiting, smuggling, terrorism, kidnapping, and drug-pushing that are genuinely villainous, but there are not many such. No vocation that does not involve dishonesty, cruelty, or destructive foolishness ought to be condemned out of hand.

The fact that moral problems are tangled up in most of what goes on in civilization does not mean that all work done within the frame of civilization is worthless and unworthy of man. It depends on how it is done, and that in turn depends on the sort of person who does it. War may be mad and bad, but there is such a thing as a soldier-saint. Usury may have its murky side, but there are holy bankers and investment counselors. Politics may be murky too, but some politicians are good and godly persons. People may be starving, but we may not call someone like J. S. Bach a cad for writing cantatas at a time when food is short. We may not even tell the clown that he is wasting his life in foolishness; there is nothing destructive about him, despite the virtuoso clumsiness with which he wrecks things during his act, and who knows what charity is in his heart, and what it costs him to bring the gift of laughter to us?

No; what we are censuring here is not unworthy work, but unworthy workers—persons, that is, who in their hearts worship the work or its expected fruits instead of worshiping God and doing their work as service to him, and who thus bring themselves under Paul's condemnation of those who "worshiped and served created things rather than the Creator—who is forever praised. Amen" (Romans 1:25).

Not to worship God, so we maintain, is a betrayal of our dignity as his creatures, and to worship something other than God is really obscene. Obscenity means the desecrating of something sacred by failing to honor it properly. Thus (to illustrate from the most familiar and best understood use of the term) our sexuality is sacred, as being the inmost shrine of our personhood, and it is obscene to dishonor it by making general merchandise or a trivial peepshow out of it. It is similarly obscene to spit on people and treat them like cattle. And it is no less obscene to prostrate our human dignity before anything less than God—money, power, prestige, or pleasure, for instance. We were not made to worship these things; we were made for our Creator, and these things were made for us, not vice versa. And just as a great duke displays, not forfeits, his nobility when he makes obeisance to his sovereign, so do we mortal men wear our dignity most clearly and plainly when we bow before the Most High. Thus we enter into our heritage as human beings, and become human in the deepest sense of that word. For we can only achieve full humanness in and through worship of the God whose image we bear.

The Meaning of Worship

A question arises. What about the many forms of honor that we pay our fellow-mortals? What of the homage we render to abstractions like virtue, or country, or "the cause"? Does not this detract from the honor and praise of God?

Or, does it? Take, for instance, a birthday party, which is a fairly universal sort of celebration. The birthday boy or girl is the center of attention, and the birthday cake honors him or her. For the moment he or she is lifted up and shines, and the rest of us, no matter how venerable and celebrated we may be, take the back seat. We sing and applaud and honor this person for nothing more than having been born. We might find a small clue here confirming what we have said about the unique dignity of humankind, for we don't ordinarily celebrate a dog's birthday. But for a human being to have been born is a significant event, one worth memorializing and celebrating. The party and the cake mean: "On this day, so many years ago, the image of God arrived in the specific form of you—a unique and unprecedented person, different from everyone who came before or since. You are you, and you are special! Know it and be glad of it, as we are! Happy birthday!" Does this celebration rob God of his praise?

Or think how we give gold stars to first-graders for nice handwriting, and certificates to campers for swimming across the pool, and medals to athletes who win, and tasseled hats and bright-colored hoods to scholars for unearthing Hittite tablets or spurring atoms to go faster. Gold cups, silver tureens, ribbons, coronets, monuments, red carpets, ruffles and flourishes, reserved seats, titles—there is no end to the ways we have of showing honor to our fellow-mortals. Does any of this degrade or dishonor God?

On the contrary! All forms of honor paid to mortals for their achievements (even if it is only a matter of one's having been born) are not only permissible, on the Christian view, but actually desirable, for they add to the honor which we render to God—at least, if we understand what we are doing. The principle is that when you honor something I have made or managed, you honor me. When the prize is given to my poem for being the best submitted, the honor is mine as the author. When the cabbage you tended so carefully wins the blue ribbon at the county fair, you the grower bask in glory. When the performance is applauded, the producer gets credit also. As God enhances his glory (meaning his presence and power in display) by the gifts and capacities that he gives to men, so we advance his glory (meaning the adoration and praise that we owe him) as we celebrate the richness of human achievement. If man was the performer, God was the enabler, and the greater the performance the more it reflects of the praiseworthiness of the Creator who made it possible.

According to the poets and prophets of Israel, God's nonhuman creatures not only show forth his glory by their beauty, complexity, and regularity of function but actually praise him by existing in their own appointed manner. Glinting water flies with gauzy turquoise wings; whales cruising the green silence of the deep; mountain goats with their little black hoofs gathered to a point on a Canadian pinnacle; sun and moon and stars, snow and hail and wind and lightning and fire and water—all extol the glory of God. All God-given glory and splendor pay homage in this way at the throne of the Most High.

But as the homage which we humans bring to God differs from that which the lower creation pays him, so it differs from that which we pay to men and things. We may applaud men and women, and sing the beauties of the Alps and the Cotswolds and the West Highlands, and extol the perfections of some champion deerhound or Angus bull. We may not, however, worship any of these. Worship is for God alone.

What does it mean for man to worship? There is a sense in which, as we have just said, all creation, though sin-scarred, offers worship, but we are the only creatures on earth who, by virtue of God's gifts of freedom and intelligence, may worship him in a way that is voluntary and articulate. Let us elaborate these thoughts.

Man's worship must be *voluntary*; that is, it must be purposefully and resolutely offered. No thrush has ever decided to sulk and withhold its song because it was not pleased with its lot in life, nor has any thrush ever composed any song other than the one given to all thrushes. The same crystal notes go up from every thrush, aeon after aeon, taking their place in the universal chorus of praise. But it is open to men and women to refrain from worshiping, whether because they are displeased with God or because they have other matters to attend to that seem more pressing, or because they forget, or for other reasons. As we have already seen, it is in worship of our Creator that our own dignity as human creatures appears most vividly, and by neglecting or refusing to worship we demean ourselves. Our worship is not, however, automatic; either we freely choose to worship, or we do not worship, and there is no third option.

Man's worship must also be *articulate*; that is, we must use our God-given intelligence to devise words and actions that transmute all our experiences into worship. All of them? Yes, every single one. But take words and actions first. The Christian vocabulary of worship is immense, and the range of verbal options open to us is vast. One of the highroads to humanness is to make constant use of this vocabulary, joining the company of those who cry "Praise the Lord!" and who sing "Jesus! the name high over all!" and who proclaim with the seraphim "Holy, holy, holy, Lord God of hosts!" Another of the highroads to humanness is the articulating of worship by appropriate actions—actions, that is, which express adoration of God. Here again the range is immense. We may dance, kneel, clap our hands, jingle tamborines, blow cornets, sit in silence, paint a Sistine ceiling or a tiny icon, stitch a lace border, or—for that matter—sweep floors, wash dishes, or peel carrots. Anything that we do to express adoration before the Throne is received most graciously. We are familiar with the question, "What on earth are you trying to do?" In our incompetence (and who among us is not crashingly incompetent at many of life's tasks?), we get asked it over and over again. We should realize that, at one level, this is God's constant question to the whole human race and that, at that same level, the only proper answer is "Worship!"

Nor is this all. *Articulating* something means giving it shape and so expressing its nature. And it seems to be man's special and unique prerogative in God's world to articulate worship in and through all his experiences, both those which he plans for himself and those which come unbidden. To see what this means, think first of churchgoing. We get into the car and go, not because our feelings about God's glory are more intense than they were this time yesterday, but because it is Sunday morning and coming up to service time. When the next hymn is announced we join in singing it, not because we are suddenly flushed with a sense of divine grandeur or because the words exactly fit our present state of heart, but because it is the next thing in the service. Yet our purpose in being there, and in trying to appreciate and enter into all that is going on, is to articulate personal worship within the frame of corporate worship. And the effect of making the attempt in a regular, disciplined way is to find worship called forth from depths of our being that otherwise might never be tapped.

The very "second-handedness" of old prayers and hymns supplies us again and again with just what we would be groping after in vain if all we had to draw on was our own verbal resources. "I bind unto myself today/The strong name of the Trinity"— "Crown him, ye kings, with many crowns,/For he is Lord of all"—"My name from the palms of his hands/Eternity will not erase"—would our own vocabulary ever have raised us to such a pitch of exalted clarity? Would our stumbling vagueness ever have permitted such heartfelt, heaven-bound devotion as words like these call forth?

Shaping Life into Worship

But the achieving of verbal praise is not the only, nor even the chief, importance of our worship in church. For worship, from the Christian point of view, is not something that may be tucked into and confined within this hour or that. Those special and regular worship times, far from being parentheses in our busy schedules, are exact diagrams, so to speak, of what the whole of life ought to look like. Nothing happens then that ought not to be happening all week long.

What? The clutter of my life—to look like this divine service? The jumble of traffic and dirty dishes and awful people and harrying tasks and boring routines—to be a liturgy?

Yes, says Christianity. That is what you were made for. The seraphim, it seems, have the dread privilege of doing nothing at all for much of the time but cry "Holy!" and the thrushes sing, willy-nilly. But all we human beings, unlike these other creatures, bear the image of God himself. And our freedom and intelligence exhibits itself in its most awesome dignity when we are "creative" in the precise sense of taking the raw materials of experience, like the chaos over which the Creator himself presided, and forming them into offerings of praise to the Most High. Yes—the clutter and jumble itself, like that chaos, may be shaped. It may, of course, be shaped into idols to which you may then bow down; but in so doing you would turn yourselves into grunting swine like the poor men in Homer's *Odyssey* who were lured by Circe's charms. But it may also be taken and shaped as an oblation to the One from whom ultimately it comes.

No experience, save that of choosing or allowing sin in oneself or in others, is such that it must be discarded as useless material although some experiences are certainly easier to mold in this way than others. The fugitive moments when we seem to catch a glimpse of the Divine Majesty are the easiest, of course. "Alleluia!" comes spontaneously then. Joy is sometimes easy to offer to God and to thank him for. The sense of success and power and beauty are like this also. As experiences, they make us feel good in the affective, rather than the moral, sense and so make phrases like "Praise God!" easy to say. But then one must ask oneself: Am I truly offering up these experiences, and that which yields them, to God? Offerings and sacrifices and oblations are taken away from the offerer. Sometimes they are consumed by fire. Am I ready for this? Am I willing for God to take away that which I experience so sweetly at present?

Such questions could be traumatic. They could lead—probably, indeed, have led—men and women to belittle their gifts and powers and to be afraid to rejoice in them lest the gifts be snatched away by a jealous God who does not want us to have very much joy, or lest they be found guilty of idolizing something (a beautiful voice, or poetic powers, or an ecstatic marriage) that is less than God. But proper Christian faith is not fearful and squinting like this. The strong man can exult in his strength, and the soprano in her voice, and the bridegroom in his bride without becoming guilty of idolatry. Of course these are God's bounty rather than our own products or possessions. But that is precisely why we must fully acknowledge their created glory, their beauty and capacity and delightfulness. If the seraph or the thrush or the chamois or the bride or the soprano all said, "No, no—it's nothing. Don't look at me. I'm a no-good, I'm a dud, I'm a worm," they would not only be speaking falsely, they would be robbing their Maker of due gratitude. The mock-modesty that declines to accept compliments and to be gratefully realistic in recognizing God's gifts both demeans the creature and dishonors the Creator. True dignity emerges, not in our faithless and fawning demurrals of worth, but rather in our learning how to bear this truly royal mantle of humanness, and this coronet of beauty or strength or talent or relational joy.

Sometimes the mantle is a mantle of pain and loss, and the coronet one of adversity. Not from jealousy, but for purposes of love, God does from time to time take away good things that he gave, and at such times sackcloth must replace holiday dress. It is harder to exult in this regalia. To believe in the value of such experience, and to offer it to God to use, and to thank him for the way he enriches through deprivation is not easy when one is in the thick of it. Here is where Christians turn to the Son of God for their cue. He was never more glorious than when, deprived of all human rights, he was robed in mockery and crowned with thorns. His Transfiguration on the mountain exhibited his glory under the aspect of brilliance; his Passion exhibited that same glory under the aspect of love. And here the disciples must be ready to go the way their master went. That is what Christ's call to cross-bearing means.

Dignity and Sanctity

Cross-bearing is the long lesson of our mortal life. It is a part of God's salvation, called sanctification. It is a lesson set before us every moment of every day. It concerns this strange and daunting business of how strain and pain—passion, in the sense of conscious suffering voluntarily accepted—may be transmuted into glory. If life were an art lesson, we could describe it as a process of finding how to turn this mud into that porcelain, this discord into that sonata, this ugly stone block into that statue, this tangle of threads into that tapestry. In fact, however, the stakes are higher than in any art lesson. It is in the school of sainthood that we find ourselves enrolled and the artifact that is being made is ourselves.

Chisels, kilns, hammers, scissors, needles—these are the trappings we find in studios where beautiful work is being made. Translating all of this into ordinary daily experience, we see the sort of studio God has us in. We are constantly being chipped and banged and burned and cut and knocked into shape—not because the Artist hates his material but because he loves it and has an exquisite artifact in mind.

"Dear friends," wrote John, "now we are children of God, and what we will be has not yet been made known. But we know that when he [Christ] appears, we shall be like him, for we shall see him as he is. Everyone who has this hope in him purifies himself, just as he is pure" (1 John 3:2–3). And everyone whom God has appointed for this destiny he prepares for it, using afflictions along with our other experiences as his tools for sculpting our souls.

Our picture of the artist's studio reminds us that great beauty lies in all sorts of materials, beauty which is often brought out by procedures that look for all the world as if they are doing violence to those materials. That makes the picture an apt one for God's work of sanctifying us. In our case the material is the most precious of all materials—created human beings—and the end product will be artifacts of inexpressible loveliness—Christlike human beings. For Jesus Christ, who was and remains perfect man no less than Son of God, is the model to which, so far as our natures can receive it, each single one of us is going to be conformed. We purify ourselves by decision and action, and God purifies us by the refining effect of experience, particularly experience that is felt to be adverse and diminishing, and so the life of grace goes on.

The final dignity of a thing is its *glory*—that is, the realizing of its built-in potential for good. And that glory crowns the dignity its maker gave it initially. A Stradivarius violin, made so carefully by cutting and sanding and bending and glueing various kinds of wood, enters into its glory when under the player's skillful bowing it sings; that, after all, is what it was made for. The true glory of all objects appears when they do what they were made to do. A tapestry shows its glory when it hangs to enhance a room; it was made for that, rather than to be rolled in mothballs. A sculpture shows its glory by arresting what would otherwise be fleeting; it does its proper work by standing in public, never moving or changing. The violin playing, the tapestry hanging, and the sculpture on display, each gain hereby their own ultimate dignity. It is thus that their full worth appears. Now think of us human individuals. We were made to worship God. Worshiping is our supreme achievement and privilege, and our dignity is fullest as we do the thing we were made for. We enter into our own glory when we glorify God.

How then are we to worship? *First*, by praising God for every truth we know about him and by thanking him for every good gift and good experience, all of which come from his hand. *Second*, by learning specifically in and with the church to adore Christ the Savior. *Third*, by making worship out of all the materials of life, not just splendid talents and powers and triumphs and joys, but plodding routines and vexations and pains and humiliations and depressions and rejections and traumas and bewilderments as well. And as we labor to make offerings of worship out of these things—offerings of patience and goodwill and trust and fortitude and hope—so God is laboring in and with us to make us into the most glorious of all his works, namely, worshipers in the image and likeness of Jesus Christ. Christ's life displayed human dignity to the full, for he worshiped and served God the Father to the full. To the extent that we follow him in this, our lives attain supreme dignity and display ultimate glory, too. But without this, whatever we do, however striking our achievements, there is neither real dignity nor true glory, only the ignoble pseudo-dignity and the short-lived pseudo-glory of the world's applause and our own pompous conceit.

This is to say that the truest dignity, nobility, and glory are seen, not in heroes, pioneers, great rulers, great artists, or any other of the world's celebrities as such, but rather in holy men and women of God who have learned the lesson of worship. Their powers and weaknesses, their successes and failures, their exultation and grief, all go up continually to the Throne as an offering. They pray and give thanks in all things; they love God under all circumstances; they hope in him at all times. In humbling themselves before God, in acknowledging their impotence and faultiness and constant need of his grace, and in disclaiming any form of self-righteousness or self-sufficiency, they find the integrity, honesty, poise, and calm which are dignity's outward form. And from the happy knowledge of being God's redeemed children, living by his forgiveness and secure in his love, they draw the incentive and the resources to be "steadfast, immovable, always abounding in the work of the Lord" (1 Corinthians 15:58, RSV), which is dignity in full realization.

It is a universal experience to feel and know when we observe such folk, poor and undistinguished as they may be, that we are witnessing true human dignity as we witness it nowhere else. Even though in the interests of secular humanist theory we may wish to deny this, our own consciences will convince us of it, as happened, it seems, to Herod in the presence of John the Baptist, and to Felix in the presence of Paul, and to Pilate in the presence of Jesus (see Mark 6:20; Acts 24:25; Matthew 27:11–18; John 18:33–19:12). Man's lie is that our dignity forbids us to serve either God or our fellow humans, though it requires us to look for service from both—in other words, that our dignity justifies our egoism. God's truth is that our dignity is only realized as we love and serve God for himself, and mankind for God's sake, according to the two great commands in which Christ said that all the law and the prophets are summed up. The alternative is to demean and dehumanize ourselves by the sort of manipulative self-centeredness that rots the soul. The choice is ours.

What then should we say of Eastern devotees who show what looks like genuine love for gods whom we can only judge to be false, or of Western humanists who genuinely sacrifice themselves in helping and caring for their needy fellow humans? The single-mindedness of the former and the self-abnegation of the latter sometimes put Christians to shame. Are we to deny them dignity and worth because they do not worship the true God?

Two things should be said by way of reply.

First: Though we must leave it to God to read hearts, it is not wrong to raise the question whether the good pagan is as altruistic and free from self-seeking as he appears. There are, we know, many specious "loves" in human relationships—self-interest, passion, lust, avarice, ambition, vainglory, possessiveness, sentimentalism, and so forth—and all will masquerade as love in the noblest and highest sense of that word. Also, it is not impossible that a non-Christian's asceticism and a humanist's altruism should have at their heart the worm of self-serving self-assertion in some form.

The only thing that enables Christians ever to rise above egocentric motivation is the knowledge that God in love has already robed them with his gift of salvation, and only Christians have such knowledge. So it would not be strange if the best unbelievers should lapse at this point. Tertullian's dismissal of pagan virtues as *splendida vitia* (good-looking vices) was by biblical standards too sweeping, and yet it could be the right verdict in any particular case. As pride will disguise itself as humility, so egoism can fool not only observers but also the agent into thinking that he or she is an altruist. "The heart is deceitful above all things and beyond cure," wrote Jeremiah (17:9), and experience constantly confirms his words.

Second: We must also remember that there is such a thing as "common grace," the universal generosity of God from which not just Christians, but all human beings benefit. Every good and perfect gift comes from God, the atheist's genius, the agnostic's skills, the skeptic's beauty, the ability of flawed parents to give good things to their children, no less than the saint's perseverance. Love is from God, says John (1 John 4:7), and, though we may be unsure how genuine love is in any particular case, we can say with certainty that where love is, there God is at work in the lover's life, even if not savingly (though it should be noted that a commitment to love is often a step toward saving faith and repentance). So, judging as we must do by appearances, we shall acknowledge and applaud God's gifts in unbelievers, and we shall see divine enabling and true human dignity in the good that they do. "Show proper respect to everyone" wrote Peter (1 Peter 2:17). Surely this was part of his meaning.

Dignity and Moral Standards

Convictions about what is real and what is right are bound up together; what you believe about behavior both follows from and implies the way you think things are. Inevitably, therefore, the different accounts of reality which divide Christians and secular humanists from each other issue in moralities which clash at significant points. To the Christian, every human being has intrinsic and inalienable dignity by virtue of being made in God's image and realizes and exhibits the full potential of that dignity only in the worship and service of the Creator. The secular humanist, however, being a practical atheist (usually a theoretical one, too), is bogged down in a social pragmatism which measures the worth of individuals entirely by their usefulness, actual or potential, to the community. Earlier we noted some of the consequences to which this scale of value naturally leads. We now round off this chapter by pinpointing some of the moral guidelines and controls which follow from the Christian view. Thus, we shall plot at least part of the ethical fault line in our culture, the series, that is, of places where Christian and humanist moralities grind hard against each other, producing periodic earthquakes in the realm of public policy.

First: the equal dignity of all human beings as God's image-bearers both undergirds and gives shape to the obligation which Christ himself laid on us, to love our neighbor as we love ourselves. Our neighbor is anyone and everyone with whom we have contact. Our task is to value that person as we value ourselves and to seek his or her good as we seek our own good. So far, our argument has stressed the individual's response to God our Maker and Christ our Savior as if this vertical relationship is all that matters. Now, however, we would emphasize that the horizontal relationship of honoring God's image in others by seeking to give and secure to them respect, goodwill, help, protection, shelter, food, education, justice, and freedom of thought and religion—meaning liberty to differ from us without our neighbor-relationship to them being thereby endangered—is integral to the worship and obedience in which love to the Father and the Son finds expression. To serve God is to serve mankind, and to serve mankind is to serve the person who is one's neighbor at the moment.

John bluntly declares: "If anyone says, 'I love God,' yet hates his brother, he is a liar" (1 John 4:20). And no human being exists who could not in principle become the neighbor whom it is my duty actively to help, right now, according to his present need; that, of course, is the point of the Good Samaritan story. We only honor God as we honor his image in the other person by practical love to that person, whoever he or she may be: rich or poor, strong or weak, red or yellow, black or white, conventional or wild, respectable or rough, significant or unimportant in the community. To put it the other way round, honoring and loving God means refusing one's natural inclination to withhold love and honor from people whom one finds awkward, repellent, and inconvenient.

To love is not necessarily to like; it is, rather, to care, help, and serve, whether you like the other party or not. Action starts with thought, and the starting-point for all Christian action in what has been called the human zoo must be the thought of our common and equal dignity as persons made in our Maker's image, having infinite worth.

Second: Love to our neighbor requires not only the bestowing of status, goodwill, and care for material needs, but also the attempt to help him or her forward in, or toward, Christian faith and holiness, in order that the potential glory of each person's created humanity may become actual. There is of necessity a pastoral and paternal aspect to neighbor-love; one who knows (as perhaps one's neighbor does not yet know) that the true fulfillment of everyone's humanity lies in the righteousness, fidelity, courage, wisdom, and worship that constitute Christlike godliness will naturally and rightly try to smooth the path and encourage a commitment to these things among all with whom one has a relationship. And so one should. The bland benevolence that will not concern itself with people's eternal welfare is a hollow mockery of neighbor-love.

So, in an imperfectly Christian society like our own, Christians will seek to persuade the community and its leaders to enact laws and programs that will make easier and not obstruct individual movement toward godliness. The axiom to which a British action group stands committed, that "law and public policy in our country should be in harmony with basic Christian principles," is one which all clear-headed Christians will embrace. With confidence (and since they have a good case, why should they not be confident?) they will seek to persuade their fellow-citizens that since the way of life that is in line with God's revealed truth is best for all, the law should encourage it. For them to do this is as true an expression of neighbor-love as is direct care for those needy individuals who cross one's path.

Similarly, one constant issue in social policy, with which all clear-headed Christians will themselves be concerned, will be the preservation of personal dignity in the worlds of work, family life, schools, hospitals, clubs, and prisons. In this fallen world, in which manipulating and using others rather than seeking their good is as natural as breathing, all these relational structures can and do degenerate, becoming impersonal and oppressive, dehumanized and dehumanizing. Neighbor-love summons Christians to do all they can to stop this from happening and to inject into these community structures a deeper respect for the individual, who bears God's image. In the modern world, with its secularist and collectivist bias, this is an uphill task, but it must not be neglected on that account. Great need, rather, should call forth great effort.

Third: Neighbor-love, founded on recognition of the God-given dignity of the individual, entails a "pro-life" stance, that is, opposition to abortion, infanticide, and euthanasia. Though on these matters modern Christians are, for whatever reason, less than unanimous, the key principles seem clear.

Concerning abortion, there are three issues. *The initial question is whether the unborn human fetus has at any stage the value of a person,* God's image-bearer, with the same claim on our protection as will exist after birth. Few Christians hesitate to say that the fetus has this value at least by the time of quickening (about twenty weeks) or of viability (about twenty-six weeks); nor do they hesitate to oppose abortions on demand after this date.

The next question is how early this value and claim are acquired. Here differences emerge; but more and more Christians are coming to see that both the value and the claim exist from the moment of conception, when under God's sovereign control an egg is fertilized and a new genetic unit formed. The biological facts that the blastocyst (fertilized egg) is not implanted in the womb wall till a week later and that the new unit (or units, since for the first two weeks the embryo is capable of twinning) cannot feel pain till after about three months do not seem relevant. The genetic unit, with all its God-given potential of future personal life, is there. And the fact that psychologically this unit is only as yet a potential person, without consciousness, does not affect its claim to protection, any more than a child's or an adult's claim to protection would be affected by a possibly prolonged lapse into coma through accident or sickness. Being a potential person psychologically and being God's image-bearer theologically are not alternative and exclusive categories, as the otherwise excellent introduction to bioethics by D. Gareth Jones, *Brave New People,* unhappily implies. Only if it becomes clear that no personal life will ever be possible for a particular fetus (as it does, for instance, in the case of anencephalia, a malformed condition in which major

---

1. D. Gareth Jones, *Brave New People* (Leicester: InterVarsity Press and Downer's Grove, IL: InterVarsity Press, 1984).

brain centers are lacking) will this dual categorization not apply.

The final question is whose claim to life has priority when the mother's life can only be saved by aborting the baby. Roman Catholics have maintained that abortion as such is unlawful even in these circumstances, though they have allowed that some forms of life-saving ministry to the mother (for example, the ending of an ectopic pregnancy or the removing of a cancerous womb with the baby inside) may be lawful although the baby's death is then inevitable. The appeal here is to the principle that an action performed for the sake of desired good consequences is not necessarily rendered unlawful by the fact that undesired bad consequences are inseparable from it. We pass no judgment on this reasoning, nor do we offer any across-the-board answer of our own to this problem. We ask only whether on Christian principles different solutions might be right on different occasions and whether the mother's own wishes in each such case should not be taken into account.

With regard to infanticide, the principle is surely this: If the infant, however handicapped otherwise, is a person, aware of receiving and capable of enjoying the love of others (for this limited relationality is sufficient to constitute personal life), then he or she has as real a claim on our care and protection as a normal child would have. Therefore, far from killing the infant, or letting it die of starvation or neglect, we should interpret its arrival as a call to us to love it as long as its life lasts, however restricted in length or quality that life may be. We need to be clear in our minds that human dignity derives not from cleverness and ability and social usefulness, but from humanness as such. Therefore, Down's syndrome and spina bifida babies possess the dignity of being God's image-bearers no less than other infants do.

As for euthanasia, whether willed by its subject (which is a form of suicide) or decided on by others (which is a form of murder), it is ruled out by the knowledge that God gives us personal life so that in it we may dignify ourselves and glorify him through our practice of worship, obedience, holiness, love, and patience. And this is our task every day that the gift is continued. Our part is to value and preserve personal life in both ourselves and others as long as we can, rather than cut it short for escapist or any other reasons. We have no call, certainly, to keep life-support systems going when it is clear that personal, relational consciousness has gone for good; but while it lasts, we should try, as Western medicine has traditionally done, to maintain bodily life as long as possible. Euthanasia may bring death without discomfort, but it is never the path of death with dignity; death has dignity only when it is awaited patiently and then accepted peacefully, when and how God chooses.

Here we stop. We have said enough to indicate what difference the Christian understanding of human dignity will make to our moral life. Acknowledging, preserving, and responding to the dignity of the other person, as God's image-bearer—summoned to wholeness and holiness in Christ—will always be one aspect of Christian decision-making. But this constant concern for man's dignity will have no parallel where the Judeo-Christian frame of reference is left behind, and inevitably we shall then feel the draught. To be valued for oneself, as a person, is humanizing, for it ennobles; but to be valued only as a hand, or a means, or a tool, or a cog in a wheel, or a convenience to someone else is dehumanizing—and it depresses. Christianity's claim to be the true humanism is strengthened by the unique dignity that it finds in each individual. Secular humanism, though claiming vast wisdom and life-enhancing skills, actually diminishes the individual, who is left in old age without dignity (because his or her social usefulness is finished) and without hope (because there is nothing now to look forward to). Christianity compels us to humble ourselves before our Maker as the weak and foolish sinners that we are, constantly proclaiming him great and ourselves small. Therefore, since it seems that in every way Christianity forces us to put ourselves down, some, seeing no further, have revolted against it on this account. Yet Christianity reveals us to ourselves as the most precious and privileged of all God's creatures, made in his image and redeemed by the precious blood of Christ the incarnate Son. With this, moreover, Christianity sets before us Christ himself as our model of human nobility, our enabler as we seek to be like him, and our hope as we look beyond this glorious preparatory life on earth to one in heaven which is yet more glorious and will never end. Let our readers judge which of the two positions does more to establish and uphold the dignity of man.

8

Culture

Every summer tens of thousands of American students pack their bags and head for Europe. Some go with a "seminar," which means trundling about from place to place in vans, stopping in the Lake District to see where Wordsworth wrote, and at Versailles to see how Louis XIV lived, and at Ravenna to see early Christian art in the mosaics. They stand on the steps of St. Peter's or on the Acropolis or on the Ponte Vecchio and listen to lectures on the history of Western art-forms. After the lectures they may scatter to snap pictures of themselves on a parapet or next to a caryatid, stop for an aperitif or some espresso at a tiny round table with spindly wire chairs under the sycamore trees, poke into the book-stalls along the Seine, follow the tourists to Place Pigalle, or better yet find some obscure bistro that most tourists don't know about.

Others do not bother with the seminar, but set off with a back-pack and a few maps. They want to keep it simple; to get in amongst "the people"; to avoid the tourist traps; to see Europe as it really is. Still others arrange an academic year abroad. They go to Aix-en-Provence, Padua, or Tübingen; learn the language; live in the world of indigenous students; and generally become European.

What is the exercise about? The outlay of money, time, and effort shows that it is thought important. But why?

The Desire to Be Civilized

If we were to chase the answer all the way down, we would find that Americans are interested in European culture and history because that is where the roots of American culture and history are. Some, if pressed, might also admit to a certain tingling hope that some *experience* would turn up as well—some tryst on the ront Neuf, or a dash to a castle with some mustachioed young landgraf, or at least mellow ecstatic nights under a Mediterranean moon with the breeze soft in the cypress trees and the lights twinkling across the water from the esplanade. But that would be the unofficial agenda. Officially, it is the quest for cultural enrichment that has brought them here.

There is traffic in the other direction, too, of course. Every year tens of thousands of German, Nigerian, and Japanese students pack their bags to "see America." On a summer trip, they might cover Yosemite, Times Square, Wall Street, New Orleans, Disney World, and perhaps Independence Hall, Concord, and a white clapboard Vermont village. Natural and technological wonders would have a slight edge over historical monuments in most of their minds, since America does not have much in the way of history, not at least when compared with the millennia that lie behind the Europeans and Asians. If they come to America for graduate degrees, they will probably be looking for American expertise in physics, medicine, engineering, business administration, or perhaps education.

What is going on here? The answer is not far to seek. People want to be wholly awake to their own humanness. "We want some culture," they say, and this is what they mean. They think of travel as broadening the mind, and other cultures as enriching it, and knowledge of origins and backgrounds and techniques as deepening a person's insight. So they make their overseas pilgrimages and tour other lands as culture-vultures in hope of ending up, not barbarians, but civilized.

The words being used here are however slippery, and the goal toward which they point is not always clear. To start with, what does it mean to acquire culture and become cultured? *Culture* is a concertina-word which moves constantly between broad and nar-row meanings. Sometimes it contracts to signify the fine arts as such, and sometimes it extends, under the influence of the social sciences, to cover all the associational patterns and mind-sets that particular societies exhibit. Ordinarily, persons are called "cul-tured" when they seem to be intelligently knowledgeable about a fair number of these things. But one can be knowledgeable with-out either empathy or insight, simply through educational drill and social grooming. Is one cultured in this case?

Again, what does it mean to be civilized? And what is the difference between a civilized person and a barbarian? Every-one—from Australian aborigine to Austrian aristocrat—follows pretty much the same routines in basic activities like eating and sleeping and working and procreating, and so it has always been. Yet there are differences between the ways in which these un-alterable routines are arranged and festooned, and it is in these differences that the difference between being civilized and bar-barian appears. Characterizing them, however, is not easy. If we said in general terms that a barbarian lives his life with no refer-ence to the many things that "higher" civilizations have devel-oped, that would not get us far. What are these things? Do all "higher" civilizations exhibit them? And what is the criterion of being "higher" anyway? Will we insist that to eat with chopsticks or forks is "higher" than to eat with our fingers? Is it "higher" to sit on fragrant mats in silk, or on velvet cushions in brocade, than to squat naked? Is linen "higher" than a banana leaf for a table covering? Is pâté "higher" food than scorched monkey's paw?

And it is not a question of having some culture or none. Every man is already cultured in the sociological sense of being schooled in his own group's way of doing things. The man in his undershirt with a can of beer sitting in a bulging brown velveteen armchair in front of the boxing match on television is as schooled in his own crowd's way of doing things as is the lady perched on a tiny Louis XVI chair listening to a concerto for crumhorn and virginals. Anthropologists will tell us how to classify and differentiate cultures in the scientific manner, but then cultural relativists will tell us that it is no good pretending that one way is better than another. All tribes work out a way of living that corresponds to the demands of their surroundings: igloos, wigwams, or villas; blub-ber, pemmican, or soufflé; skins, loincloths, or brocade—these are neutral items, they say. "Higher" and "lower" are thus not words that fit.

Let us for the moment grant all this. Nonetheless it cannot be denied that the question of being civilized is an important one for all of us. Christianity and secular humanism have no quarrel at this point, at least not on the surface. Both agree that the question reaches close to the center of what we human beings are, and what goals we set ourselves. For example, we want our children to be able to use a fork, and to know how to greet adults. We want them to get into the habit of brushing their teeth and taking a bath. We expostulate with them for belching in company; we think it offensive for them to do that, though in other cultures a belch is a compliment to the food and the cook. We try to suppress their screams in church or in public. We tell them not to get dirty fingerprints on the white doorjamb, to wipe the chocolate ice cream from their chins, to keep their hands to themselves in the antique shop, not to cut into the waiting line (jump the queue, as the British say), and to give that lady a hand with her suitcase. In all these matters we try by means of instruction and example to lick them into what seems to us to be proper shape.

It appears, then, that being civilized has something to do with thoughtfulness, or politeness, or courtesy. But what are these? Are they not just names we give to the attitude which lies at the root of all civilizations, namely, recognition of the rights and dignity of others, and reticence about imposing oneself too freely upon them? All of our efforts at cleanliness, for instance—all bathing and spraying and powdering and gargling, and the whole industry thereof—say in effect, I won't ask you to live with the miasma that floats so persistently from my body; this should be neutralized so that we can enjoy freedom in each other's company. Clothes say the same thing: I won't ask you to cope with my nakedness. Polite conventions of eating and conversation testify likewise: My habit of gobbling food and talking with my mouth full will introduce a difficult note into this group at the table here, so I will curb it. My strong opinion that you are a bore or a fool shall be hidden away behind polite inquiries after your tennis, your children, or your studies. (The conventions of course work both ways: By suppressing my boredom and asking a few nice questions, I may find out that you have something to say after all.

And if your answers only confirm my initial thought about you, then I can at least learn patience and forebearance through the exercise.)

Technology and Taste

It is, no doubt, more common to measure civilization and to offset it against barbarianism by its greater technological sophistication. But this is a less decisive criterion than it looks. Are we to assess the richness of a civilization by the extent of its *technology?* We can all agree that it is a good thing to have fire and the wheel and the pulley and the lever and so forth. But is it *better* to be propelled by a sleek piece of aerodynamic engineering at 1200 miles per hour from Paris to Washington than to cross the Atlantic by steamship?

Is it always best to travel as fast as one can? But then someone will raise the question of the steamship itself as opposed to the clipper ship. And while we might agree that the old sailors were a doughty lot and that much romance and grace lie in the picture of those princely vessels surging across the Atlantic, nonetheless, we must admit that great gains in comfort and convenience accompanied the advent of steam. No matter how nice they may look in Christmas cards, the same would have to be said about the jolting and swaying of stagecoaches when compared with the Orient Express or the Super Chief. Concrete, the internal combustion engine, radio, television, computers—no questions arise if we are thinking of them as means to comfort, convenience, and efficiency, which in this materialistic age are major values for most of us. The questions only come when we step aside and ask ourselves whether the *quality* of our life is now better than that of our forefathers.

Sentimentalism tends to sigh "No" here; and all forms of romantic primitivism decry the noise, speed, metal, fumes, and plastic that bedevil modern life. Indeed, we need not be romantic primitivists to feel this way. Only the most brassy of us will actually admit to preferring neon and din and polystyrene foam to creaking old inn signs, earthenware, and silence. Yet not one of us wants to return to the plumbing, surgery, and hygiene of the pretechnological era. We know that at these points we have something better. But does that mean that the overall quality of our life is better? The question is one on which a debating society might well chew for a whole winter and still be divided.

How then, in relation to all this, are we to identify, and protect, and nourish, and perpetuate our humanness? Could technology engender barbarism, rather than a richer quality of human life? In the interest of being civilized, we go to an art museum. There we see a van Ruysdael painting with a rutted road running through the middle of it, and we envy the tranquillity of those cottages. The experience leaves us feeling that the bulldozer and the cement truck are somehow raping both the landscape and us when they growl up and start work on new roads. But we would not wish to be digging our cars out of mud and sand all day. We must admit, then, that the bulldozer and the cement truck have made life easier for us. Again, our hearts sicken when we see a mountain valley, the home of elk and marmots, all torn to pieces and turned to slag heaps when the mining company moves in with its rattling conveyor belts and diesel engines. Yet we are glad enough to have this copper wiring installed in our home. Who likes the look or the smell of an oil refinery? But which of us will put his car up on blocks and get out the surrey or the dog-cart?

The questions jostle and elbow each other, and most of us try to have it both ways, decrying filth and smoke and noise while merrily whirring along in cars that only exist by virtue of filth and smoke and noise. But it is difficult to doubt that the questions are really idle. Nothing can put a stop to the curiosity and genius that have flogged us along from the discovery of the wheel to the harnessing of steam to the splitting of the atom and the cracking of the genetic code. In our reveries and on greeting cards we like dirt roads; under the tires of our cars we prefer pavement. So what should we do?

On this, Christians and secular humanists have no quarrel with each other, not at least in their character as Christians and anti-Christians. Some from each camp will be found, no doubt, driving the bulldozers and some of each will be found trying to wave them back, but that is another story. The question, how far to push ahead with technological development of any particular front, puzzles all of us and divides all sections of the community, and plain personal preference plays a large part in determining our point of view.

Certain questions of preference do seem to reach deeper than mere inclination, however. Especially is this true when it comes to what we call matters of *taste*. Whatever one might like to think and wish to say in debate, polystyrene foam is not, in fact, as worthy a material as earthenware or gold. And somehow polyester cannot hold its head up next to wool. Or can it? The one certainty is that when we start making remarks like this we raise hackles. Accusations of snobbery or tackiness fly back and forth, and everyone goes away angry and unbudged.

The truth is that taste is no small matter. Think again of our students tramping around Europe. It is not simply dates and names that they are after. What they hope for (though they might not say it like this) is that the experience will make them men and women of taste. For taste is a facet of wisdom; it is the ability to distinguish what has value from what does not. The fact that most of us invest a great deal of ourselves in these ventures of travel to cultural centers shows that we really do regard taste as something crucial to our authentic humanness. And in this we are right. It is.

Humanists, both Christian and secular, see this. When you get any group of people talking about what gives full quality to human life, sooner or later the conversation turns toward this matter of taste. Words like *simplicity* and *integrity* and *authenticity* crop up; they stand for the qualities which should mark the way that we dress, talk, and festoon our doings. To say that a painting, a pair of shoes, a belch, or anything else, is *in poor taste*, implies eventually that it is unworthy of our humanness. It does us a disservice; it has a coarsening effect. Whatever its surface-level appeal, it numbs and atrophies our sensitivity to value. That painting, for example, is tasteless; it sentimentalizes life; or it is garish; or it appeals to mere sensation. And that pair of shoes! Doesn't he know that no one with any shred of taste would be caught dead in such horrors? And—my *dear!* No one bat an eye . . . keep talking . . . but, yes, that was a belch.

Here caricature is hard to avoid. But there are serious undertones, all the same. Is it proper to make value judgments in these matters that determine the shape and flavor and tint of our mortal life? Lord Clark, in his television series on civilization, said that if he were really pressed to name one time and place that in his view brought civilization to its finest peak, he would pick out the Renaissance court of the dukes of Urbino. Is that snobbery? Must we have courtyards and cypress trees and slashed sleeves and pages and conversation about Neoplatonism over the wine? Can we not be civilized otherwise? To state the question in a more general and positive way: What items make up the list of things contributing to, or detracting from, a developed, civilized humanness? And what is the real importance of these things?

The first part of the question takes us back to the obvious: clothes, courtesies, food, habits, furniture, decorations—all the things that show up in our routines of life. Not many of us are rich or leisured enough to have much leeway here. We make do as best we can with what we can afford or with what has been handed down to us. But it is very far from being a matter of money, really. The simplest apartment or farmhouse can exhibit flawless taste, and the splashiest townhouse or villa can be a nightmare of foolishness. The thing we call good taste does seem to have something to do with a sense of *appropriateness*. It's grotesque for me to borrow somebody's porcelain and crystal if I'm having you in to supper at my little cold-water, walk-up flat. An omelette with brown bread and a green salad on plain crockery is in much better taste here than an extravaganza of pheasant galantine, sturgeon, and peau-de-creme.

By the same token, the clothes that I choose for my daily work ought to take some account of what is customary in this part of the world as well as of my own self-image. If I cannot bear robin's-egg blue for my jackets, then by all means let me put on something in neutral-colored corduroy, even if everyone else in the office is sporting blue. Understated colors and designs may be in far better taste—far more appropriate, that is—than that which is slick, ostentatious, and gaudy. But to come to the office in swim trunks or pajamas or a clown suit would quite definitely be bad taste.

We used the word *ought* a minute ago. My clothes *ought* to take account of convention. And we said that the omelette is in *better* taste than the galantine. This brings us to the second part of the question, namely is any of this important? Should lapses of taste on our part and that of others bother us? Why should we think that they matter?

Some people would insist quite loudly that such lapses do not matter in themselves and should not matter to us. Come, they say, can't we just accept people as they are? Must we be forever assessing and squinting and sizing them up? Do we really want to be caught running our fingertip over the invitation to see if it is engraved and not just printed? Is it not viciously snobbish to behave in this way? And besides, some of us have more important things to think about. We have tasks at hand that demand our whole attention and energy, and we cannot be harried by these questions about social window-dressing.

At surface level, this has force, particularly in an age like ours which is paranoid about snobbery and unreality. The protest would seem to pit hard work, simplicity, necessity, responsibility, and perhaps poverty over against luxury, leisure, money, sophistication, and overrefinement. Who will see the latter items as hallmarks of authentic human life? If ever those who lacked them were thought of as a little less than human, it is not so now, and the uncultured hick who runs rings around well-heeled top people has become something of a folk hero in our time, popping up in films and paperbacks constantly.

Plainly, too, we must grant the validity of any style that has been imposed on people by economic or environmental necessity; it is not lack of taste, for instance, when brutalizing poverty drives people to sleep out of doors and ransack trash cans for food. Yet it is a fact that just as taste may lapse among the wealthy, so it may triumph even in poverty. When one's wretched lean-to is kept tidy and one's unsuitable clothes, other people's castoffs, are kept clean, good taste is appearing (for it is always fitting that homes and clothes should be spick and span). And with that good taste—indeed, in it—there appears a degree of humanness which muddle and dirt can never show forth. It really does seem, as one thinks about it, that those who urge that taste does not matter are missing something. One way of being a barbarian is to have bad taste, or no taste; the other way is to dismiss questions of taste as irrelevant to our humanness. Either way, there is loss, just as in vision marred by astigmatism or color-blindness there is loss. Therefore, as Christians, we applaud taste.

Christianity Transcends Culture

So far, the secular humanist would probably agree with most of what we have been saying. But now he might wish to chip in, to challenge our right to say it. Surely (he might object) all major religions forbid us to be preoccupied with the immediate, visible world. That is one of the things wrong with them! They tell us that this life is only important as preparation for the life to come, even if that life to come is no more than oblivion and absorption into the All. Christianity, which posits personal life in that eternal future, is emphatic in requiring us to sit loose to what is around us. Nonreligious people (he might continue), we humanists, and others, who believe that this is the only life there is and the only world we shall ever know, may well stress the importance of taste, since nothing outside mortal life may be brought in to rescue it from the drudgery, ennui, and brutishness in which lack of taste will speedily submerge it. Therefore we value the Western cultural heritage, the legacy of Greece and Rome and the Renaissance and the Enlightenment, very much indeed. But what right have Christians to say that culture and taste are important? For Christians, if we understand the matter aright, nothing in this world is important except the saving and preparing of one's soul for the future life. So it is inconsistent, not to say disingenuous, for Christians to claim to value culture and taste in the way that this chapter has done so far. A negative stance, affirming the irrelevance of culture—a barbarian stance, in other words—is all that is consistent with the Christian faith.

A fair challenge! We shall try to meet it with a full and fair response. To this end, we would distinguish two quite separate questions, which the challenge has run together.

First: Is it true that biblical Christianity is indifferent to questions of taste and culture?

It might seem so; and indeed there is an important sense in which it certainly is so. Aesthetics, good taste, and cultured enrichment are not direct or explicit biblical concerns. So far, the humanist is right, and we may without embarrassment develop his point for him. Look first at the Old Testament. Its law is entirely ceremonial and moral. When it is not specifying strictly religious observances, it is spelling out canons for behavior; all its imperatives are liturgical or ethical, and all its interest centers on these two aspects of godliness. If there are any artistic, architectural, or domestic specifications, they are all determined by religion (diet, for example, or the various washings and purity rituals, or the design of the tabernacle and temple, or the tailoring of the priestly uniform). Questions of taste are not raised, not at least in that form.

(We ought, however, to note in passing that it is difficult to fix the frontier between the moral and religious realm and the realm of taste. For example, the prohibition of opulence in the law and the prophets meant that the baubles, combs, crisping pins, and cosmetics that we find in Egypt were to have no counterpart among the Jews. Arguably, this was a lesson in taste, directing Israelites toward a simple style of life marked by a depth of integrity in dealing with God, men, and things that those who spend their lives in the lap of luxury cannot ordinarily match. But even so, it was godliness rather than taste that was being taught.)

When we come to the New Testament, we find that apart from a few specific prohibitions in the interests of modesty there is a complete absence of anything that might be called cultural awareness, or cultural concern. Not a line in the Gospels or Epistles encourages us to attach the least importance either to the culture we have or to the quest to become cultured, which was so major a concern among the Greeks. It is as though for Christ and the apostles such things as geography and race and economics and class—all the factors that separate us out from each other and make our cultures visible and various—did not exist. When Paul talks about Jews and Greeks, or Greeks and barbarians, he is not thinking of these people as an anthropologist or historian might do. He is talking of one thing only—mankind's need of Christ. The Jews are privileged in having been chosen as God's people, and in having been drilled in devotion by Moses and the prophets, and in now being blood brothers to the Messiah. The Greeks are outside that pale, but they have a lively interest in the gods and in moral and philosophical questions. Very good, for the gospel is what both Jews and Gentiles need. The barbarians are outside the sphere of Graeco-Roman civilization altogether, but Paul is not curious about their cultures. To him they represent potential converts. They, too, need to be saved. That is the focal point of his interest in them.

We may huff and puff that this is no way to think about people and the fascinating range of styles in which they live. Isn't God interested in people just as they are? we ask. Wasn't it an expression of his own creativity to make us capable of shaping life in all these varied and colorful ways? Doesn't lack of interest in cultures, therefore, argue failure to appreciate the work of the Creator? What is Paul thinking of? Heavens! Let's not stir everything down into one gray porridge of *converts*.

What is implied here is that Paul is missing something—that, to put it bluntly, he is culturally color-blind and is the worse for it. But in reality he is seeing something that his critics do not see. He is seeing and expressing the universality of the Christian religion: the fact that it is good news, not just for some, but for all. All human lives, and all human cultures, are vitiated; all need to be changed, and can be changed, by the saving power of Jesus Christ. Nothing human can stand before God without being re-made, but every human being who is willing is a candidate for redemptive renewal, and every culture may find renewal through the input and influence of renewed human beings. Paul's reason for being negative about nature and culture is his passion to high-light the positives of grace.

Culturelessness is in fact one of the piquant paradoxes of Chris-tianity. The gospel is the great leveler. It is not interested in whether I am a Laplander or a Filipino, a Hebrew or an Aryan, a garbage man or a millionaire. My race, my history, my family, my brains, my prestige, my taste are not seen as credentials, or ac-cepted as qualifications, at any stage. Paul brings the matter to a head when he tells us that in Christ there is neither Jew nor Greek, slave nor free, male nor female (Galatians 3:28). That sounds like a final blow against any interest in culture and the cultural aspects of relationships; it also, at first blush, sounds like nonsense. Do Christians actually forfeit their racial, social, and sexual identities and become deracialized, classless, and sexless? The answer of course is no. Paul's point, stated in a nonparadox-ical way, is that racial, social, and sexual distinctions are no longer determinative of behavior patterns in the new community that Christ creates, because they no longer control the way that peo-ple regard each other. What is determinative is their common relationship to Christ, which requires of them a new way of relat-ing together.

Why then does Paul choose to wrap up his meaning in this paradoxical, and even silly-sounding form of words? Partly for emphasis, because the point is so important; partly to jolt us awake, lest we miss it; partly to make us think, since without hard thought we shall not fully grasp it. Paul's words are, in fact, a shatteringly radical declaration, crystallized, Jewish-style, into three specific instances of the difference that the vertical of know-ing Christ must make to the horizontal of meeting people.

Take Paul's words about sex—*"neither male or female."* These words do not point to any disregard or overthrowing of sexual distinctions. Christians are not androgynous, nor are they required to hanker for that dull state. They see that, far from destroying sexuality or rendering it unimportant, Christ through the gospel raises and frees it from all the sludge, surfeit, and shame into which it slides when we mortals are left to our own appetites. He restores it to us in freshness, fascination, richness, and variety, as part of the spice of our created life. (*Vive la difference!*)

Christians know that virginity and even vows of celibacy, no less than holy marriage, testify to true maleness and femaleness by extolling the body as the shrine of a man's or woman's real identity and by protecting this shrine from being made into a flea market. And Christians experience life as sexual (at least, they should); for sexual awareness is part of what is involved in the virtuous habit—of noting in what ways each person we meet is like us yet differs from us, and seeking to help that person accordingly. (You ask, with some amazement perhaps, where do Christians get all this from, and the answer is, from Scripture, largely from Paul himself: see 1 Corinthians 5–7, 11:2–16, and Ephesians 5:15–33).

But—BUT—we only enter into this Christian apprehension of sexuality through learning to know and treat our fellow-Christians trans-sexually, as simply our equals in Christ—that is, as redeemed persons who are not to be used and exploited, sexually or in any other way, but rather to be honored and served, because they are children of the Father who loves them no less than he loves you and me, and because they with us are members (limbs and organs) of the body of Christ, who is the Savior and Elder Brother of us all. (Paul points to this when he finishes his sentence in Galatians 3:28 by saying: "for you are all one [man] in Christ Jesus.") As one forms the habit of treating one's fellow-believers, and others, too, in a trans-sexual, honorific way, at least honoring God's image in them, in cases where one sees no redeemed identity to honor, one's sense of the reality and glory of their sexuality is increased rather than diminished. Thus, as it is the pure in heart who will see God in heaven, so it is the pure in heart, and they alone, who appreciate sexuality on earth. But only the living Christ, the Christ of the gospel, can make and keep the heart pure; so if the secular humanist, or anyone else who does not

know Christ, felt left behind at this point in our argument, it
would be no wonder.

Now take Paul's words about race and station—*"neither Jew
nor Greek, slave nor free."* Though Christianity abolished slavery
in the end (twice, in fact; first in Western Christendom and then,
more than a millennium later, in the British colonies and America), it has never sought to obliterate racial or social distinctions as
such, so long as they do not become occasions of exploitation,
inhumaneness, or denial of honor where honor is due. Paul's first
point in context is that neither of these types of distinction, any
more than maleness or femaleness, either qualify one for or disqualify one from acceptance by God in and through Christ. They
are simply not relevant to the issue. Acceptance, according to the
gospel, is by faith alone, and the only thing that can disqualify one
from acceptance is one's own unwillingness to respond to God's
message. Then Paul's second point in context is that no racial,
social, or sexual distinction should be allowed in any way to re-
strict mutual acceptance within the company of those whom God
accepts, those who call on Jesus as their Savior and Lord.

As Christians, we are to cultivate, and be enriched by, the
fascinating unity that we find in Christ within the equally fascinating diversity and variety of our natures, roles, and social identities. So all of a sudden the queen and her chambermaid, the
philosopher and the simpleton, the boss and his Girl Friday, the
gourmet and the churl, find themselves on exactly the same footing. They go through the same water of baptism and eat and drink
at the same holy table. Pride of place, or face, or race, or grace (or
family, or intellect, or money, or power) is banished in the name
of Christ. A new society, with a new bond, is formed. Here is the
holy company: Jews, Greeks, women, men, freemen, slaves. A
ragtag and bobtail? Yes—and a noble retinue too, for they are all
new creatures in Christ Jesus.

What we are surveying is the absence of any "cultural" limitations in the gospel—a quality without which it could not be the
truly universal message that it is. If we think of its universality as
glorious, we should think the same of the culturelessness that
makes this universality possible; and we should rejoice that biblical Christianity is in this sense so entirely unconcerned about
cultural achievements, heritages, and restrictions. But to say that

obliges us at once to raise our second question—a different issue altogether, as we shall now see; and the exploring of it will take us to the end of this chapter.

Second: Is it true that biblical Christianity requires Christians to be indifferent to questions of taste and culture?

Christianity Generates Culture

First, let us note that as a matter of fact there has been a Christian culture in the West for the best part of two thousand years. As a witness to the gospel it has, we grant, been spotty. Emancipation, integrity, mercy, and good work are part of the story. Hospitals, universities, and schools have been pioneered; slavery, as we said, has been abolished; prison conditions and judicial barbarism have been reformed; ideals of moral integrity in rulers and bureaucracies, and of fair trading, thrift, and philanthropy have been established; and home life has been enriched and stabilized (though for the past half-century this latter gain has been largely squandered, even in professedly Christian countries). Lives without number have been cleansed and freed and redirected and energized and hallowed. The fine arts have been put to service: frescoes; mosaics; basilicas; cathedrals; the poetry of Dante, Donne, Spenser, Herbert, Milton, Charles Wesley, Hopkins, and Eliot; the music of Palestrina, Bach, Handel, Franck, and Bruckner; and the fiction of Dostoevsky, Solzhenitsyn, Defoe, Chesterton, Lewis, Greene, Tolkien, and Williams spring to mind at once.

The other part of the story, however, deals with tortures, religious wars, anti-Semitism, simony, extravagance, oppression, forcing of consciences, callous colonialism, and a thick-skinned exploitative disregard of others' needs that can only be called hypocritical. Christians must hang their heads when these things are mentioned and admit that they have not always made a good showing. Christian culture, though carrying within itself a principle of self-criticism and change for the better (that is, the biblical truth by whose light we ourselves have just condemned these evils and by which they were largely purged out before our time), has at each stage been a flawed product, and doubtless where it survives it is so still.

Yet, however damning the Christian crime sheet might appear, it would be an error of judgment to treat it as canceling the significance of the cultural positives listed above. Insofar as Christians were perpetrating horrors or stopping their ears to the cry of the needy, they were disobeying the gospel. And if the biblical diagnosis of the hardness and perversity of the sinful human heart is true, the reality of such disobedience, whether unconscious or uncaring, and of persistent blind spots in Christian societies, should not cause surprise, just as the parallel failings of individuals, however disappointing and shocking, should not cause surprise. Total moral awareness and full moral strength, like every other facet of human perfection, will not be experienced till we reach heaven. Certainly, each Christian generation, like each Christian individual, should be growing toward it, and God sends many holy and prophetic spirits to further the process, but neither individually nor corporately is sinlessness arrived at in this world. And it is always the case that alongside moral issues to which Christians are sensitive lie others to which we are not as sensitive as we should be.

So the truly significant thing here is just the startling and sustained upsurge of moral vision and energy over two millennia. And this upsurge, whatever the defects attached to its qualities and whatever the parallels to any of its particular moral ingredients in isolation, was and is in its totality quite unparalleled in world history. What should impress us about it is not its incidental shortcomings, but the extent and strength of its civilizing passion. In this it outstrips ancient Greece, Rome, and China completely. This moral upsurge was not self-generated, and nothing around us today encourages us to share the humanist's confidence that it can be self-sustaining. No; Christian culture, in its historical development as an offspring of the gospel, remains a wonder of God's "common grace."

Second, let us note the basis on which from the first this cultural enterprise rested. Christians have always believed in the goodness of creation, and historically the cultivating of the created order (which is what the word *culture* on Christian lips signifies) has been seen as one side of our service of God. As against the Gnostic and Manichean dualism of early Christian days, which regarded bodies and material objects as valueless if not indeed malevolent and pictured the good life as concerned with the mind only, Christians hold that God likes the matter he made, and we must not be too proud to like it, too. All created things reflect eternal realities and embody divine values (as Plato with uncanny intuition had gropingly guessed), and we are to study and value them accordingly. Also, we are to serve God by developing their latent capacities—which is what the creating of a civilization, with its arts, sciences, pooled know-how, and cooperative patterns of learning, acquiring, and distributing, really amounts to.

The picture of Adam set to tend God's garden says it all; for gardens are cultivated by planned hard work based on acquired knowledge of natural growth processes which the gardener seeks to direct and control. Consider Psalm 8:6–8, "You made [man] ruler over the works of your hands; you put everything under his feet: all flocks and herds, and the beasts of the field, the birds of the air, and the fish of the sea." These verses hark back to God's "subdue [the earth]. Rule over . . . every living creature" in Genesis 1:28. When man harnesses the powers and resources of the world around him to build a culture and so enrich community life, he is fulfilling this mandate (the "cultural mandate" as it is often called).

Thus, the Christian estimate of cultural activity is that, far from being an irrelevance or a snare and a sin, it is one of the ways in which we serve both our neighbor and our Maker. The humanist idea, that for Christians nothing can matter but preparing their souls for flight to heaven, is a mistake born of an unduly man-centered outlook. Biblical living is God-centered, and is concerned with obedience and the furthering of God's praise in this world, and cultural activity is abidingly relevant to both.

So, *third,* let us be clear that—in addition to being called to faith, hope, love, righteousness, worship, and witness—Christians have a vocation to develop taste (that is, a sense of fitness and value), to become civilized themselves, and to play as positive a part as they can in the ongoing civilizing process around them. Redemption is God's restoring of what he created. And his commands to the redeemed, though now applying in a redemptive context (signalized sometimes by calling them "kingdom ethics"), are in essence the laws of creation, of which those embodied in the Decalogue number ten and the "cultural mandate" is an eleventh.

The fact that the Bible concentrates, as we saw, on the knowledge of redemption and the practice of righteousness and religion should not blind us to the cultural implications of its teaching. It does not, to be sure, teach us standards of beauty or ideal voting patterns, any more than it teaches us how to use a knife and fork or to split atoms or to compose music. But it charges us to use our creativity to devise a pattern of life that will fitly express the substance of our godliness, for this is what subduing the earth, tending God's garden, and having dominion over the creatures means.

It thus belongs to the Christian vocation to be world-affirming, and those who out of a sense of divine pressure adopt a world-renouncing lifestyle (poverty, celibacy, or any form of withdrawal) must acknowledge the goodness of the world they renounce and the exceptional nature of their own calling. For centuries Christians idolized the monastic life of celibacy and poverty as higher and holier than any other, in a way that let Manicheism into Christian minds by the back door; that must not be allowed to recur. To affirm and bask in the goodness of the world, to praise God for the wonders of creation, to practice responsible stewardship of this small planet, and to honor its Maker by using its resources wisely for the welfare of the race and the enriching of human life are all integral aspects of the work that Christians are charged to do. Any idea that consistent Christianity must undermine or diminish concern for the tasks of civilization should be dismissed once and for all. Biblical teaching sets this concern on a different footing from that put forward by humanists, but requires that the concern itself be no less vigorous than theirs.

Christianity Critiques Culture

But how is Christianity's mission as a generator of culture to be fulfilled today? The short answer is: by letting loose the biblical message to assess, critique, purge, and remodel the manifold forms of culture that surround us.

The first thing to say here is that there is no one Christian culture, in the sense of a universal community lifestyle to which ideally everyone would conform. Indeed, there is, strictly speaking, no *Christian* culture at all. What you have all round the world is a fascinating variety of local, ethnic cultures, which Christians should seek not to sweep away but to appreciate. They are all expressions of human creativity, having their own history and integrity, and are fascinating in their variety. Though they are marked by the evil of man's rebellion, the first thing to say about them is that in and through them the creativity of God himself bubbles up like a great fountain, splashing in glory over all the world. Indigenous cultures are thus to be respected, and Christian concern should be limited to making sure that the fullness of Christian truth finds expression within them, both intellectually and behaviorally. *Contextualization* is the name given to this process, and it is a major theme in present-day missionary thought.

There is, of course, a sense in which all who live by faith in Christ as their Savior and who seek to love the Lord with heart and mind and soul and strength, and their neighbor as themselves, will look alike. The Savior himself, though as Jewish as can be, is at the same time the ideal man for every culture, and wherever he is trusted and loved his moral image—that is to say kindness, generosity, mercy, honesty, patience, and purity—will emerge. But, because the cultural creativity of mankind is so diverse and sumptuous, these qualities will show up in each community in a form shaped outwardly by that community's cultural distinctives—Japanese or Slavic or Welsh or Indian or whatever. Godliness, which as we have seen is the only true humanness and which is always the same for substance, will take to itself any number of cultural styles and indigenize itself in countless different ways, adapting to itself existing behavior patterns of many kinds. This is one measure among many of the power of gospel truth when blessed by the Holy Spirit.

It is only in recent years, since the study of cultural anthropology got into its stride, that the rich and dazzling pageant of cultures round the world has been appreciated in a positive way. In the last century it was generally taken for granted that all non-Western styles of life, however venerable or quaint, were inferior and that total Westernization was the best thing for everybody. This cultural imperialism is often blamed on the Protestant missionary movement, which generally made its converts wear Western dress, receive a Western type of education and worship with Western hymns and prayers in Western-type buildings, thus in effect deculturalizing them and projecting an image of

Christianity as essentially ethnic, a foreign religion rather than a universal faith. But in fact the assumption of Western cultural superiority was common to all the Protestant nations from which the missionaries came, and the only reason why the missionaries stand out as exponents of it is that in their greater charity, they worked harder than anyone else to share the supposed benefits of Westernism with their flocks.

The secular imperialists were less concerned to raise native people to Western standards, so they took less action than the missionaries at this point. The missionaries' cultural imperialism, like John Calvin's initiative in having Michael Servetus burned for anti-Trinitarian heresy, should be seen as the fault of an age rather than of any individual. (Nor should we suppose that their exporting of the lineaments of Western Christian culture was an unmixed disaster; it wasn't, and it is a hypocritical sop to the Cerberus of latter-day nationalism to beat one's breast and talk tragically as if it was. Today, however, a stronger doctrine of the goodness of creation and of God's common grace is teaching Christians not to undervalue indigenous cultures, and to graft the gospel into them if possible rather than trying to replace them. And seeing this shift we should be glad.)

However, this does not mean that the pendulum may swing to the opposite extreme, that of justifying everything in each culture as if it were of equal and absolute worth. Cultural relativists who censure Christianity for undervaluing and sweeping away the marvelous artifacts and traditions of pre-Christian cultures show their unbelieving bias at this point. Ethnic and pagan cultures always bear marks of human sin and are often as closely bound up with what Christians cannot but call idolatry as Western culture is with Christianity. When idols are part of a culture, the Christian attitude toward them will seem culturally disruptive. The apostle Paul, pioneer evangelist of the non-Jewish world, called on his hearers to "turn from idols to serve the living and true God" (1 Thessalonians 1:9, cf. Acts 14:15), making at this point a clean break with the religious side of their Hellenistic culture. One result was the riotous demonstration staged by the idol-makers of Ephesus, who feared for their business (Acts 19:21–41). A further result of the same stance (which was not peculiar to Paul, but common to the whole early church) was that for over two centuries Christianity was an outlawed cult (*religio non licita*), and its adherents were exposed to persecution throughout the Roman empire because they would not share in the formalities of emperor-worship, Rome's civil religion. Granted, the idols and false gods were very much part of the fabric of established culture, so the gospel seemed to import sacrilege and outrage against precious and colorful customs. But, no matter how highly prized and exquisitely characteristic of the genius of this or that people the idols were, the gospel judged them to be false gods, delusive and dehumanizing, which as such must be challenged, condemned, negated, and excluded. There could be no compromise here.

This scenario has been repeated many times, and many Christians down the centuries have suffered abuse, ostracism, and even death for declining to acknowledge local or ethnic gods. Such has been the fruit of the inexorable critique of all cultures and all religions which the gospel mounts with regard to the question of *truth*. For Christianity does not see itself, as Hinduism and some Western thinkers would see it, as one of an infinite number of symbolic expressions of mankind's sense of an ineffable divine reality; Christianity sees itself as revealed truth, absolute and final, and judges accordingly, justifying and protecting all that is true, honest, just, pure, lovely, and praiseworthy, but expunging the rest.

The passion for God's revealed truth, which has historically been part of the Christian ethos and which at one period led to rigid intolerance and persecution of misbelievers, is balanced nowadays by respect for the individual conscience and recognition of our duty to secure to the other man the right to be wrong. Toleration as a principle, and tolerance as a mental habit, have thus come to characterize Christians generally. This is something else of which we may be glad. It does not mean, however, that the Christian truth-claim is any less peremptory than it was or that there is any call to silence the Christian critique of notional error, or of intellectual and moral relativism, or of dehumanized and dehumanizing features of our own culture (for instance: the provision of abortion on demand; the readiness for infanticide and euthanasia, built on an implicit denial of any duty to protect the weak and unfit; the systematic weakening of the family unit; the unisex syndrome; the eclipse of integrity in politics and public administration; and the forward creep of bureaucratic statism). The battles against these things must go on. The Christian program must always include monitoring current cultural developments and maintaining (hopefully, by actual dialogue) a prophetic critique of the idols and idolatries that disfigure all cultures and civilizations, not least our own. And Christian people must be willing to lay themselves on the line in this cause, for such critiquing is an integral part of the job that as practical humanists—that is, as God's chosen humanizers—we are called to do.

Goodness Has Priority

We have made it sound as if there are reforming crusades that need to be mounted and supported, and we will not hide our conviction that that is indeed so. But where does the Christian individual fit into all this? We think it important, as we conclude our sketch of the cultural task which the Bible lays on us, to remind ourselves that cultural concerns, however important, may never come first in our lives. What must always come first for us is the quest for goodness. Our most cherished preferences and pipe dreams, our most carefully cultivated tastes, and our most carefully worked out plans of campaign to recapture our civilization for Christ, must always take second place to Christ's requirement that we should be, quite simply, like him in humble love and service to our neighbors in their various personal needs. And matters of taste, and cultural strategies, are largely irrelevant to this. We may prefer Shakespeare or Bach to other kinds of poetry or music, but that has not much to do with discerning and meeting someone's need of a cup of cold water or a listening ear or a helping hand—and we may not despise, spurn, or patronize the needy one if it turns out that he or she would rather read comic strips to the sound of Muzak. We may regard junk food as a poor alternative to vegetables and cream soups, but that should not make us any less ready to run errands and buy meals for those who prefer Kool-Aid and Twinkies and instant hamburgers.

Snobbery about one's tastes and preferences is as nauseous as snobbery about anything else, and forcing your taste on others is always an insult, however good your taste and however bad theirs. Again, you may have a fine plan for effective agitation against some great social evil, yet the priority question for you might be whether you take time out to help your son with his homework. Not by hearing testimony to things cultural, but by bearing one another's burdens, do we fulfill the law of Christ (so says Paul, Galatians 6:2).

Has any single person ever had so great an influence, long-term, on human culture as Jesus Christ himself? Yet he had no cultural program to implement, nor did he clash with his contemporaries on cultural as distinct from moral and religious matters. The secret of his cultural influence lies in what he was—marvelously perceptive in moral matters, marvelously dignified in human relationships, marvelously ennobling in his compassion, marvelously liberating in his love. Some of us have our cultural programs and our cultural battlefields, and it is right, placed as we are, that we should. But if we want to exert a genuinely humanizing influence, programs or no programs, we must embody and model true humanness as our Master did; there is, in God's ordering of things, no other way to do it. We influence others culturally either by this means or not at all.

9

The Sacred

"Nothing is sacred!" So, it seems, oldsters always cry as they watch youngsters ignoring the taboos and conventions of their own youth. Their cry expresses the conviction that some things, in fact, are sacred, but their sacredness is being ignored. And such casual dam-busting by a new generation can be a traumatic and even tragic spectacle to those who identify with the older values.

Convention and Taboo

Take, for example, something on which we touched before, the sudden lurch in the 1960s to informality in dress and etiquette. Up to about 1960, one wore "traveling clothes" for train and air journeys—coat and tie for men and boys, tweed suit or demure dress, stockings, hat, and maybe gloves for women and girls. But nowadays any file of passengers shuffling into an airplane will be a pageant of sartorial self-assertion. Their clothes will say, not "Here is how you dress when you travel," but rather "This is what I feel like wearing right now"—shorts, sandals, jerseys, sunsuits, denim jeans, jogging gear, overalls, or whatever. No convention seems to operate, and most would find incomprehensible the idea that any should. What? Dress up? What for? I'm comfortable like this.

Has anything that matters been lost by this change? Well, perhaps. Once people thought that dress was as much a matter of compliment to everyone else as it was an expression of one's own inclination. One dressed for others, not to win prizes in the best-dressed sweepstakes but out of deference to their sensibilities. Rather than force everyone to inspect all the contours of my torso I'll wear a shirt or blouse and jacket; rather than oblige them to cope with the sight of my skinny legs or pudding-like thighs I'll swathe myself in trousers, or skirt and stockings—such was the reasoning implicit in the earlier, less free-and-easy way with clothes. What was the value of this attitude? Was it of any importance? Should it have been kept sacrosanct? Older folk will say that they think it should. Are they right?

Or take etiquette, by which we mean not a demure and finicky delicacy but a considerate way of organizing one's behavior toward others. For example, it used to be the rule that people got up and gave their seats to older riders in crowded subways and buses, men took the curbside of the pavement when walking with a woman, and children at table with adults were discouraged from dominating the conversation. All of these customs seem quaint now, and to many people objectionable. We are well rid of them, they would say. Older people saw them as courtesies expressing one's awareness of others; you set your own convenience, or inclination, or interest on one side when it encountered someone else's. But to people unfamiliar with that social atmosphere, these courtesies look like artificiality and repression. Again we ask: Has anything that is truly sacred been lost?

The matter is complicated. It is easy and no doubt correct in some sense to conclude quickly that everything is going to the dogs. How can slovenliness, self-centeredness, and boorishness possibly be as good for society as neatness, consideration for others, and reticence? And of course the answer to the question put this way is that they can't. The elusive factor, though, is this: when in the more distant past it has seemed that things were slumping into utter piggishness, the human spirit and its graces have in fact survived. To the woman of 1900, the pert mincing of the woman of 1920 would look brazen. To the woman of the fifteenth century, the brittle extravagance of Tudor brocades and frizzed hair might look brazen. To the woman of 1945, the jogging shorts and clogs of 1960 could look brazen. To those who in 1909 arrested her on the beach for wearing only a solid one-piece bathing costume instead of standard swim gear (bonnet, long-sleeved skirted dress, bloomers, stockings, and shoes), Annette Kellerman undoubtedly looked brazen. But, in truth, no one can say when the human spirit is actually being damaged by changes in fashion and convention; the fact of change regularly proves to be more of a shock than the substance of it, and what is brazen for one era (the one-piece swimsuit, for instance) is demure for another.

Purists might argue that this just goes to prove the bleakest point of all, namely, that things do grow worse and worse, and that to acquiesce in this downhill slide is to admit disaster. Once more, however, the plain fact is that good and modest people in any era do dress and behave in ways which would have shocked their ancestors. Does the sight of a woman's ankles, or knees, or arms, or midriff even, really cheapen her and us? Is this degree of undress incompatible with modesty? Some eras have thought so. Have we lost anything by ceasing to agree?

But wait a minute, says someone; what has all this to do with the sacred? Are we not going astray from our theme by talking of shorts and swimsuits? No, we are not. The words that have cropped up in our review of changing fashions have been *convention, taboo,* and *reticence.* These words express a notion, common to the human race, which is as potent on the boulevard, at the table, and in the world of dress, as it is in the temple or shrine. It is a notion that turns up constantly in every stratum and segment of society, and in connection with every human activity. The notion is of obedience and of awe and of subordinating oneself to something outside of oneself. It is an idea of there being a standard, or an authority, to which one is bound to submit. It is a sense of reality which everyone who is not a psychopath knows well. To this notion the word *sacred* always points.

On the boulevard, the notion prompts dressing according to the public code, which in the past has been fairly peremptory and static. So in a North African bazaar we would for centuries have found men and women clothed in the same predictable way—convention required it. There was a prescriptive dress code in Genghis Khan's empire and Charles II's England, too. In Caroline England it was possible to outrage public taste and incur punishment for it—if not by being flayed or put in the stocks, then at least by being told you were a hussy or a fop. This was not because everyone was puritanical or squeamish, heaven knows; it was because of the dress and behavior codes that operated. The convention said, do this; the taboo said, don't do that. Reticence then required that I set these do's and don'ts ahead of my own whims. Dukes and laborers, shopkeepers and scholars were all bound to follow the code. And it is always so in every society. There are customs, traditions, conventions, codes, rules, taboos, behavior patterns, courtesies, constraints of etiquette, yardsticks of good and bad manners, which are felt to have authority, and you put yourself outside the pale by ignoring or defying them.

What then of our time, in which so many of the old behavioral landmarks have vanished? Are there no conventions, taboos, and restraints operating anymore? Not at all. It is an illusion to say that these things can be jettisoned; all we can do is replace one set of them with another. If we won't wait for others to be served at the table, then the new convention is every man for himself and all four feet in the trough. If we won't dress formally to travel and eat, then the new convention is open necks and tee-shirts everywhere. If we won't cover ourselves in public then the new convention is high exposure—breasts and bellies and buttocks and thighs all bobbling in full view of everyone. The only question to be asked is: Which way of doing things does a greater service to what is truly human in us? Are we closer to genuine humanness when we are all laced up in corsets or when everything tumbles out? The one judgment that we may with complete confidence pass on the 1960s is that the advocates of change in that decade were naïve to suppose that one can do away with conventions. That can't be done—and they couldn't and didn't do it. They just devised new ones, which then became as binding as those that went before. Some things can never be changed, and the potency of convention is one of them.

So there are always conventions and taboos of one sort or another; and that is a highly significant fact. For if we trace back to its source our sense of fitness and unfitness, of decency and indecency, of there being things that one ought and ought not to do in society, of our being *bound* or *under obligation* to act thus and so, we shall find ourselves in very solemn precincts indeed. What we have here is a secular expression of our awareness of the sacred, the inviolable, the authoritative, the "numinous" as it is nowadays called—in short, the divine. In the customs, taboos, and reticences that we accept we see what might be called the footprints of the gods.

God and the Gods

Does that seem a fanciful way of putting it? To some it would certainly argue a primitive state of mind. Anthropologists speak of the gods, but only as an ingredient in others' mentalities; they do not undertake to endorse the beliefs they describe. Humanists may speak of gods this way, but not any other way, for they do not themselves believe that there are any gods in reality. So, too, Christians will speak of gods this way, but not any other way, for Christians believe that there is only one being to whom divinity may properly be ascribed. However, using the word this way we may make a point which seems to us crucial, namely, this: You can no more have a tribe, community, or civilization without gods than you can have one without customs. To try to imagine such a thing is like trying to imagine a square without sides or the spectrum without colors. It can't be done.

The immediate objection here will be, of course, that it can. Look (someone might say) at the French Revolution—indeed, at the whole eighteenth century. Or look at the Bolshevik Revolution, or Mao's China. Don't we see in these immense spectacles the very thing we are denying, namely, the plain fact that one *can* get a civilization with no gods? What was the Enlightenment all about if it was not the supplanting of all gods by human reason? What did the Jacobins and Bolsheviks insist on if not on the autonomy and solitude of Man? If religion was allowed to go on at all in those societies it was only as a sort of sop to a hopelessly childish populace who would keep saying their prayers although intelligent folk knew that no one was there to hear them. Thus the Catholic Church went on in France as a minority grouping; the Bolsheviks and Mao made an enormous effort to extirpate religion forcibly, but it would not go away, and so for the present it is tolerated as being fairly harmless. The gods, however, have officially been shown the door.

But our answer to that is: Not so. Our point goes deeper. What we are saying is that wherever any custom or convention, or attitude, or convictional system or point of view is felt to have binding authority, so that to disregard it is taboo (at worst, a crime against society; at least, a social gaffe, like wearing a suit on the seafront in Venice, California), there you have what we called the footprints of the gods—an intuition, however anonymous and unidentified, of the divine. The closing of shrines by revolutionaries in the name of reason is simply a shuffling of the cards, we might say. This god, or that one, might have been sent packing, but now we have a new icon in its place. The Crucifix is no longer paraded through the streets—but what is this gigantic bronze thing coming along? The Worker? Oh. The icon of *Christos Pantocrator* is taken down from the wall—but whose face is this looming so titanically over Red Square? Nikolai Lenin? Oh. The New Testament may be suppressed—but what little book is this that everyone is required to master? *The Thoughts of Chairman Mao?* Oh.

It may seem clownish to set things up this way, but it is not as absurd as we might wish it were. We may tell ourselves that we have gotten rid of the gods and hence of religion. But we cannot and will not live without paying ultimate homage to something. It may of course be something as brutish as mere pleasure—though the besottedness that attends this depressing cult is as disgusting to humanists as it is to Christians. It may be power that becomes our god; but once again, who of us can see this spectacle of egomania without pity and horror? It may be an abstraction like Reason, or Art, or Sport, or Freedom, or Humanity, The Dictatorship of the Proletariat or The Aryan Race. So be it; but sooner or later our homage, whatever its object, will bring out the regalia of religion. Icons reappear, and symbols, and sacred books, and a gallery of saints, and holy places. Pilgrimages are made and rites observed. The solemnity with which the presidium greets the slowly rolling caissons bearing the latest warheads through Red Square is as weighty as the solemnity with which the hierarchy of Spain might greet the hearse bearing the relics of St. James of Compostela. The Nazi salute to the icon of Hitler was as punctilious as the sign of the cross made by the peasant in front of the Sacred Heart of Jesus. It only remains to inquire just what, in fact, is being extolled in the differing systems, the religious character of which is so plain.

There is, of course, an obvious difference between cults that posit something or someone "there" and those which are built on loyalty to an idea. Religion regards its gods as real; nonreligion knows that Voltaire and Lenin and Mao are only men, and dead men at that. The old lady in Russia trusts that Jesus will hear her prayers, but the Marxist does not suppose that Marx will. But the difference here is superficial, and we are training our sights on something deeper. We are speaking of what animates the human spirit, which can no more live without worship than our bodies can live without food. Ideas only become the food of the spirit as they exert authority over the spirit—in other words, as they establish themselves in the category of the sacred. From this standpoint the agnostic old Oxford don who spends his days in the lively exchange of ideas without committing himself to any of them is nearer—much nearer—to final spiritual death than is the suburbanite who in the Oxford sense has virtually no ideas at all, but who worships and serves the game of golf, and labors with passion and devotion to lower his handicap. Yet both the golfer, with his unconcern about ultimate truth, and the don, with his refusal of commitment to anything, are starving their souls and diminishing their humanity, and the old lady in Russia saying her prayers is more alive in the deepest sense than either of them.

For human beings are worshiping beings, we are saying, made to acknowledge the sacredness of God our Maker by sacred responses of worship and devotion. When our modern, post-Christian world declines to do this, two things inevitably happen. First, we produce, willy-nilly, substitute religions for ourselves; and, second, we shrink and maim our souls—our personal selves, that is—by reducing them to the measure of that which we give ourselves to serve. That is one reason why Bible writers, echoing the second commandment of the Decalogue, are so hot against idolatry, even when the idols (Aaron's golden calf, or Jeroboam's bull images) purport to represent Israel's God. Paul diagnoses it as the initial and basic folly of the human race to have "exchanged the glory of the immortal God for images made to look like mortal man and birds and animals and reptiles" (Romans 1:22). And one can see his point: A debased theology will produce a debased religion, and debased religion will shrink and deform the souls of its devotees. If that is true within the Christian camp, where worship is still directed, however deficiently, to the Father and the Son through the Spirit, much more is it true of the alternative religions and quasi-religions (like the service of art or golf) and counter-religions (like atheism and humanism) to which our sense of the sacred so often gets transferred in this post-Christian era. It is ironic, pathetic, and tragic that so many pursuits which are meant to enrich the soul, and would actually do so if practiced in a spirit of love and gratitude to the Creator, are followed today in a way that shrinks us, parches us, and leaves us spiritually drained and starving. But that is what happens when the human instinct to worship is focused on the wrong thing.

This has already become evident in those parts of the world where the most vigorous efforts of this century to stamp out religion have been made. Two generations after the Bolshevik Revolution you find not only old ladies in Russian churches saying their prayers, but also young communists, weary to death of dry Marxist stubble, crowding into Baptist congregations and wondering if the Virgin of Kazan is an icon of something worth looking into. Marx offers no crown, and a crown is what we want; it will do more for us than the cloth cap. They told us that redemption was a fairy tale, but why does the fairy tale touch deeper and richer chords in us than politics and economics? Is the bowed head or the raised fist the more profoundly human gesture? Could it be that we are missing something? And in China after Mao, tens of millions of Christian believers have emerged. The spiritual enervation of the atheistic scheme has been felt, and this is the result.

It may be, though, that what Stalin and Mao could not do by force, we in the West are doing more effectively (or perhaps we should say, having done to us) through drift and by guile. Without guillotines, pogroms, deportations, or desecrations, we are well on our way to full-scale secularity. Despite the religious boom in the United States and the slight improvement in churchgoing figures for Britain, public legislation, educational theories and textbooks, the steady progress of affluent materialism, the ongoing gallop of technology, the trivial sensationalism of the media, the general sense that unlimited tolerance and permissiveness are the supreme virtues, and the bland, unresisting pragmatism of leaders in church and state, all combine to ensure a further slide down the secular slope in the coming generation. Today's centers of influence on Western minds are the restaurants where TV magnates and anchormen talk together, the editorial board rooms of the big syndicated dailies, the parties where journalists clink glasses with intellectuals, the faculty clubs of universities, and the committee chambers where laws, liturgies, and reports get written. It is hard to find out all that goes on there, but this we know: A hundred thousand people demonstrating in Washington or London do not have one hundred-thousandth part of the influence exercised by (say) a circular to publishers specifying what sorts of story and picture will and will not be acceptable in kindergarten literature. A denominational committee may tinker with statements of faith and forms of worship, and a hundred mass meetings and a million mail-outs can do little about it. It is not possible to doubt that in our time slogans about scare tactics, pressure groups, and reactionary minorities have been infinitely more effective in silencing threats to secularism's present agenda than the guillotine ever was in relation to the agenda of the Jacobins. So secularism creeps on in the modern West, and the tide will not be turned back yet awhile.

Sacredness and God

The secular humanist's claim is that whereas religion binds us and arrests our development, secularism liberates and leads toward full and authentic humanness. The Christian replies that, on the contrary, Christianity charts the way to full and authentic humanness, first and foremost by linking our appetite for the sacred, to which all conventions, taboos, and recognized reticences bear witness, to its proper objects. Secularism, however (so the Christian continues), frustrates and deforms us within by forcing that ineradicable instinct to focus on objects that are inappropriate and unworthy, and that breed such irrational superstitions as the belief in inevitable progress, or in the absolute value of the humanist liberation program. Then these superstitions themselves are invested with a sense of sacredness, and the convictional circle is complete; but the whole thing, as the Christian sees it, is the spiritual counterpart of an obsessive neurosis, a departure from rationality rather than an achieving of it.

The secularist is resolved to see all the gods of the religions, with their shrines and required routines of worship, as so many projections of our need to have something utterly mysterious, inviolable, and priceless as a sort of anchor point for all of our values. We need something that will validate and hallow all that we hold to be true, and that will be beyond the reach of criticism, decay, and misfortune. Hence the gods. They are a very ingenious device, and have no doubt been valuable and perhaps necessary components of human development up to this point. But adult realism requires us to dispense with them now, as illusions that we shall be better without.

No, it is the other way around, says Christianity. We and all things were made by God and for God, and this is the fountainhead from which our indestructible awareness of the sacred derives. Far from being our own projection onto entities outside us, sacredness is a real and eternal property of things, an intrinsic quality that belongs to them, and we are made with the capacity to sense this. Dogs aren't. They lope into shrines and pick bones from the very altars and run off to gnaw them. We, on the other hand, find ourselves compelled to pause and lower our voices, even in the shrines of gods in whom we do not believe. Despite ourselves we feel that there are titanic immensities presiding over our life, and the shrine is a celebration of them, and we are reluctant to swagger too much in the presence of anything so awesome and mysterious.

When we are in a shrine, we are at least confronted by an idea of the ineffable, even if we think that this particular shrine has it all wrong. Or to put it another way, here we are made vividly aware of our littleness and mortality. With an array of test-tubes or graphs in front of us or with legal books and telephones at our elbows, we shall fancy that control is vested in our fingertips. But facing sacred vessels and sacred books, we feel that, out of courtesy if nothing else, we should make the gesture of being quiet, for we realize that we are far from being in control.

We have made no inroads on death, for example (vaccines and surgical techniques merely defer death's march). We can do nothing about the stars. We cannot reorganize the wind. For every photon we harness, two more particles seem to swim across the screen. It is, of course, possible to tell ourselves that we will one fine day gain complete control. But do we believe it? No, we do not. When we stand on the edge of the abyss, we have no question as to whether the bowed head or the raised fist is the more fully human posture. There comes a point when the most plucky secularist will want to mutter to the old woman in the babushka, "Pray for me."

Does this sound like the rhetoric of intimidation? Like the small child who warns his opponent of the imminent arrival of his big brother, it seems to say, "Just wait till the Grim Reaper has you in his bony hands—you'll see!" But we are not trying to threaten; we simply state facts. Unless we are total imbeciles there will come points in our lives at which there is nothing to do but stop in our tracks and fall on our knees. We are told that the very devils believe—and shudder (James 2:19). No tyrant or ego-maniac is invulnerable here, and certainly no person of ordinary sensitivity. King Nebuchadnezzar was made to scrabble and slob-ber and eat grass in order to learn that he was entirely in the hands of God, and he duly learned it. So, sooner or later, shall we all. God himself will see to that. As they said in the first World War, there are no atheists in the trenches, and equivalent moments of truth, here or hereafter, await everyone.

However, we digress. Back, now, to our argument.

The Meaning of Sacredness

Sacred is a word with a double reference. On the one hand, it points to the intrinsic worth of God and the value that inheres in the things he has made. He and they are sacred—that is, pre-cious, awesome, and worthy of praise—whether we acknowledge them to be so or not. On the other hand, the word points to our recognition of sacredness when we discern God, and when we view things as made by God and for God, and treat them accord-ingly. Not to do this, but to deny the Creator, or refashion him imaginatively in our own likeness or the likeness of something that is less than we are, and to treat things around us either as our own or as worthless, is to desecrate and profane the sacred. As we saw, each of us has an instinctual appetite for sacredness, just as we have for food and drink, and as hungry and thirsty folk may grab at solids and liquids that are really poisonous, so we may focus our urge to acknowledge sacredness on corruptions of truth and value in God's world, rather than on the Creator and created realities as they were meant to be. All sorts of sincere supersti-tions, in secular as well as religious forms, result from doing this; the world, alas, is full of them, and many views, programs, ac-tivities, customs, and projects are treated as sacred quite im-properly. But we have said enough about that already. It is the proper acknowledgment of sacredness rather than the pathology of the matter that concerns us now.

God, to start with, is sacred—that is (to break the thought down into its two components), he is holy, and he is inviolable. His holiness is a quality highlighted throughout the Bible, where the basic use of the holiness vocabulary is to mark him out. Holiness, the attribute of all God's attributes as it is sometimes called, signifies everything that God is—all that sets him apart from us and makes him different, all that sets him above us and makes him awesome and worshipful, all that sets him against us and makes him fearsome as the Judge of our sins. If one thinks of holiness as a circle embracing everything about God that is unique, the center of the circle is certainly God's moral and spiritual purity, contrasting sharply with our own twisted sinfulness, and sometimes when Christians speak of God's holiness this is all that they have in mind. Thus, for instance, the Shorter Catechism of the Westminster Assembly, using a formula supposed to have come off the top of the head (it would be more biblical to say, the top of the heart) of one of the members as he led in prayer, answers the question "What is God?" as follows: "God is a Spirit, infinite, eternal, and unchangeable, in his being, wisdom, power, holiness, justice, goodness, and truth." Though no words are adequate to mirror God, it would be hard to find a less inadequate set than this, in which holiness signifies specifically the moral purity which God's righteous acts express.

As God is holy, so he is inviolable. He cannot be injured, diminished, or unseated from his throne as ruler of all; and he is not to be profaned, insulted, defied, or treated with irreverence in any way. This is the point of the Decalogue's third commandment, "You shall not misuse the name of the Lord your God" (Exodus 20:7). God's sacredness implies his claim to veneration, the adoring worship that will naturally and spontaneously arise when our appetite for the sacred focuses on his divine reality.

Such is the sacredness of God. What, now, of the sacredness of things? Since Christianity is not pantheism, and does not see all things as divine (indeed, it sees no *thing* as divine at all), admiration directed toward any of God's creatures or toward any human artifacts and performances must be kept distinct in our minds from worship of the Creator. Yet the two ought to go together; admiration of anything created should always be, as it were, the underside of our praise to the Creator for making it, or letting it be, the glorious thing that it is. All created things, being made by God and for God, have value and in that sense are sacred in themselves; and all are to be appreciated and used in a way that shows their value and harmonizes with their Maker's purpose, for it is in this way that they will be sacred to us. More specifically, however, it is our habit to use this word *sacred* to refer to things that have been specially and consciously set aside to honor God, and for him to use, and which then become inviolable because they reflect or convey something of special significance about God and his laws. Sacredness of this sort needs to be understood well, so let us illustrate it.

Take, as an example, bread. We can do any number of things with bread: toast it, cut it into fancy shapes for afternoon tea sandwiches, crumble it for the birds. It is God's gift to us, sacred in the broad sense that as a gift it should be valued, but not requiring of us any such ceremonial observances as tiptoeing up to the grains of wheat to gather them, using incantations as we grind and bake them, or eating with bowed heads and washed hands. We do regard waste of bread as a pity, but here our thought is of good stewardship and of hungry people who could be fed with what we are wasting. By the same token there is nothing intrinsically wrong, we suppose, with rolling up bits of bread and throwing them across the room as spitballs. It may be out of place, and vulgar, and tiresome, and argue a bad spirit in us who do it; but no sin is occurring as far as the bread goes—unless, indeed, the game takes up too much time and bread, in which case we are back to our point about stewardship and waste. In general, however, we may treat bread as ours to use, under God, any way we wish.

But sometimes bread is set aside to be one of the two elements used in the Lord's Supper, the Christian Eucharist. Any bread will do—mass-produced white, stone-ground whole grain rolls, saltines, little white discs that look and feel like paper—it does not matter. But when the minister, acting for the congregation, takes this bread to use it in the unique rite that Jesus instituted, and proceeds to recite the formula, "This is my body, which is given for you," then the bread is sacred in a richer sense than was the case a minute ago. We need not here raise the question of what, if anything, "happens" to the bread itself. We need only observe that, once these words have been spoken over it by a recognized officiant, no Christian will grab it and gobble it up by mouthfuls, or throw it round the room. While the rite is on, Christians will handle the plate of crackers or wafers or the single loaf with a certain solemnity and restraint. Why? Because it is now specially sacred, in virtue of the special significance that it has been given. The only thing that is proper to do with it now is to eat it in thankful remembrance of the Lord whose saving sacrifice it has been made to symbolize.

Christians see the Eucharist as a sort of diagram of what ought to be true constantly—namely, that the recognizing and receiving of gifts from God (in this case, the bread and wine) becomes the occasion of our giving ourselves and all that we have to God, to whom we and what we see as "ours" belong in any event. In bringing this to a bright focus in our experience now, the rite anticipates the state of affairs at the end of time when the torn fabric of heaven and earth will have been knit back together by Redemption, and God will be all in all, and there will be nothing but Eucharist (thanksgiving, with self-giving), because Eucharist in this sense will have become the whole of every Christian's life.

By carrying this weight of theological meaning, as part of the action of the Lord's Supper, the eucharistic bread acquires a degree of sacredness beyond that which bread has in everyday life. And this illustrates what it means for created things to gain special sacredness by being specially set apart to establish or express some special aspect of the Christian's relationship with God. Here are some further examples.

Think of money. What money we have comes to us as God's gift, and we are free to use it to feed and clothe ourselves and our families, to buy cars and bubble gum and holidays in the Canary Islands and a thousand other things. But Christians, following a principle enjoined in both Testaments, reckon to set aside a proportion of their money as a special offering to God, and in doing that they let go of it entirely and forbid themselves to spend it on themselves. The Bible suggests the tithe as an appropriate minimum, and an old book commending tithing was well titled *The Sacred Tenth*. For a special sacredness attaches to money given to God in this way: The gift proclaims that all our money comes from him, that we are aware of this and grateful for it, and that we want all our use of it to render him homage in the way that this specific offering does. Thus it becomes a sacred token of a sacred relationship.

Again, when we set aside time for God (an hour for prayer or worship or spiritual reading; a weekend, or a week, or more for a retreat, a conference, or something similar) it becomes specially sacred, both as a vital necessity to keep our own relationship with God in shape and as a witness to our awareness that all our time is God's, and a witness to our desire to use it all for him.

Places, too, may be set aside for special spiritual purposes which give them special sacredness: the corner of the room, perhaps, where we pray, or the chair where we sit or the spot on which we kneel for the purpose. They are sacred because the relationship with God which my prayers are meant to further is sacred. And shrines, temples, and church buildings are sacred places because of the worship offered in them and the experiences of the presence of God that are enjoyed within their walls. Granted, some Christians decline to regard any places as sacred, on the ground that God does not dwell in temples made with hands. But even so they build churches and take care of them and object if any irreverence is exhibited in them. Even if we may not speak of the building as housing God, nonetheless it speaks to us of God in a way that the gas station next door does not. And is it fanciful to sense an aura of the sacred, of God himself, in buildings where earnest Christians regularly worship? Answer that question with another: Is it fanciful to feel at places like Gettysburg or the Tomb of the Unknown Soldier or Westminster Abbey a sense of nearness to the events or people celebrated, long gone though they are? Secular locales are felt to be special, and our language often proclaims that—"*sacred* to the memory of so-and-so," we say. Places where God is worshiped are similarly felt as places of his special presence—sacred, then, in a most basic sense.

Objects, too, may have this character of special sacredness by virtue of having been set apart, either because they were used at some hallowed event or because we have made a special point of consecrating them to God. In the latter class might be a house given for use as a retreat center. In the former we might find the Shroud of Turin, or the great Richard Baxter's pulpit in Kidderminster. If the shroud were proved to be that of Christ, one would hesitate to tear it up for dustcloths, just as one would hesitate to chop up Baxter's pulpit (about the genuineness of which there is no doubt) and use it as firewood. Involvement in hallowed events confers a sacredness which we shrink from violating. And inviolability, as we said earlier, is part of what sacredness means, in the case both of God and of things.

Inviolability

Inviolability is a part of our perception when we sense sacredness: what is sacred, we feel, must be treated with proper respect. To flout this requirement is taboo, and we must restrain ourselves from any such action. Here we are back again with the certainty that some things are sacred, which, as we saw, is a pervasive and incurable state of mind in all normal persons, and in the final analysis is a witness, willy-nilly, to the reality of God, even when it is centered on things that are not God. The sense that this or that is inviolable breaks surface constantly in ordinary life. For example, what would we say if we found someone snatching up George Washington's hat from his desk at Valley Forge? "Put that down?" we would shout. "Guard—guard! There's a thief here!" But if our pilfering friend insisted on wanting to know why he should not have the hat, since it is very old and hardly worth sending to the Salvation Army—if our friend were this naïve, what would we all try to tell him? "But that's *George Washington's* hat, man! Don't you know that we can't run off with relics like that? They belong to the public." Such things are hallowed, not because some divine threads were woven into the fabric, but simply because a great man wore them. When you are talking of relics, it does not make the slightest difference whether the hat is a battered old sou'wester, a cloth cap, or a crown. Its value derives from its connection with some person—some China clipper captain, or Washington, or Lenin, or Ivan the Terrible; these are, so to speak, the ghosts which haunt the hats, and thereby hallow them.

All sorts of things are looked upon as inviolable for all sorts of reasons. "Oh help—be careful! That was Great Aunt Emerald's fan! It is all in tatters—don't touch it!" Here the inviolability has something to do with sentiment, which is one aspect of memory, which itself is a servant at the shrine of antiquity. A fan, a pair of spectacles, a cane, a bundle of letters—they need not be very old; but one way or another they keep alive now something that has gone and, in the case of sentiment, something to which we attach great value, sometimes for no other reason than family.

Great Aunt Emerald was dead long before I was born, so I cannot pretend that I miss her; and no one beyond Beacon Hill had ever heard of her, so I cannot pretend that her fame invests the fan with value. This fan's special ("sacred") character derives wholly and solely from family sentiment. But what is family sentiment? It won't restrain vandals—they'll trample the fan as insouciantly as they will smash plastic toys in Woolworth's. And it won't impress the antique dealer: "Oh yes—how very interesting. You know, of course, that there are thousands of these fans on the market? I can offer you $4.00 for it." And even my close friend will have to suppress a yawn while I go on about Aunt Emerald and her fan. Of course, being kind, he will grant me my sentiment and understand why I feel the old fan is sacred, and he will honor it by leaving it on the table and only bending judiciously to peer at it. But he doesn't want it, he doesn't feel about it as I do, and he would demur if I tried to enlist him to get up subscriptions for its preservation after I die.

Sentiment, then, or some august connection, will bring to the surface a sense of the inviolability of particular objects. So will monetary or symbolic value. The Kohinoor diamond, for example, won't break if we touch it, or even if we juggle with it and drop it. But it is the world's largest, and belongs to the British Crown jewels; we wouldn't juggle with it if we were asked to; something restrains us as we face its silent twinkling. Other qualities will also confer inviolability. Awareness of painstaking labor has this effect. Look at the clipper ship in a bottle; someone spent hundreds of hours making it; so we don't shake the bottle till the whole thing is a heap of matchsticks; we respect it, we don't violate it. Recognition of genius will restrain us too. Why don't we spray a mustache on to the Mona Lisa? It would be a great lark, wouldn't it? But we know that everyone would be outraged rather than amused, for the Mona Lisa is a work of genius. Thus our joke would be violating the inviolable. It would do us no good to protest that it was only a joke. Humor must back away in this territory. Three cheers for jokes, but our idea was obscene.

We are illustrating the sense of inviolability which all of us in fact have in relation to some objects. We can illustrate it further from the realm of social solecisms and taboos. Travelers know the perils here. Who addresses whom first? What gestures are insulting? If offered a plug of tobacco, must I chew it? Which side of the road should I drive on? What should I wear for this occasion? Am I allowed to whistle? A rising scale of inviolability attaches to the various taboos, breaches of which will accordingly be more or less serious. Some blunders are mere gaffes: "*Hush!* The princess has to address *you* first, dummy!" Others are worse: "You offended them by refusing the tobacco. They won't befriend you; you had better go." Or, worse yet: "You weren't allowed into that tomb. Flee for your life. No white man is safe here now." Subcultures, too, have their taboos. A drunken beach party at Fort Lauderdale may hoot a local householder into terror and shame over his protests, feeling that no one has a right to be so uptight and insistent on peace and quiet. For them his complaints violate all canons of decency. Tattling is taboo in schools, and jailed child molesters are ostracized by their fellow-prisoners. The sense of there being inviolable limits attaches to different things in different human minds, but in itself it is a universal human fact.

Always, however, the sense of inviolability and the sense of value go together. That which we regard as inviolable is that which we feel to have value, whether the value lies in the fact that it is mine, or that we love it, or that it is old or expensive or full of history, or that it represents a lot of work, or some ancient custom, or this year's fashion, or our right to fun, or that it is in some permanent and transcendent way glorious and sublime. To flout that which is inviolable is taboo, for the inviolable is sacred. Such is our concept of inviolability, whatever particular items we view as instances of it.

The Law of God

We said earlier that for Christianity it is part of the holy Creator's sacredness to be inviolable. Now we must sharpen this statement. *The first thing to say* is that inviolability, as applied to God, is a moral, no less than a metaphysical, notion. It means not only that God cannot be challenged, but that he ought not to be. As holy love—tripersonal and self-sustaining, infinite and eternal, joyous and outgoing—God has supreme value. And the knowledge of value always entails the duty of respecting, celebrating, and preserving it—which is the positive analysis of what treating something as inviolable means. So the knowledge of God's value is in itself a call to pay him honor, homage, and worship, as well as one which prohibits any defiance of him or rebellion against him.

The next thing to say is that we know God's value by revelation—self-revelation, in fact, made in history, embodied in Scripture, transmitted in the church, and brought home to mind and heart by the Holy Spirit. From this source we learn: *First,* that God made us in order to love us, sharing with us his own joy as we respond to his love by obedience and worship; *second,* that, being made as we are, it is in this response to the specifics of revelation that we become fully ourselves, in righteousness, maturity, and joyful contentment; *third,* that the specifics in question take the form of directives (standards commanded, with sanctions appended), all of which are predicated on facts about God and his doings, and all of which together constitute God's *law*—"the perfect law that gives freedom," as James calls it (1:25).

The Hebrew word for law is *torah,* which means not so much public legislation as fatherly instruction, given out of goodwill for the neophyte's benefit, and that is precisely what God's law in Scripture is. In this sense, all biblical teaching about faith and life is law, not just the Decalogue or the Pentateuchal legislation. The gospel commands to repent and believe (and to serve and praise and imitate and love and commune with Jesus Christ) are part of "the perfect law" of which James is speaking.

God's law in this broad sense, set forth in Holy Scripture, is, as the Moderator of the Church of Scotland tells the British Monarch when presenting the coronation Bible, "the most valuable thing that this world affords." The Jewish people glory in that part of God's law which they acknowledge; Christian people, who acknowledge the whole of it, should glory in it even more. Not only does it reveal God to us (showing us what pleases and displeases him, and how he acted in the past, acts today, and will act in the future), it also reveals us to ourselves. It shows us what we were made for, how we have swerved from it, and how incapable we are of knowing spiritual reality aright without God's own instruction (his Word) and illumination (his Spirit). In addition, it shows us what we must do and what we must have God do in us if we are to enjoy the destiny for which we were designed.

Whatever problems of detail some Christians may have with the Bible, all will agree that in its preciousness as God-given wisdom and truth, divine light shining into our darkness through the Holy Spirit's ministry, this biblical teaching which is God's *torah* (law) is sacred and inviolable in the fullest and most absolute sense. It is not to be challenged, but rather to be set up as the yardstick for challenging the inadequate ideas of what is sacred that infect our benighted minds. Applying this yardstick, we shall not attach sacredness to any fashions in dress, or amusement, or taste; nor to the goals of profit, pleasure, and preeminence, of physical health and material wealth, of power, influence, and domination, which capture so many minds; nor to any one local cultural pattern as against any other; nor to any traditions and customs (however time-honored) that are cruel, immoral, demeaning, or simply uncaring; nor even to the quest for truth, beauty, and morality when these are pursued as an alternative to seeking God (though we shall insist on the sacredness of these values for Christian disciples). Instead, we shall honor God's inviolable law as the sacred rule over our lives, and the sacred light for all lives, and we shall insist that only diligent observance of it can bring us to full stature and to true happiness.

I don't believe it, says someone. Law as such is impersonal, and law-keeping as such is legalism (you see it in the Pharisees), and human maturing is a relational process which any form of concentration on law is bound to impede.

Not so here, we reply; for, in the first place, what we have referred to as the law of God is itself, finally, God in person relating to us, telling us who he is, what we are, what he has to give us, and what he wants us to do to receive it. The law is not simply what God *said*, but it is what he *says*, here and now, to you and to us; it is to be received as God's present message, and our response to it must be a directly personal response to him, rooted in and growing out of prayer.

In the second place, Pharisaic legalism is the wrong model. The Pharisees seem to have thought that their law-keeping was a meritorious performance, earning or enhancing their acceptance with God; that is the principle of legalism, and it feeds pride. The gospel says that on the basis of Christ's atoning death God freely forgives, accepts, and adopts sinners the moment they turn to him, so that Christian law-keeping becomes an expression of the adoring gratitude of the humble poor for an undeserved salvation already given. That is something very different from legalism.

In the third place, we have in Scripture a series of transcripts of the attitude of godly folk to the law of God which they were busy obeying: these are the Psalms. The attitude which the psalmists express to the law is not vexation or frustration or resentment, but love—hilarious, boundless, thankful love. Evidently they had discovered that the law is itself the very pattern, safeguard, and guarantee of all that is most precious in created humanity. Far from stultifying or brutalizing them, the law sensitized, ennobled, liberated, and opened wide their hearts. As God's word to them, it raised them up to fellowship with him, the most exalted privilege that man can ever know, and aroused in them both joy and compassion of truly awesome intensity. The psalmists, not the Pharisees, are our models of humanity humanized by God's *torah*.

Finally, in the fourth place, we must realize that relating to God means relating to the Father and the Son through the Spirit; and the Son, God incarnate, the Word (personal self-expressive utterance) of the Father, may truly and properly be described as the law incarnate. What we see in him is the law that was given with rumblings and smoke at Sinai, and amplified with grimmest warnings by the prophets, now at last embodied in a perfect human life. Here is what law-keeping, living by God's message, really looks like, says the gospel; and it points us to Jesus. We look, and we see in him more of peace and joy and ripeness and wholeness than we have ever seen in any man, notwithstanding the pain and sorrow of his compassionate empathy, and of his being misunderstood and rejected, and of the final agony and shame of his cross. We see in him the closest and most sustained communion with the Father in worship, obedience, and faithful endurance that ever was. And we see in him the sublimest spiritual insight and authority.

Jesus showed an infallible sense of what was deepest and neediest in the humanity of each person that he met. If ever anyone knew, in depth as it were, what both humanness and sacredness are, he did. When (as often) he violated supposedly sacred Jewish taboos and customs in the interests of inviolable divine truth, his touch was sure, his dignity commanding, and his moral penetration breath-taking. We feel that his own sacred person ought to have been inviolable, and the restrained, low-key, matter-of-fact passion stories in the four Gospels, telling how he was in fact violated in the worst possible ways, are the most shocking and traumatic pages in literature.

Now our own law-keeping, whatever else it involves, is first and foremost the relational business of hearing Jesus' word, shouldering our cross, and following him through the daily death of self-denial into his moral likeness now, to be crowned with a fuller likeness on resurrection day. This is the humanizing process to which we have been referring throughout this book. Law-keeping is a true way to describe it, but we do not properly understand it till we see that it is essentially a matter of discipleship to the living Christ, God incarnate, crucified Savior, risen Lord. If we will hear him, and obey, we shall learn from him what all true sacredness has always been about, namely, knowing God and finding eternal life; and that will be our portion, now and forever.

Sin Is Sacrilege

One sacred thing not yet mentioned in this discussion is the image of God in which we were made. God's sacred law, uttered at Sinai and embodied in Christ, has the office of guarding this sacred image and ensuring that, instead of using our powers and resources satanically, we use them to grow up into the Christlikeness which is total humanness, the moral potential of our created humanity completely fulfilled. Don't steal; don't lie; don't kill; don't commit adultery; don't covet; worship God alone. Why these restrictions? The answer is: To preserve us. These restrictions mark off the path of life that we should walk in from the way of death that we should avoid, and so teach us to honor God by honoring and not sullying his image in us. So they are not like a cage for a canary, to keep it from flying free; they are like railings at the edge of the cliff, there to keep us from falling. They are fences which guard all that is most truly us, and landmarks which enable us to see our proper way. They are the Maker's handbook, showing us how our humanity is meant to work and warning us not to misuse it. They are the rules of God's house, which is the place of his presence where we are called to live and where we find his fellowship. They are fixed and rigid, for they are showing us what sorts of action God loves and what sorts he hates and that he does not change; what he hated yesterday he will continue to hate today. If, as forgiven sinners and adopted sons, we want to show our gratitude to him by pleasing him, then we shall take our cue from the law and be glad that its guidance is so clear.

But suppose we break the rules, jump the fences, kick over the traces, and leave the law behind—what then? Then we rebel, transgress, disobey, fall short, go astray, defile ourselves, become guilty (so Scripture pictures sin in its various aspects). We also commit sacrilege, for we profane and defile the sacred reality of God's image in us. In that regard, sin always has a boomerang effect. Thus if we fiddle our tax return, we not only violate the law of God and of the nation, we commit sacrilege against our own being, made as it is for truth not lies and for honesty rather than its opposite. If we abuse or insult another person we not only break the law of charity, we violate God's image in him and sully God's image in ourselves as well. If we commit adultery we flout the law of God, commit sacrilege against the sacred institution of marriage, violate the shrine (that is, the personhood) of our accomplice, ignore the shrine which is our spouse and to which we have sworn to be the faithful attendant, and once more defile God's image in ourselves. Strong language? Yes; but in the strong light of holiness and truth that Jesus Christ shines on our experience, this is how these things show up.

We have to realize that as the sacred reality of God's image in us gives us enormous dignity, so it imparts enormous significance to every moral decision and makes guilt great when we sin. Surprise has sometimes been expressed at the severity with which God in Scripture reacts on occasion to what strike us as quite small sins, but this realization makes sense of it. There are no small sins in the sight of the great God whose claim on our obedience is absolute, and whose image we bear. To be sure, this is not the typical modern way of thinking, let alone the secular humanist way of thinking. The widespread denial of God's reality, or at least of his holiness, has trivialized the moral life of Western man and encouraged a blasé, "laid-back" attitude which declines to treat any moral lapses seriously. But this is devilish. Where biblical faith has failed and sophistication, urbanity, levity, mockery, and moral frivolity reign, human individuals cannot know themselves or their true dignity or the issues of their lives; nor can they find reason to treat anyone else with respect or restraint; nor can they expect to be so treated themselves. And so the human zoo becomes a moral jungle. If God is dead, then indeed nothing is sacred—then our cry of outrage at the start of this chapter will have become a metaphysical truism; and our instinct for the sacred, running blind as it were, will be absolutizing irrationalities as long as our life lasts. From such a negation of true humanness we should pray to be preserved.

10

Esteem and Identity

"Nobody knows my name!" cries the title of a once popular book. No wonder it was popular; who does not feel the force of that cry? Even those who are garrisoned and coddled with all possible affection and recognition will have felt the dark chill of solitude and anonymity at least in nightmare. How awful to be nobody. How horrible to find that no one cares whether you exist or not. How ghastly and destructive not to be esteemed.

It is hard not to gulp convulsively when we see the stage production of *Oliver Twist* and hear the waif-like Oliver sing "Where is love?" as he stands among the coffins. Oh, it is sentimental, we say; words, tune, and scene combine to break through our defenses. True, but that is exactly the point about sentimentalism; it is something that touches us. Our objection to mawkishness is not to the situation that calls forth the tears, but only to the self-indulgence of the tears themselves. If orphanism is as bad as this, then action, and not just tears, would be the proper response; but a sentimental song about it invites us to weep and then pass on. There was, however, something to weep about here. It is pitiable beyond words for any child to be orphaned.

Why is that? Last century orphanages, such as Oliver experienced, were chillingly prison-like, but nowadays someone will be sweet to the orphans, and they will be housed and fed and clothed well. What more do they need? We all know the answer. They, like the rest of us, need affection and esteem. But could not a kindly matron in an orphanage give them this? Yes, she might; and God alone knows what heroic and saintly mothering has been carried on in all sorts of dismal situations by aunties, nurses, nannies, matrons, and guardians down the centuries. But it is not quite the same as having one's own parents.

Name and Affection

One index of the difference is the use parents make of family names and diminutives—their name for their child. Such names express affection and valuation in a way that a number, a surname, or even a baptismal name (especially if it is one that sounds formal and grand, like Leofric) can hardly do. When father or mother say "Chick!" or "Buster!" a whole world of love is invoked. They may be calling us to supper, soothing us, teasing us, or summoning us to some accounting. But whatever the situation, the use of the affectionate name tells us that they care for us and we matter to them; and this gives us a real and substantial identity in which we rest content. Long before the word *identity* enters our vocabulary our sense of identity is fed this way. Long before we ask the question, Who am I? we live off the fat of the harvest of our parents' answer to it; namely, you are you, known and loved without measure for no other reason than that you are you and that you are ours. That is what the family name is expressing. To miss this experience through absence or loss of parents is bitter deprivation indeed.

"You are ours"—does that make us some commodity that our parents possess?

Oh, no. The words *ours* or *mine* spoken by love have none of that calculating proprietorship that we feel toward commodities. When spoken wisely and truly, they express something infinitely more potent, while yet in one way weaker, than owning a possession. *Ours* said by parents to children implies all the value that affection can confer, and in that sense it is a word of power. But it should not imply that the parents will hang on to the children and refuse to let them go, as they will hang on to their house, jewelry, stocks, and bonds. For the whole purpose of nurturing and training our children is that in due course we should let them go—just because they are they, and we love them.

For a thirty-year-old to be tied to parental apron-strings like a thirteen-year-old is grotesque to see, just as it is grisly to experience. Such "smother-love," as we call it, is as gruesome a non-recognition of personhood as were the Beadle's sadistic sallies to Oliver Twist; and "love" is as false a description of it in the former case as it was in the latter, even though the smothered soul is "*darling* Jimmy" or "*dear* Liz" to its smotherer. There is no esteem in either attitude, only deep egoism and real if unconscious cruelty. The love that confers identity on children as distinct from destroying it must be ready at the appropriate time to let them go. Esteem for them will respect their adult right to self-determination, and not try to break their spirit or possess and exploit them in a way that really reduces their humanity. Such esteem is embodied in our Maker's way of dealing with us, and we should likewise embody it in all our dealings with each other.

Name and Identity

The cry, "Nobody knows my name!" certainly expresses the sense of not being loved and cared for; but that is not all. It also expresses the sense of not being *known*—the sense that nobody calls me anything that shows awareness of who and what I am, what makes me that person, and how I tick. My individuality is disregarded; I am just a cipher, a cog in the social machine. What we want here is to be called a name that is ours in the sense of truly setting forth what we are. From that standpoint, titles and semidescriptive, half-facetious appellations like the Brown Bomber, the Great Defender, the Iron Lady, Flash Harry, and Elvis the Pelvis please us more than they offend us; for even when uncomplimentary, they show some knowledge of what our life is about. The name by which we are known, so we feel, should be, not just a label, but a true token of our identity in this personal way. If no such name can be had, it is a pity.

In the world of religion, names have always had great significance, just because they are felt to embody knowledge about their owners. In all religions it matters, to start with, what you call the gods; if one does not get the name or descriptive formula of invocation right, one may not get the favorable response that one seeks. If you do not show proper esteem for the gods, they will not esteem you, and one basic way to show esteem is to use their names correctly. If, on the other hand, a god lets you know his name, that implies his availability for a relationship with you, just as when our fellow-mortals give us their names in ordinary life; and if he gives you a name, that is his name for you, expressing his knowledge of you.

This universal sense of things in religious past and present is taken up into the revealed religion of the Bible. In the Old Testament the Creator gives Israel, his covenant people, his name, designated by the Hebrew letters YHWH, and explains it to them as proclaiming his free, self-sustaining, sovereign life (I AM WHAT I AM and I WILL BE WHAT I WILL BE are both signified by the Hebrew formula of Exodus 3:14). The Jews were to call on him by this name, though it appears that after the Old Testament period they ceased out of reverence to use it.

Again, we read of God giving men names to point up something about their destined role in his plan (Abraham, meaning "father of many," Genesis 17:5; Israel, meaning "he who struggles with God," Genesis 32:28; Jesus, meaning "God is Savior," Matthew 1:21; Luke 2:21; and then God incarnate changes Simon's name to Peter, meaning "rock" [Rocky!], John 1:42). The whole creation was called into being, apparently, by being named (Genesis 1), and the first man's dominion over the animals was established by his discharging the dignity of naming them (Genesis 2:19).

Then in Revelation 2:17 we read that to those who "overcome" in the war with Satan God will give "a white stone with a new name written on it, known only to him who receives it." In other words, the overcomers will find out at that point what their real name is (meaning, their own real identity). The longing for a name which is mine in the sense of specifying me, indicating exactly and fully who and what I am, will be fulfilled at last in the discovery of what God's hidden work of grace has made me into. Our new redeemed identity will be finally disclosed to us, thus revealing the measure of God's esteem for us. These are the significant ways in which the thought of naming appears in the Bible.

"To him who overcomes, I will give . . . a white stone with a new name written on it." The suggestion seems to be that the Christian's new identity in Christ is a prize of such measureless worth that it cannot be comprehended save by persons matured through the experience of conflict and victory on the spiritual battlefield. The purpose of our life, we may truly say, is to become in Christ what in one sense we have been from the first moment of our union with him. We are to grow up into the persons that God means us to be—the persons whom he knows through and through, since he made us, redeemed us, and has fully planned our futures: the persons whom he alone knows at present, since we ourselves remain largely ignorant both of what we are and of what we will be. To receive the stone engraved with our name is evidently part of the same event as being crowned (an image used in parallel to the naming in Revelation 2:10, 3:11), and the thought behind the one image illuminates the meaning of the other.

A prince's training has one thing in view, namely, that when the day comes he should be ready and worthy to carry the crown on his head; and the crown, when placed there, will, like any other accolade, testify to what is already a fact. The fact in the prince's case is that he is already king, and the crowning proclaims it. So, too, the gold medal is given to the person who has already won the race, and the epaulet on the shoulder proclaims that its recipient has already become a full colonel. But the public bestowal blazons abroad these facts and so confers a public identity. The new name, we are told, is going to be a conqueror's name; after we have conquered we shall receive it; it will celebrate us as victors. Then we shall know as never before just who we are and just how much we are esteemed and loved. Here, then, the awareness of identity and of being esteemed are joined together; and so, in the nature of the case, they always must be.

A Problem for Humanism

On the human level, psychologists assure us that the achieving of a strong sense of identity is bound up with the experience of being esteemed and (to use the jargon) "affirmed," particularly in childhood. They assure us also that possessing a strong sense of identity and (to use the jargon again) the "positive self-image" that springs from this is basic to emotional maturity. The marks of emotional maturity have been formulated as the capacity (1) to deal constructively with reality, (2) to change, (3) to live without being crushed by symptoms of tension and anxiety, (4) to find more satisfaction in giving than in receiving, (5) to relate consistently, with mutual satisfaction and helpfulness, to other people, (6) to sublimate and redirect anger to creative ends, and (7) to love. As this analysis (which comes from the post-Christian psychiatrist Karl Menninger) bears an obvious relation to the Christian moral ideal, so it is also obvious that the grace of God as set forth in the Christian gospel provides for its progressive attainment through the strong sense of identity and the new self-image (beloved child of God, pilgrim, warrior, imitator, and embodiment of Christ) which the knowledge of Christ begets. If Christians, who know God's love, do not advance toward emotional maturity, they are evidently like people who do not tan in the summer because they will not expose themselves to the sun that shines all around them. The reason is in them, not in the sun. But this analysis of emotional maturity poses a problem to secular humanism, of a very acute sort, because secular humanism runs on antireligious reaction as its fuel, and, as a system, it has nothing in it corresponding to the sunshine and warmth of God's redeeming love. Its bleak doctrine can never produce the maturity so badly needed today.

Secular humanism seeks a new and better society. Good; so do Christians. But one cannot have a better society without better people, and that means people of sufficient emotional maturity to sustain constructive relationships across the board. Lack of emotional maturity has been diagnosed, however, as the number-one defect of modern Western society, and the problem appears to increase rather than diminish as the twentieth century goes on. To Christians, this appears as the natural and inevitable consequence of the drift from Christian faith in the West; for if, as they believe, human nature is radically flawed through sin, it is only where Christian values and God's common grace irradiate family and community life (not to mention his special, saving grace in the lives of believers) that significant emotional maturity can ever be expected on any large scale.

Humanists, of course, dispute that at the level of theory, but when the question is put: How, with only the resources that secular humanism commands, is it proposed to produce the better people who alone can form and sustain the better society?—then the humanist difficulty begins to appear. Humanists around the world have at various times put their faith in education, moderate affluence, centralized planning, technological advance, genetic engineering and selective breeding, and behavioral control through what would ordinarily be called brainwashing to produce the new inhabitants for their brave new world, and some of these suggestions are still being closely examined. But if the psychologists are right, none of them touches the root problem of modern societies, which is our communal lack of emotional maturity—a lack that is rooted in too frail a sense of responsible adult identity, which in its turn is the fruit of experiencing insufficient love and esteem from others, particularly in the family. The question here is not whether humanist altruism is a sufficiently noble ideal, but whether humanism can provide sufficient motivation and resources to fulfill it.

Putting it bluntly: Where is the missing factor of neighbor-love to come from? Family life among us gets more brittle, not less so, and the emotionally immature, by their own inability to love, ensure that their own deficiency will be passed on. We note, indeed, that many humanists, molded already by the Christianity they deny, are sensitive, caring people who find it hard to see that they have a problem here, but it cannot be doubted that they do. There seem to be no resources at all in humanism to generate neighbor-love where it is not already present. And, as we saw earlier, there is nothing in humanism to create and sustain esteem for another human being save the likelihood or actuality of social usefulness, so that if humanist influence grows one can expect less mutual esteem among us than at present rather than more. Altogether it is a daunting prospect, and we continue to think that continued Christian influence in society will prove more fruitful.

Christ and Our Quest for Identity

The lack of a clear sense of who we are which is so common today often comes to a head in crises of identity, sparked by the discovery that the roles we play in society, and the masks we wear as we play them, are not, as we say, "me." Why does the athlete throw his medal across the room? Why does the famous actress attempt suicide? Why does the playboy go into a monastery? The answer each time is the same: It is because of the alarming realization that what they have been doing is not all there is to them and is, in fact, throttling the real person inside them. But how can we identify that "real person"? All we are sure of is that our innermost selves are sick and starving as a result of our way of living up to this point. So something must change; those inmost selves must be located and cherished and fed; the final harbor of true personal identity must be sought and found, and anchor dropped there. The quest for our authentic identity must begin in earnest.

Many voices today tell us that seeking one's identity is in fact life's most serious task, and top priority for all. The problem of achieving an identity out of a prior state of alienation, isolation, noncommunication, and unfocused guilt is one of the staple themes of modern novels, which of itself shows that this is a major concern of our time; and, indeed, the testimony of psychologists is conclusive on the point. When the late Peter Sellers said, in response to a request, that he could not make records of the Bible, reading it in his own voice, because he did not know well enough who he was, he spoke as a typical man of the modern West.

Once folks left home to seek their fortune; now we do it to seek our identity. Whole armies of counselors, therapists, analysts, exponents of actualization, and gurus from the mystic East teaching the techniques of Hinduism or Buddhism stand ready to help us find out who we are. Their common assumption is that once the phony pretenses in our personal lives are identified and jettisoned, and the short-circuiting wires in our psyches are uncrossed, and the routes to inward relaxation are known, tranquillity and new *joie de vivre* will automatically result. Sometimes this appears to happen; more often, it seems, the pain of living is lessened without anything that can be called joy emerging; certainly, however, these methods, encouraging self-absorption as they do, are not able to produce more neighbor-love than was there before. They give some help to some people, but whether they give all the help that is needed is a very different question, and one that requires more thought than it usually receives.

Does Christianity speak to this concern for finding one's true identity? We have already seen that it does indeed; but it does so in a way that sets it apart from all the approaches just mentioned. Here we find a paradox. While, as we have seen, the gospel promises Christians knowledge of who we are at the end of the road, it practically forbids us to bother about the question of our identity for the time being, demanding that we direct all our attention elsewhere. This makes it sound like one of those magic spells which will be invalidated if you think of a camel's left eye when saying the formula; knowing that, you cannot get camel's left eyes out of your head, so you can never make the spell work. But it is not quite like that, as we shall see.

The gospel, we must remember, consists not only of words about Jesus but centrally of the words of Jesus himself—Jesus, whom Christians believe to be divine, and alive, and by his Spirit ubiquitous, and addressing mankind still in the same terms as when he was on earth. So we learn the Christian approach to the problem of finding our identity first and foremost from Jesus' own utterances. And what do we discover? Just this: Not a syllable can be found in all of Christ's words encouraging us to explore our individuality or to feel the slightest interest in knowing by introspection who we are. Instead, Christ tells even the most needy, broken, and confused people that there are things for them at once to *do:* go wash and present yourself to the priests; go and sin no more; go and tell your neighbors; stretch out your hand; have some breakfast; follow me; fold up your bed and walk; be born again.

None of these needy ones hears anything about finding out who he is. Nor do they hear Christ dilating upon how he accepts them for what they are, and affirms them, and so forth. He does accept them, of course; it is clear, indeed, that he esteems them and sees value in them in a way that others have not done; but he never makes anything out of this, and he always has specific activities in mind for them from the start. His acceptance of them is a tacit starting point for a new life of action now that they have met him, and it is on their activities as beneficiaries and disciples that interest should now center.

Also, we find that to those who go on with this new life Jesus' words become progressively more difficult, mysterious, and even harsh—so much so that they probably would not have been able to bear it if he had told it all to them at first. Rude shocks come to the disciples as Jesus talks to them on his last journey to Jerusalem. Now they find that it is not just freedom and health and ease and royal glory that are ahead; they must obey him and follow him and suffer with him, and leave their families and be rejected and exiled and hauled up before kings and magistrates and no doubt killed.

There is something peremptory and cryptic about the way Christ talks to disciples who ask for encouragement. When they inquire what the rewards might be if they do pay this daunting price, he suggests in effect that this is not really their business. When John the Baptist, the greatest man on earth in Jesus' view, is in extremity in prison and sends for some little reassurance that he has not been deluded, he is only told that it is a blessed thing not to stumble over all the enigmas that surround his cousin. When two of Jesus' intimates (or their mother, really) want him to promise them front seats in heaven, they are only pointed to the sufferings in store before they get to heaven. A call from his own mother is turned aside by the statement that everyone who does God's will is his mother.

All are required to negate themselves, to take up their cross daily (i.e., accept the position of condemned prisoners walking to execution) and to be ready, if need be, to cut off their hands and feet and gouge out their own eyes. The impression left is that the closer we get to Jesus the more severe discipleship becomes and the less comfort of any sort there is for us. Certainly, there is not a word spoken about finding out who one is as a way of arriving at serenity, courage, cheerfulness, and freedom here and now. Jesus' interest is clearly elsewhere.

This is all so remote from the psychologically oriented subjectivity that marks the modern outlook on life and religion that we can scarcely cope with it. Our first reaction, perhaps, is to suppose that when it sets before us the ideal of forgetting ourselves in the task of honoring Jesus and doing his will, so that we never bother to ask whether or not we feel okay, it does not mean what it seems to mean, but is somehow exaggerated for effect. We would like to read in between the lines our own programs of self-help and self-actualization and claim Christ's blessing for them. But it can't be done.

Heavens, we say, it's no wonder that Christians get neurotic; look how Christ beats them down!

But wait a minute. We are not the first to hear this teaching of

Jesus; we have the privilege of inheriting two thousand years of testimony from others who, having heard it, actually embraced it and lived it. The typical thing we get from them as we listen is not an angry record of bickering, frustration, neurosis, and self-hate—nor of misery. Rather, the whole train of them, poor specimens as well as robust ones, seems to call out to us, this *is* the way of life! Try it, and see! Never mind your anxiety over whether the things you have and love—your identity, perhaps, especially—will be kept intact. In your sense of that word, none of them will, and you must abandon your claim on all of them. Letting go is the rule of God's house: Everything, and everyone, gets utterly changed here. What you will receive, having let these things go, is more than we can tell you; for it is outside your experience at present. But don't let that keep you from doing what you ought to do, and responding to Jesus' word.

New Creation

Now at last, perhaps, we can see what we are looking at and hear what we are listening to. The speaker is the Son of God, our Maker and Redeemer, who made this priceless reality called *me* in the first place and gave his incarnate life to retrieve me from the ruin of my own making. And what he has in mind for all who receive his word is something more radical than anyone can imagine, or than anyone has ever been able to measure or map out. By becoming Jesus' disciples we become candidates for new creation. That is Paul's phrase in 2 Corinthians 5:17, and it is literally meant. "If anyone is in Christ, he is a new creation; the old has gone, the new has come!" Jesus proposes to take us with him through death into resurrection, in a three-stage operation.

First there comes the stage of initiation, pictured by Christian baptism. Baptism, as Paul expounds it, is essentially the symbolic rite of going under water and coming "out from under," as we say, as the sign of one's former, egocentric, Christless life ending and a new life in Christ beginning. The water is water of death, like the Flood, and also water on the far side of which is new life, like the Jordan River. Anthropologists would call baptism a rite of passage, and so indeed it is. It signifies our exit, with Christ, from all the old relationships and the identity built on them, and our entry with him into a new frame of relationships, attitudes, and obligations, in which we are at no point our own, but belong utterly to our Redeemer and under his direction live to God.

C. S. Lewis developed the baptismal picture in terms of having to dive through an underwater tunnel, invisible from the pool edge, into a new world which turns out to be the old world, differently seen, valued, and used. Adult conversion always has this awareness of things at its heart, though the initial crystallization of it may be felt as violent or gentle, agonizing or liberating, shattering or integrating, according to what has preceded it. It is in this God-wrought change, often called new birth, of which the human side is called faith and repentance, that the new creation starts, and the two further stages complete it.

Next there comes the living of the new life, the baptismal life as we may properly call it, in which the pattern is of constant deaths, large and small, followed by repeated resurrections. The *death* experiences are the denials of self in which we consent to go God's way, whatever the pain and loss, rather than our own; thus we look after our neighbor at the expense of not indulging ourselves. The *resurrection* experiences are the joy, calm, and contentment which come through the testimony of a good conscience (this tells us that we have, in measure, pleased God) and the fresh energy being given to us to love and serve again. The conviction that Christ himself walks with us in both types of experience comes unbidden and is not to be denied. The severe-sounding words of Christ to those closest to him, of which we spoke earlier, can now be seen in their true light as words of love directing them (and we with them) not to waver in their readiness to live the baptismal life in all its many aspects.

Lastly there comes the sometimes long-drawn-out business of physical dying, with the promise of bodily resurrection in God's immediate presence undergirding us as thus we go home.

Such is the new creation. If God is true and Christ is true, then this is true, for this is the central New Testament message. And we have evidence of its truth, as we said, over and above all the compelling reasons there are to receive Scripture as revelation and Christ at his own estimate of himself. We have two thousand years of amazingly consistent testimony from mortals who have taken the plunge of faith, repentance, and commitment to the new life. What do we see in the merriment and fortitude and serenity and freedom and goodwill and contentment and (note this well) self-forgetfulness of the saints, if it is not the crop—the characteristically glorious, more-than-natural, humanly inexplicable crop—that follows their implanting into Christ in new creation? Bad Christians, as we have already observed, need no explanation; it is not hard to say why they are as they are. But good Christians need explaining, and the objective reality of new creation is the only explanation that accounts for all the facts.

Here, for instance, is a brilliant, cultured Lutheran clergyman named Dietrich Bonhoeffer. He is just thirty-nine. At twenty-four he was teaching theology in Berlin University, at thirty he was running an informal seminary, and at thirty-three, when war broke out, he had returned from America to Germany, to continue his ministry there. "I shall have no right," he had written in a letter, "to participate in the reconstruction of Christian life in Germany after the war if I did not share the trials of this time with my people." Once a near-pacifist, he had come to think of active resistance to Hitlerism and the encompassing of Germany's defeat as part of his Christian calling, and understandably he was arrested in 1943.

For two years his fellow-prisoners in various detention centers had found him brave, unselfish, and generous, tireless in comforting the depressed and in sharing his own faith. "I am sure of God's hand and guidance," he wrote; ". . . I am thankful and glad to go the way which I am being led. My past life is abundantly full of God's mercy, and above all sin stands the forgiving love of the Crucified."

Now it is April 8, 1945, the Sunday morning after Easter. He has just led an informal service for his fellow-captives, preaching on the scriptures: "By his wounds we are healed" (Isaiah 53:5), and "Praise be to the God and Father of our Lord Jesus Christ! In his great mercy he has given us new birth into a living hope through the resurrection of Jesus Christ from the dead" (1 Peter 1:3). Straight after this comes the message that he must leave, and he knows what that means. "This is the end—for me the beginning of life," he says to an English airman who had become his friend; and early next morning, after being seen praying in his cell, he dies with dignity on a Nazi gibbet.

He had announced the baptismal life, writing in 1937: "When Christ calls a man, he bids him come and die." He had labored to live that life, saying no to ease and escape from conflict all along the line. Now he crowns it, as his Master did, by enduring a criminal's death at the hands of a criminal regime. Some few Christians have wondered about his priorities, but none can doubt his holiness, nor his martyr status. Only new creation, so we argue, explains a man like that.

Esteem and Identity in Christ

The questions of esteem and identity now appear in a new light. What the psychologists and gurus offered us was self-discovery through introspection, self-scrutiny, and self-love. What Christ in the gospel offers us is, in effect, self-discovery through self-abandonment to God's love. This is self-discovery not in isolation, but in relationship; not by shutting oneself up to keep the world out and withdrawing into some inner sanctum of the psyche, but by opening oneself up to the invading Savior and letting him lead one's heart out into the world in sympathetic care and concern for others. The esteem which creates and shapes our identity, and thereby leads us to a strong and joyful sense of identity, is the redeeming love of our Creator to us his sinful creatures. We deserve to be shaken off into hell, as one shakes an insect off one's hand into the fire, and here is God seeking to love us into heaven at the cost of the death of his Son. And the gospel affirms that all avenues to self-discovery apart from opening myself to God's approach are blind alleys, for the notion of myself to which they lead me, however agreeable, consoling, bracing, and fascinating it may be (and what can be more fascinating to sinners than the study of themselves?) is precisely not "me," any more than the notion of myself which by its collapse sent me flying to the shrinks and gurus was "me." In telling me how I function in terms of my make-up the counselors are *not* telling me who I am; that is something which only God makes known to me. There is no way in heaven, earth, or hell that I may know myself without knowing the One who made me, and for whom I was made in the first instance, and from whom I should never have lapsed.

But there is more to the matter of my identity than just this. From Jesus Christ I receive a new identity, which is henceforth my true identity as a sinner now redeemed, an identity which I may truly know as the real "me." This new identity has two aspects, just as my natural identity does: namely, the relational and the dispositional. The relational aspect has to do with commitment and identification. As Christian marriage changes a woman's identity, because she commits herself to her husband as leader and identifies with the task of furthering his welfare and his interests, so Christian faith changes the believer's identity; for, having committed myself to follow Christ, I am now bidden to identify with him in such a way that the pattern of his life, death, and resurrection become the pattern of my own existence henceforth. His laying aside of his prerogatives, rights, dignities, and interests, here on earth and his laying down of his life for others must be reproduced in me here and now at the level of motives, goals, and strategies. I am, in short, to imitate Christ, to model myself on him, to walk as he walked, indeed to *be* Christ in my attitudes to other people.

The dispositional aspect of our new identity springs from the reality of our new creation. People who become Christians may look the same from the outside as they did before, but they are not the same inside. They are new people, radically altered—though they themselves may not fully at first appreciate this. Deep down within them, however, deeper than depth psychology can plumb or sustained introspection can reach, God has changed the motivational core of their personality—what Scripture calls the "heart"—in such a way that now there moves within them a longing and love for God: God's will, God's truth, God's service, God's fellowship, God's honor and glory. It is a desire to know and please and enjoy and share the God of one's salvation, and only as this desire is satisfied is their heart at all contented. So, whereas before it was one's nature to live to oneself, it is now what may almost be called an instinctual drive to live for God, and worship becomes the deepest joy of one's heart. This is the family likeness of all God's children; it is a description to which Christians have all answered from the beginning, nearly two thousand years ago. The New Testament describes the condition as being risen and alive to God in union with Jesus Christ.

In Galatians 2:20 Paul capsules this condition in words that combine the deep theology of personal renewal with direct witness to the new identity that renewed people consciously possess. The apostle is explaining the words *"that I might live for God,"* with which he ended the previous sentence. He speaks in the first person singular, but he speaks for every Christian; what his words express and model is not only the standard for, but also the experience of, all believers in all places at all times. His words are these: "I have been crucified with Christ and I no longer live, but Christ lives in me. The life I live in the body, I live by faith in the Son of God, who loved me and gave himself for me."

"*I have been crucified with Christ,*" he writes. That means: Across space and time God has linked me with—or, as Paul says elsewhere, grafted me into—the historical event of Jesus' dying on the cross, and has thereby terminated what I was before. "*And I no longer live.*" That means: The egocentricity, self-sufficiency, and independence of God, in terms of which my former identity was to be defined, are no longer the determining factors of my life. Though I have not ceased to be, the old Adamic "me" has gone.

"*But Christ lives in me.*" That means: My life is now shaped and controlled by a new allegiance. God has linked me with, or grafted me into, the risen Jesus, in such a way that the purposes and attitudes, the loves and the hates, which were and are personally his, now spontaneously through the Spirit seek expression in me. And I aim to give them that expression, so that it is indeed the life of Christ that I live out.

"*The life I live in the body, I live by faith in the Son of God, who loved me and gave himself for me.*" That means: Don't misunderstand "Christ lives in me" as if I were saying that I am not the same individual that I was before, or that I have become Christ's robot, with him animating my limbs in a way that bypasses my self-awareness, my mental processes, and my powers of decision-making. Understand the statement, rather, as declaring that I am now under the control of a new and all-embracing relationship, faith in the Son of God. Understand *faith* as a knowing trust in the divine Savior with whom I am now vitally linked in the manner just described. Faith is an attentive, adoring apprehension and appreciation of him. Faith watches him, listens to him, learns from him, sees his redeeming love for myself as an individual as the most wonderful thing ever, and lives henceforth utterly under its constraint. Understand, therefore, that my identity henceforth is not that of a rebel and a scapegrace, but of a redeemed sinner and a disciple of Jesus, renewed by his risen life and mastered by his dying love.

The living of this new life, which is what all the apostolic letters and all Jesus' moral teaching are really about, inexorably directs our attention away from the "problems" which our unregenerate egocentricity formulates for us. They are not life's real business. The call of Christ is in truth so remote from our modern agenda of self-discovery and self-actualization as to be almost incomprehensible to us. We want to paw Christ's arm and say, "But wait . . . I have this problem . . . I'm not ready for all that heavy discipleship stuff . . . I need some attention myself . . . what about me, I'm miserable . . . I could do right now with a bit of special care"—and so forth. So speaks our residual egoism.

How does Christ react to such thinking and praying? Well, much of it he ignores, or seems to slap down, as we saw earlier. But he is very generous and kind and does not cast us off in impatience or disgust. Having made us, he knows our weaknesses—our fear, our self-pity, our self-regarding anger, our moral paralysis, our randomness, our indiscipline, our suicidal self-loathing. As gently as a shepherd taking up a lamb out of the brambles or a mother taking her infant to her breast, he will take us up and work with us—not to indulge our egoism, however, but to cure it. We must realize that we are in the hands of the Great Physician, whose goal it is, not to make us comfortable invalids, but to restore us to moral health and wholeness. And we must understand that his principal method of treating us, his petulant patients, is hard and constant exercise in a world which under his providence becomes a moral and spiritual gymnasium for us.

That explains the following testimony, which we have read in a number of forms:

He asked for strength, and God gave him difficulties to make him
strong.
He asked for wisdom, and God gave him problems to learn to solve.
He asked for prosperity, and God gave him brain and brawn to work.
He asked for courage, and God gave him dangers to overcome.
He asked for love, and God gave him troubled people to help.
He asked for favors, and God gave him opportunities.
He received nothing he wanted; he received everything he needed.
His prayer is answered.

Exactly! So often it is like that.

Our life of grace, then, is a life of action and of growth. And our growth is a matter of developing our new identity in Christ, by becoming increasingly Jesuslike in our attitudes and spirit. And the essence of Jesuslikeness is self-denying love to God and others. Here, more than anywhere else, we learn by doing—that is, we learn to love by loving; for love in essence is not a matter of how we feel about people, but how we treat them. Knowledge of our identity, as new creatures in Christ, carries with it this knowledge of love as our duty and destiny, our true fulfillment as the new selves whom we now are.

But love, as Paul describes it, is patient and kind, free from envy, conceit, and pride; not rude, self-seeking, touchy, or unforgiving, but trustful, hopeful, protective, patient, and persistent; it is essentially a matter of sustained goodwill and generosity in giving help, and it takes a lifetime to learn. So the summons to master the art and craft of Christian love is both a high calling and a daunting privilege; it directs us to a pilgrim path, the end of which is at present out of our sight. And it can be said with confidence at the outset, and also at any subsequent stage on the road, that learning to love all the different sorts of people whom God sends across our path, in all the different sorts of situations he shapes up for us and them, is going to prove the hardest discipline we shall ever face. For in God's gymnasium that is how it always is, as long as life lasts.

Finding Identity in the Church

Yet there are encouragements for us as we travel God's road. First, the thought of God's esteem for us—sinners whom he has sought, found, ransomed, healed, restored, forgiven, and taken as his children and heirs for all eternity—cannot but evoke peace, joy, and detachment from worldly goals, attachment to our heavenly Father, shame at our apathetic lovelessness, and constant fresh commitments to the task of loving others as our Lord has loved us. Second, there is a promise of being enabled by the Holy Spirit to do more than we are naturally able to do, and one of the recurring joys of the Christian life is to prove that promise true. And, finally, there is the help and support we get from other members of what we may call God's gang, limbs in the body of Christ as Paul describes them; in other words, the human units of that organized organism of divine life that goes by the name of *ecclesia*—the assembly, the church.

The church, we say—and the word dies on our lips. Is that all? Anticlimax! We think of Gothic barns, mildewing pew cushions, shabby walls, varnish, choir jealousies, screechy soloists, Thursday circles, ratty-haired seminarians, unctuous preachers, boredom, cliques, intrigue, snobbery, philistinism. We have heard that the church is terrible as an army with banners, but in our experience it has been terrible in an earthier sense than that. What help, for realizing our identity in Christ or for anything else, can we hope to get from the church?

There is a secret here—an open secret, something which should already be obvious from what we have said; but a genuine secret nonetheless, which unfortunately remains hidden from many people for whom the way of Christ holds some real attraction. The secret is this. The church is people, and, as we have seen, people are to be loved and served. So the church as such is to be loved and served. It is God's family gathering, and it is therefore the proper place for us, his children; also, it is Christ's body, and that is a picture precisely of love and service within the fellowship. How then are we to find help and encouragement in the church for the furthering of our identity in Christ? Not primarily by listening to sermons and paying our dues, but by loving and serving as best we can, in whatever way we are able.

Just as the eye, so exquisite and marvelous a thing in itself, does not come into its own by sitting isolated in a jar of formaldehyde but rather by being at home in the socket, doing its work together with the brain and the whole network of nerves; and just as the hand, so fragile and yet so strong, is not seen in its best light severed from the arm, but appears most gloriously itself when it works together with the arm, brain, and whole system of nerves and muscles; so it is with us. Left alone we hardly know who or what we are. But brought into our place in Christ's body, and put to work, we begin—perhaps only begin—to find out. So awkward at first, and so maladroit, we find that not only are we helped by being involved in something so vital and ample as this. We also become presently aware there is something significant for us to do, and that this task itself unplugs wellsprings in us we did not know were there at all. We may never come to the point where we would be ready to say of ourselves, "Oh—I'm an eye," or "Yes, I'm the kneecap"; indeed we probably shall not, for the further we go in this way, the less we think about such things.

Perhaps I came into the church wondering who I was, or worse, convinced that I was nobody, and hurting at the thought. But now, years later, having been helped to know what it means to be accepted by God through being accepted as a brother and a genuine part of Christ's body, I have more or less lost interest in that frantically and suffocatingly subjective question of who I am. No doubt the process took a long time. But now it is as though I do not need to stir up the question, any more than I need to stir up the question of hunger. I am fed. I am at home. God loves me, I know; for he sent his Son to save me. And the acceptance—call it esteem—that I get from church folk confirms God's love and makes it vivid to me.

Who am I? Oh well now, let's think. I'm not sure that I know in any full way; but this is my home, and this is what I do, and I do know that the matter of my identity is in absolutely safe hands. But more than that, I know that the matter of my identity does in fact have something to do with what I am learning and doing now. Only God knows who I am. But in this body he is making me ready to bear with power and grace the noble reality of who I am when it is time for that to be unveiled.

Until then, I am en route, with all these others who are learning to love me, and whom I am learning to love day by day. We love; we give; we share; we serve; and as we do so, focusing habitually on the divine Lord whom we praise and the human friends whom we help, we cease to think about our identity, just as healthy people never think about their internal organs. You only think about aspects of yourself that are causing you pain or anxiety in some way. Nonthought about our identity, like nonthought about our bowels, argues simply that at that point we have no present distress.

Thus the church's life helps us with our problems of esteem and identity—not by addressing them any more directly than the gospel does, but by drawing us into a discipline of worship and service that takes us beyond them. As we give help, so we get it. But the process is usually indirect, operating by a kind of spiritual osmosis, and it is only afterwards that we realize how the kinks in our screwed-up, spasm-ridden subjectivity have been straightened out. If some miss this in top-of-the-heap churches because they are there only to get and not to give in active service, others find it spectacularly in very run-of-the-mill churches just because they have come in to give and serve first and foremost. The benefit does not depend on the size or quality of the church. It depends on whether or not we commit ourselves in the church to the way of Christlike love.

Is this the path of true humanness? health? maturity? freedom? joy? What do you think? Once more, we rest our case. You, the reader, shall be the judge.

11

Upside-Down Is Right Way Up

The foregoing chapters have set out our response to the secular humanists' claim to be charting the best way for every one of us to go. In reply we have offered, not an argument for the truth of Christian belief, but rather a vision of Christian life as the only true, full, and authentic humanness; and we have pointed out where secular humanism falls short of this. We have not labored to demonstrate that Christian belief has objectivity, coherence, integrity, and explanatory power, which are the prime requirements for credibility from an intellectual standpoint. There is a place for doing that, but this book was not it. Instead, we have tried to show that the highest personal values and the noblest ethical ideals are bound up with Christian belief, which is a demonstration of its credibility from a moral standpoint.

We have been illustrating how what the gospel offers, and what the human heart in blindness and pain cries out for, fit each other as key fits lock and glove fits hand. From that perspective, we have been writing a footnote on Augustine's dictum: "You made us for yourself, and our hearts are restless till they find rest in you." In biblical terms, what we have been trying to establish is not that Christianity is *truth* as opposed to falsehood, but that it is *wisdom* (the good life for man) as opposed to folly. We have on occasion enforced our claim by bringing in the alternative standards and ideals of humanism for comparison and contrast—not in order to attack them directly, but to highlight the distinctiveness of Christianity. And our enterprise has, we think, made two things clear.

Two Conclusions

The first is that the Christian notion of the good life for man, shaped as it is by Christian beliefs, really does rise above the humanist notion, which is not so shaped. The moral seriousness of humanism is undoubted, but its standards are so much more self-regarding and so much less exacting than those of the biblical ethic as to seem at times almost disreputable by comparison with it. Nor is humanism the only non-Christian position of which this has to be said; as a matter of fact, the Christian moral ideal shows up shortcomings in every other ethical system that the world has ever seen. For in truth there is nothing higher or nobler than grateful, trustful, worshipful love to God and humble, patient, wise, brave, fair-minded, self-effacing, self-sacrificing love to others—not just to one group, either, but to all others, according to their needs.

And let it be said explicitly: All the words in that formulation are to be understood in their full Christian sense. It has to be recognized that by taking them out of their context in Christian belief and making them stand on their own feet, so to speak, in a conceptual vacuum, our society regularly reduces these words to vague incantations in a ritual rhetoric of uplift, so that, as commonly used, they no longer convey any specific meaning. But Christianity forbids and condemns that (to cultivate fuzziness of mind is always sin, most of all when it is done by smudging revealed truth), and the fact that it has occurred among us is cause for shame. Here once more, as has happened many times previously, so-called "Christian" culture has dissolved away something that is at the very heart of the Christianity that produced it and that it claims to be upholding.

Now to state the present matter positively, Christianity requires us to anchor these phrases about love in the teaching of Scripture about God's action in creation, providence, and redemption. Specifically, we are to anchor them in the model of goodness that is given us in the earthly life of Jesus Christ, whose temper we are charged to imitate, whose instincts for living to God the Father are in fact implanted in us by new birth, and whose Spirit indwells us to change us into our Master's image. Then the meaning of the Christian ideal will be clearly seen, and, by the same token, Christianity's claim to be the true humanism will be established.

We know, indeed, that Christianity has sometimes been misconstrued as Manicheism, which denies the goodness of matter and of ordinary everyday pleasures. We know, too, that Nietzsche the clergyman's son and the neopagan Nazis regarded Christian love and humility as unmanly. Nonetheless, we hold that anyone who looks at the Christ-centered Christian ideal in a straightforward way, so as to see what he is looking at, will recognize it as the highest and noblest design for living that he has ever met. The dictum that we must love the highest when we see it seems to us doubtful—sinfulness of mind and heart may well be too strong for that—but we are confident that the highest, once recognized, will at least be remembered. Therefore we venture to hope that the biblical vision of freedom, hope, health, dignity, maturity, and identity, all being found in the exercises of Christian faith and worship—the life of love and service through Christ to God and men—will long stay in our readers' minds. We think that it should.

The second thing now clear to us is that the humanist attempt to devise a way of life more humane than its Christian counterpart actually produces one which is less so: less compassionate, less free, less hopeful, less dignified, less respectful, less patient; one that is more bleak, harsh, savage, gloomy, and—let us face it—dull altogether. We do not deny that, as indeed we said earlier, there are many humanists whose conscientious goodness puts Christians to shame, humanists who are in fact much better than their creed. Our concern is only to affirm that where the excitement that comes with Christian doctrine—the excitement, that is, of knowing God's love—is missing, any view of life will seem by comparison drab, harsh, and chilly; and humanism is no exception. That is not, of course, an argument for anything, merely a statement of fact, and it is one that needs no proof, for humanists admit the chilliness of their view very readily.

Bertrand Russell, a clear-headed liberal humanist, wrote as follows about what he called "the night of nothingness": "There is darkness without and when I die there will be darkness within. There is no splendor, no vastness, anywhere; only triviality for a moment, and then nothing."[1] That says it all. Whereas for the Christian nothing is finally trivial, for the humanist everything becomes finally trivial, death, as Russell says, producing precisely that effect.

Therefore, within this dismal frame of reference, it can hardly surprise us if standards relating to, for instance, the protection of handicapped human life, truth between man and man, and the responsibilities of relationships (particularly those between the sexes) should fall below, or at least be set lower than, those of Christianity. That this has actually happened in all forms of post-Christian humanism (liberal, scientific, existentialist; Marxist, Freudian, Nietzschean) is a matter of plain fact, and of general knowledge, on which we need not dwell any further.

Upside-Down

The Christian understanding of the humanist ethic and lifestyle can be summed up by saying that there are limits to what is possible when you are upside-down. Sin, by leading us to worship and serve ourselves rather than God, turns us, so to speak, upside-down in relation to our Maker's first intention for us; and humanism, negating the Creator, sees this egoistic upside-downness as both natural and necessary. But human individuals cannot fulfill their potential as God's creatures while they are upside-down, denying their creaturehood and trying to process all their perceptions of what is, what might be, and what should be within a God-less, egoistic frame. Christian conversion, by which we mean self-commitment to the saving ministry and lordship of Jesus Christ, is often and rightly pictured as an event that turns one's life upside-down, and in this it is the healing corrective; for if you invert something that is upside-down already, it finishes right way up, able once more to function in the way that it was made to do. Christianity claims that Christians, and Christians alone, are in this sense right way up, and so are able to appreciate

---

1. Bertrand Russell, *Autobiography*, vol. 2 (London: George Allen and Unwin, 1968) p. 159.

the tragi-comic oddity of the rest of the race, who unwittingly live upside-down the whole time.

This paradoxical vision of fallen humanity as being upside-down, so that common notions about fact and value constantly turn out to be absurdities that one can only achieve by standing intellectually on one's head, was the inspiration of half a lifetime's writing by journalist and apologist Gilbert Keith Chesterton. The paradoxes for which he was famous, indeed notorious, were so many attempts on his part to turn already inverted thinking right way up, and his Father Brown detective stories, in which God's spokesman is the one who distills the *prima facie* incredible truth behind the illusions, were written not just as *jeux d'esprit* but as parables of life in this fallen world, where repeatedly things are not what to our upside-down gaze they seem to be, and folly passes for wisdom while wisdom is judged to be folly. Chesterton's vision is in fact the central Christian view of the human condition, and the proclamation of Christianity as the true humanism cannot be separated from the summons to conversion: the call, that is, to all who are biologically human to become human in personal, spiritual terms through a life of repentance and faith in Jesus Christ. Readers will observe that we ourselves have sought to make this connection throughout our book.

The Proof of the Pudding

The chief obstacle to believing that Christianity is the true humanism that this book has claimed it to be is, of course (as we know and have said already), its spotty track record. What sets heads shaking skeptically over our claim is knowledge, second-hand and first-hand, too, of bad Christianity, past and present— the Christianity of hypocrites, zanies, boors, and self-absorbed nincompoops; of tyrants, manipulators, and exploiters; of freaks, fanatics, and weirdos; of neurotic, obsessive, cruel, and otherwise loveless personalities; of people like Pilate who wash their hands of their responsibilities, and people like Ananias and Sapphira who curry favor and feather their nest at the cost of dishonesty to God; of the bitter, the discontented, and the restless; of the unctuous, the unfriendly, and the unfeeling; of snobs, racists, misers, powerhunters, self-promoters; and of all the rest of the Christian fraternity who have not taken their own professed Christianity with sufficient seriousness. It was observation and experience of the bad Christianity of a church (Roman Catholic, allied to a corrupt power structure) that produced the anti-Christian hostility of the French Revolution. It was observation of the bad Christianity of churches (Protestant: the Prussian state church, and later the Church of England, both of which were stagnant and aloof from working people) which convinced Marx that religion is the opiate of the masses, needing to be abolished; and it was a similar experience of bad Christianity in the Russian Orthodox Church that set the leaders of the Russian revolution to work carrying out Marx's program. The badness of bad Christians and churches gets remembered (things that offend and hurt stick in our minds), while the humanizing achievements of the gospel get forgotten. This, unhappily, is how it always goes.

Since Christianity is a faith that claims to change lives, and since the proof of any pudding is in the eating, we cannot regard inspection of the Christian track record as inappropriate; nor can we be other than abject about the amount of evidence that there is on the debit side. But at the same time we can point to people like Origen, Augustine, Francis of Assisi, Bernard of Clairvaux, John of the Cross, Martin Luther, Richard Baxter, John Wesley, John Newton, Hudson Taylor, George Müller, Sundar Singh, Charles de Foucauld, C. S. Lewis, Mother Teresa, and countless others whose lives Christ made new for all to see, and whose mature humanness in Christ, free, humble, patient, and loving, none can doubt. And (a point we made earlier) bad Christians, however large their numbers, are really no counterweight to the evidence of lives like these. For no one disputes that we can profess Christianity without being transformed by it, or tell ourselves that we love Jesus without letting him change us. Chesterton's dictum applies: It is not that Christianity has been tried and found wanting, but that it has been found hard and therefore has not been tried. But the question is, whether faith in Jesus Christ when taken seriously has a moral and spiritual transforming effect that is natural to it and that cannot be explained in naturalistic terms. We think that the devoted love of God and men which we see in such lives as those cited, expressed as it constantly has been in what might be thought extravagances of prayer and service, shows quite decisively that it does. Christ himself, God incarnate, is the model of perfect, unmatchable humanness, and what we see in those whom we call saints is a growing Christlikeness. And while the saints continue to lay down their lives for others, the claim of Christianity to be the true humanism will stand. One cannot quarrel with transformed lives.

One final point. Secular humanists sometimes take a leaf out of the Marxist book (some of them, of course, are Marxists anyway) and flay Christians for not having in their back pockets great and compelling programs of social, political, and economic action. What the humanists imply is that the worth of any convictional system may be known by the quality of the proposals for sociopolitical and socioeconomic change that it makes. Sometimes, indeed, Christian bodies try to produce such programs, offering them as the Christian answer to the world's problems, and specifying "humanization" as their goal. About all this, however, two things should perhaps be said, very briefly, as we round off our essay.

First: Programs for action are compounds of proposed goals and practical wisdom about means. Christian leaders, who have only limited opportunity to learn wisdom for managing public affairs, constantly give hostages to fortune, launch boomerangs, and make God's enemies blaspheme, by producing amateurish blueprints for public policy in the name of Christianity. Also, their blueprints divide the Christian community in the way that political proposals always do (that is, by offering as practical wisdom what to some seems folly), and thus they disrupt and erode unity in their own immediate constituency. The true Christian task here is to maintain a Bible-based critique of evil in all its forms and to pinpoint in God's name what in society needs changing, but not to behave as if Christian faith guarantees sufficient practical wisdom to upstage professionals in formulating policies. Christian bodies should cultivate modesty here, and not politicize their faith in this way, lest they put needless stumbling-blocks in people's paths.

Second: the idea that humanization depends on socioeconomic and sociopolitical programs is itself one of the illusions (a modern illusion, post-Marx) that is born of mankind's upside-downness and is accordingly not to be assumed, but to be challenged. Technological civilization is on balance a blessing, and collectivized procedures in society are necessary to it; that is surely beyond dispute. But, as we have seen in our own century, technology and greater affluence do not of themselves humanize, and can actually (if we may coin a word) barbarianize; whereas Christian faith will humanize, as our argument has shown, in any socio-politico-economic context whatever. That is what needs to be stressed. Christianity, as we have sought to state it, is good news—the best news of all time—for all mankind, in all places, and at all seasons; and no preoccupations of a secularist and materialist sort must be allowed to obscure that glorious fact.

Appendix

A CHRISTIAN HUMANIST MANIFESTO

In our time the word "humanism" has been claimed by those who explain human existence without any reference to God. We are unwilling to yield the term to those views that are least able of finding depth of meaning in the life of mankind.

We regret that Christians have rarely offered a clear alternative to secular humanism, and we seek now to set forth the salient points of what for centuries has been called "Christian" humanism. To this we stand committed.

The Starting Point

The proper study of mankind is not man alone, but God and man together. The triune God—Father, Son, and Holy Spirit—is the Creator of the Universe and of each person within it. God, who is the ultimate meaning of the universe, is eternally self-existent, though the created order is not.

By thus acknowledging God, the Christian view of reality embraces more than does that of the secular humanist.

The following document appeared in *Eternity* Magazine, January 1982, pp. 16–18, as part of an article titled "Secular vs. Christian Humanism." The present authors were among the many consultants who helped to determine its final shape and content. It is here reprinted by permission of *Eternity* Magazine copyright 1982, Evangelical Ministries, Inc., 1716 Spruce Street, Philadelphia, PA 19103.

Who We Are

Human nature combines physical and spiritual, natural and supra-natural characteristics. To the physical, sexual, and social aspects of normal human life, in which we rejoice, must be added the understanding that human beings alone of all creation are made in God's own image.

We can, therefore, create, love, assert, reflect on our past and future, communicate with words, and distinguish good and evil. Even more fundamentally we can worship the One whose image we bear. This gives man an intrinsic dignity beyond mere animals. Human beings can never be understood only as animals, however complex, for at heart they are religious beings.

Value of Life

Because human beings, male and female, bear God's image, their life, which is his gift, claims our care and protection throughout, from the time of conception to the furthest point at which it can continue. Neither abortions of convenience nor euthanasia when social usefulness has passed can therefore be justified.

Why We Exist

The meaning of human life is moral and spiritual: moral, in the performance of God's will, which is both just and loving; spiritual, in a fellowship with God and other persons. No human life, however prosperous, healthy, or devoted to others is complete when this moral and spiritual development is lacking.

The Human Task

From his creation, man as male and female has been given stewardship over nature, commanded by God to develop a culture and nourish human life from the productive earth.

Labor and leisure, science and art, family and state, belong to human life as God meant it to be. Yet the meaning of life is not found in these activities but in the God who enables them.

Science and Art

God created and maintains pattern and consistency in the universe, making science and technology possible. Secular humanism, lacking this ultimate foundation for science, must posit the consistency of the universe as a mysterious "given."

The form and materials of his creation also make art and beauty possible: human creativity thus echoes God's own.

Truth and Error

Something of God's character and will may be known by all people, even if dimly and with confusion. An awareness of God and of moral standards is natural to mankind, and the urge to worship, though often misdirected, is indestructible.

God the Creator has clearly revealed his character and will in history, culminating in Jesus Christ. This revelation, in which God interpreted for us the whole of human life and met in principle the whole of human duty, is now permanently available in Holy Scripture; and no one who lacks knowledge of it knows enough for a fully human life.

Though we know only in part, God's revealed truth is absolute, not relative. Because truth can be known, error can be identified, and a path is thereby opened through the contemporary religious and philosophical confusion.

Evil
Human life is blighted by the alienation from God introduced by human disobedience after man's creation. Moral evil, though universal throughout history, is therefore abnormal. Its root lies in human rebellion against God's Lordship and the rule of his law.

Ours has become a bent world: selfishness, violence, injustice, pride, self-destructiveness, and inhumanity everywhere pervade human life.

This evil may appear in individuals or institutions. It is manifest in governments, businesses, and families. The human will, rather than social conditions alone, however, is the decisive factor in evil. No explanation of human brutality that omits sinful choice is adequate.

Providence
In the face of this pervasive evil, God maintains a governance of human affairs that sets limits to evil, prospers human life, and preserves his purpose in history. The end of history, like its beginning, is under the sovereign control of God.

Human Restoration: Reconciled to God
To end our alienation from him and to restore human life to its original design and purpose, our Creator has acted in the life, death, and resurrection of Jesus Christ, a first-century Jew who was, in truth, the second person of the Trinity, God incarnate.

The appearance of Christ, therefore, is the most important event in all human history. By his sacrificial death, he paid the moral debt of those sinners who submit to his transforming reconciliation.

The loving service of God and man which Jesus taught and practiced perfectly is the model of true humanness.

The Kingdom of God Begun
From the ministry of Christ sprang an international, multiracial community of forgiven sinners. They acknowledge a common calling to proclaim Jesus as King and to bring all human life under his sway. This community, the Church, despite failures, inconsistencies, and hypocrisies, has pioneered a many-sided humanitarianism.

The Christian movement has been the cultural matrix of the modern Western world. Christian fruit, however, cannot continue in society without Christian convictions.

World Crisis
Current social and political problems are overwhelming: international tensions, crime, family breakdown, abuse of the powerless (including the unborn and the aged), scarcity of resources, nuclear threat, and more.

Christian humanism offers, not a program to solve these problems, but a framework for their solution—truth linked to spiritual power.

Pessimism, Optimism, Realism

Human life is not perfectible and progress is not inevitable, but despair at the human prospect is no more justified than is naive optimism. Hope for mankind lies in the knowledge that Jesus Christ, the Lord of all things, will make all things new at his Second Coming. The Christian Humanist therefore avoids both the pessimism and the over-optimism of secular humanism.

The individual Christian, facing death, can likewise know that conscious friendship with God and other persons is forever. Death can destroy the body, but it does not destroy the person or meaning.

In contrast to secular humanism, therefore, Christian humanism does not hesitate to speak of absolute truth, goodness, beauty, love, morality, the sanctity of life, duty, fidelity, hope, and immortality. These are not empty religious sentiments but the natural language of those who know even if partially, of their creation and redemption by a loving God.

> *"God has made everything beautiful in its time. He has also set eternity in the hearts of men; yet they cannot fathom what God has done from beginning to end."*
> Ecclesiastes 3:11